W9-BNH-697

The Golden Pharaoh

by

PHILIPP VANDENBERG

MACMILLAN PUBLISHING CO., INC.

New York

First German edition *Der Vergessene Pharao* Copyright © 1978
C. Bertelsmann Verlag

English translation *The Forgotten Pharaoh* first published 1980
Copyright © 1980 Hodder & Stoughton Limited

Macmillan Publishing Co., Inc.
866 Third Avenue, New York, N.Y. 10022

Library of Congress Cataloging in Publication Data
Vandenberg, Philipp (date)
    The golden Pharaoh.
    Translation of Der vergessene Pharao.
    Bibliography: p.
    Includes index.
    1. Tutankhamen, King of Egypt—Tomb.
2. Excavations (Archaeology)—Egypt.   3. Egypt—Antiquities.
4. Carter, Howard, 1873-1939.   5. Archaeologists—Egypt—
Biography.   6. Archaeologists—Great Britain—Biography.
I. Title.
DT87.5.V3413   1980   932′.01   80-16391
ISBN 0-02-621580-2

First American Edition 1980

10   9   8   7   6   5   4   3   2   1

Printed in the United States of America

Contents

Illustrations

Between pages 104 and 105

Tutankhamun's gold mask[1]
The Valley of the Kings after a water-colour by Howard Carter[1]
The entrance to the tomb of Tutankhamun[1]
A painted wooden casket[2]
A pendant from the Treasury[2]
Howard Carter accompanied every find under police protection[3]
Tutankhamun's dismantled chariots[4]
Lord Carnarvon and Howard Carter break open the sealed wall to the burial chamber[5]
The excavating team[3]
Howard Carter and his assistant Callender at the opening of the last shrine[4]
The golden throne of the forgotten pharaoh[2]

———————————

Wall painting in the burial chamber of the tomb[2]
Carter and Callender remove part of the roof of the first shrine[1]
The present state of the burial chamber[6]
The re-opening of the tomb[4]
Lid of a chest inlaid with ebony and ivory[2]
The king as the god Horus harpooning hippopotami[1]
A portrait head of Tutankhamun[1]
Dr. Douglas Derry applies the scalpel[7]
The bare mummy of Tutankhamun[7]
The forgotten pharaoh in his gold coffin[4]

Acknowledgments

1 Vandenberg
2 Hirmer Fotoarchiv, Munich (both)
3 *The Times*, London
4 Bilderdienst Süddeutscher Verlag, Munich
5 Bildarchiv Preussischer Kulturbesitz, Berlin
6 Lehnert and Landrock, Cairo
7 Griffith Institute, Ashmolean Museum, Oxford

1 Howard Carter: the apprentice excavator

*With archaeological work the
reverse of what is anticipated
almost always occurs.*

Howard Carter

On Thursday, 30th November, 1922, *The Times* reported the
resignation of the Egyptian Prime Minister, the occupation by
Communists of the town hall in Wunstorf near Hanover, and a
visit by Queen Mary to the exclusive London department store,
Harrods. The Royal Opera House advertised Humperdinck's
Hansel and Gretel, and the New Gallery cinema in Regent Street
the film *Fascination*, with the silent star Mae Murray. On page
one were the family announcements, births, deaths, silver
weddings, in accordance with *Times* practice for over a hundred
years; the sensation came later, on page thirteen. There, the
Cairo correspondent of the paper reported news, brought to
Luxor 'by runner', of 'the most sensational Egyptological find
of the century'.

These were big words, especially at a time when the century
was only twenty-two years old, but they are still valid today,
half a century later. In fact, today we are inclined to go further
and call this find, the discovery of the grave of Tutankhamun,
the find of the millennium.

The remarkable discovery announced today [reported *The Times* proudly] is the reward of patience, perseverance, and perspicacity. For nearly sixteen years Lord Carnarvon, with the assistance of Mr. Howard Carter, has been carrying out excavations on that part of the site of the ancient Thebes situated on the west bank of the Nile at Luxor. From time to time interesting historical data were unearthed, but nothing of a really striking character was found, although Deir el Bahari and Drah Abul Neggar were diligently explored. Seven years ago work was started in the Valley of the Kings, after other excavators had abandoned the Valley. Here, again, the excavators had little success. At times they almost despaired of finding anything, yet they did not lose heart.

The search was continued systematically, and at last the dogged perseverance of Mr. Carter, his thoroughness, above all his *flair*, were rewarded by the discovery. . .'

Concealed between these lines is the destiny of a man who spent his life looking for a pharaoh who had been forgotten, and it is the greatest adventure in the history of archaeology. It began exactly thirty years before this sensational announcement, and anything but sensationally.

Howard Carter was only seventeen when Lord Tyssen-Amherst sent him to Egypt. He was supposed to take part in the British excavations. In sending him, however, the generous lord thought less of research than of his collection of valuable manuscripts and antiquities, which Carter was intended to supplement. For a few weeks Howard tried to make himself useful at the excavations at Beni Hasan, and then went to Amarna, where Flinders Petrie needed help.

When he arrived at Amarna, a lanky figure with sketch-blocks and boards under his arm, the impression he made on the excavators, who had been working there for years, was that of a parlour tourist, and Flinders Petrie, the leader of the excavations, was doubtful, as he later admitted, whether this young chap would ever be able to make himself useful to archaeology. The one qualification which the newcomer brought with him was his talent for drawing.

Since his patron had not sent him to Egypt to paint, however, Carter expressed a wish, the very next day, for a claim of his own, in order to try his luck. This ingenuous request from a beginner provoked some indignation among the experienced archaeologists, but Flinders Petrie nevertheless assigned him a plot on the outer wall of the Great Temple to Aten. No more than the foundation of this wall was in fact to be seen, but young Carter set to work feverishly; he had to find something, for he couldn't, after all, disappoint his patron.

Flinders Petrie was a wily old bird. He had been digging in Egypt for the treasures of the past for over a decade now. Who could blame him if he assigned to this young protégé of Lord Tyssen-Amherst an area which his own assistants had long since been through with a sieve? Petrie watched with mixed feelings how Howard Carter, unsuspecting, naive and enthusiastic, went to work with true tenacity.

The first working-day went by without result. But this failed to discourage young Carter – quite the contrary, on the second day he went to work with even greater zeal. And on the third day, just as Petrie's conscience was beginning to trouble him and he went to look for Carter, shovelling away to exhaustion, in order to assign him a new, as yet untouched area to excavate, the latter, beaming, held out to him the fragments of a queen's statue, and on the very same day he recovered several torsos from the supposedly sifted rubble. The yield from that one day was sold in 1921, twelve years after Lord Amherst's death, by Sotheby's, the distinguished London auctioneers, for several hundred pounds.

With his capacity for enthusiasm and his youthful energy, Carter had soon won a new friend in Flinders Petrie. But what sort of man was Petrie? At a time when archaeologists were accustomed to appear at digs in brushed frock-coats, with hats and stiff collars, he worked, ragged and dirty, in shirt and trousers, with dishevelled hair standing on end and feet grubby and bare in frayed sandals.

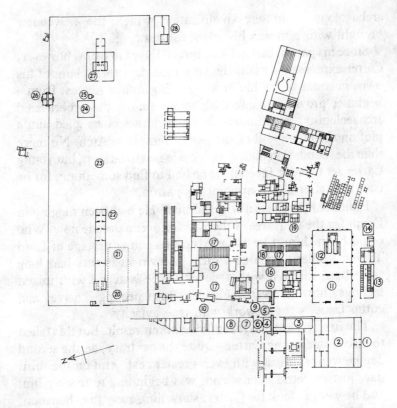

Plan of the inner city of Akhetaten.

1 Throne room	11 Altar	22 Gem-Aten
2 Great hall of	12 Sanctuary	23 Great temple
pillars	13 Temple store	24 Slaughter
3 Store	14 Lake	house
4 Southern harem	15 Royal	25 Stele
5 Window for	residence	26 Hall in which
public	16 Garden	tributes were
appearances	17 Store	received
6 Court	18 Tank	27 Sanctuary
7 Northern harem	19 Archive	28 House of
8 Garden	20 Per-hai	Panehesi
9 Bridge	21 Sacrificial	
10 King's street	stone	

The most distinguished of all in those days was the Oxford archaeologist Archibald Henry Sayce, of whom Petrie remarked that he 'paid more attention to luxuries than to . . . science, and had the gout in consequence'. He himself, on the other hand, lived in a primitive fashion almost contemptuous of life, and he demanded the same stone age standard of his assistants. Carter had Spartan days in front of him.

Petrie's appearance, his extremely simple way of life, were not the consequence of his activity but its precondition. At any rate, that was what he preached. 'One must rough it,' was one of his favourite sayings. 'And part of that,' Petrie explained to the newcomer, 'is to eat sparingly. We eat no better than the natives; after all we don't work any harder.' Carter nodded agreement. Eating had never meant all that much to him. Last year, Petrie went on, he had spent 'just five shillings a week for provisions for himself and his assistant'. The amount was derisory, and so it was not surprising that some of the team had to vomit after the atrociously bad food, or secretly left the camp to scrounge from the natives boiled beans or one of their little flat loaves of bread.

William Matthew Flinders Petrie, from Charlton in Kent, is regarded as one of the most successful archaeologists of the world. He excavated in the Near East for forty-two years, and in so doing made more discoveries than any other explorer before him. His scientific work comprises some thousand books, articles and reports.

He found his way to Egypt, oddly enough, in a roundabout way via mathematics. His father, William, was an engineer, who roused in Flinders an interest in measurement and weights.

Among his father's friends was the Scottish astronomer Piazzi Smyth, and one day young Petrie saw a work by this acquaintance in Smith's bookshop in Charlton: *Our Inheritance in the Great Pyramid*. Flinders bought the book and devoured the contents. In it Piazzi Smyth put forward some bold theories, according to which the construction, measurements and angles of the Cheops pyramid contained significant prophecies about the history of the world.

Constructing angles and calculating the courses of the stars had long fascinated young Petrie; now he suddenly saw all this linked up with history. He made himself a sextant, with a telescope and map table, and conducted surveys. When he was nineteen, he went with his father on a visit to the neolithic sun observatory of Stonehenge, near Salisbury, and decided to become an archaeologist.

Without proper education, he occupied himself for years with the prehistoric remains of constructions in Southern England. 'I used to spend five shillings and sixpence a week on food,' he wrote late, 'and beds cost about double that'. In this way he got to know the country and its people; he slept in barns and in village inns, and maintained, 'All this was the best training for a desert life afterwards.'

Young Carter was fascinated by this self-willed man. If only he might some day be like him! A lifetime in search of adventure, one's whole life a single adventure!

Petrie, who seemed to guess Howard's thoughts, shook the young man awake. 'Hey, now tell us *your* story!'

But there wasn't very much to tell. After all, Carter was only seventeen and had never been out of England before. His childhood had been anything but happy. When he was seven years old, his mother thought he ought at last to be sent to school, but his father thought otherwise. 'The boy's far too frail!' So a tutor was engaged, who took the place of primary school for the sickly Howard. His mother, Martha, was constantly running after him, to see that he was always warmly dressed and didn't catch cold. He was not allowed to play with other children, because according to her they were all street urchins. It should be said, however, that the 'street' in which the Carters lived was the genteel Richmond Road in the high-class London area of South Kensington, and that the Carters were not so superior as his mother liked to think.

His father, Samuel John Carter, enjoyed moderate success as a painter of animals. Because photography was still very expensive, the nobility, obsessed with the Turf, liked to have their racehorses painted, to preserve their memory for posterity by hanging them on the walls of their country houses. Since animals were the only company allowed to him, Howard spent most of his spare time in his father's menagerie at the back of the house in Richmond Road. His tentative efforts at drawing the caged birds there, following his father's example, were judged by the latter to show inherited talent; so from then on his father gave him drawing lessons. 'At that time,' Howard confessed later to his friend and teacher Percy Newberry, 'I made my pocket-money by painting portraits of pet dogs, cats and parrots for some of my father's clients.'

The Carters used to spend the summer in the country, at Swaffham in Norfolk, where in fact Howard was born. Young Carter then used to wander from village to village with his painting materials, on the look-out for worthwhile subjects. One day in the summer of 1891, in the neighbouring village of Didlington, he met Lady Amherst of Hackney. The noble lady took an interest in the seventeen-year-old's work.

Did he want to become a painter, asked the Baroness.

Howard shrugged his shoulders. He didn't know yet. It was hard to earn a living from painting.

Lady Amherst said she might have a job for him, a commission. The well-known excavator Flinders Petrie and his young assistant Percy Newberry had brought back thousands of pencil sketches from an expedition to central Egypt the previous winter, and now poor Newberry was sitting day and night in the British Museum in London making finished drawings: would Howard like to help him?

Would he indeed! Howard travelled to London with his father and presented himself at the British Museum. He was engaged for three months. The copying of drawings suited him, and his employers were satisfied.

In October 1891, when Percy Newberry was preparing a new expedition, commissioned by the Egypt Exploration Fund, he told the Committee that it would really be more economical to take young Carter along with them to Egypt. There he would be able to make copies on the spot, and the excavators would have more time for their researches. That meant creating a new post, and that, of course, was above all a matter of cost. Lord Amherst declared himself ready to sponsor young Carter, if the latter, besides drawing, might also do some digging. His lordship was a collector of antiquities.

In the past two months, Carter related, he had worked with Newberry on the rock tombs of Beni Hasan and Deir el Bersha. He had been drawing only, drawing from morning till night; there had been no question of excavating. But here in Tell el Amarna he hoped to be able to dig for Lord Amherst.

Young Carter's story reminded Petrie of the start of his own career as excavator. He had been twenty-seven years old when he was sent to Egypt through the mediation of Amelia Edwards, at that time a famous writer and Egyptologist, the 'Queen of Egyptology'. In 1883 she secured her protégé a post with the Egypt Exploration Fund, which she had founded. What he lacked in school and university education, Petrie rapidly made good. With his wilfulness it was to be foreseen that sooner or later he would fall out with his patrons. This duly occurred after two years, and from then on Petrie worked under his own management. He founded the Egyptian Research Account, which was later expanded into the British School of Archaeology in Egypt. In the end, however, he returned to the Egypt Exploration Fund and worked for that foundation for a further ten years.

There is hardly a place of historical significance in Egypt where Petrie has not dug and made important finds. He began his work at Tanis, Naucratis, Daphnae, Nebesha, Arsinoe and Hawara, and then went to Illahun, Kahun, Medum and Abu Gurob; he dug at Tell el Amarna, and also in Thebes; at Dendera and at Abydos; in Giza, Memphis and Heliopolis; in Sinai and in Palestine.

Howard Carter could not have found a better teacher than Flinders Petrie. And the latter recognised, after only a few days, that a great talent for excavation stood at the beginning of its career. Carter was allowed to lodge with Petrie and the British excavators. They had built themselves primitive huts by the high surrounding wall to the north-east of the village of El

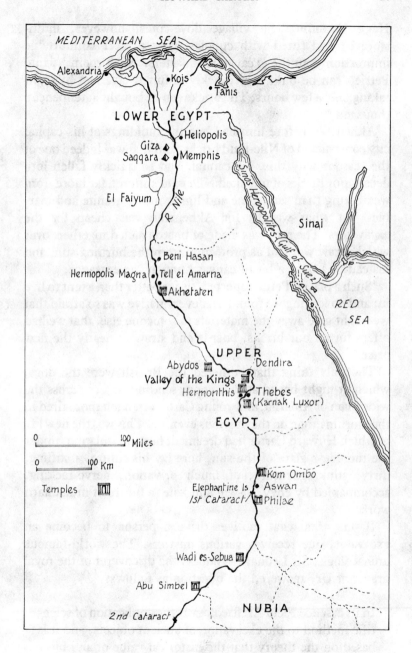

Hagg Quandil. The village dove-cotes, however, multi-
storeyed and fitted with cupolas, gave a more comfortable
impression than the excavators' quarters. 'Such room,' wrote
Petrie, 'can be built very quickly; a hut twelve feet by eight
taking only a few hours. The bricks can be bought at tenpence a
thousand.'

Akhenaten before him had had the buildings of his capital
city constructed of Nile-mud bricks, and that was indeed one of
the reasons why this, his capital, had so quickly fallen into
decay. For bricks of unbaked Nile mud suffered far more from
weathering than sandstone and limestone or granite and mar-
ble. Yet what was fit for Akhenaten was cheap for the
excavators. The roof was made of boards nailed together, over
which straw was laid as protection from the burning sun, and
instead of a door a bit of canvas hung at the entrance.

'Such a place,' Petrie reported, 'is far better than a tent to live
in; and on leaving we found that every native was so afraid that
we might give away the materials to someone else, that we had
offers for all our bricks, boards and straw at nearly the new
price.'

The only thing that bothered the British were the dogs,
which at night bayed at the moon, sending echoes across the
wide plain of Amarna, and young Carter often felt more tired in
the morning than on the previous evening. This was the new life
of which Howard Carter had dreamed; here, in isolation, under
the merciless glare of the sun, here lay his future, a stifling,
dirty, stinking future, of much privation, nerve-racking,
accompanied by envy, ill-will and hate, a future of much hard
work.

If one asks what motives drive a person to become an
excavator, one receives various answers. The world-famous
archaeologist Sir Leonard Woolley, the discoverer of the royal
graves at Ur, answered the question as follows:

In its essence Field Archaeology is the application of scientific method to the excavation of ancient objects, and it is
based on the theory that the historical value of an object

depends not so much on the nature of the object itself as on its associations, which only scientific excavation can detect. The casual digger and the plunderer aim at getting something of artistic or commercial value, and there their interest stops. The archaeologist, being after all human, does enjoy finding rare and beautiful objects, but wants to know all about them, and in any case prefers the acquisition of knowledge to that of things; for him digging consists very largely in observation, recording and interpretation.

Seen thus, Howard Carter was anything but an archaeologist; he was a treasure-hunter, forced by chance into that role. He was under the obligation to look for treasures for his patron, for excavated objects whose historical significance mattered less than the fact that they looked nice – back home in a glass case. A figurine, of virtually no historical significance, would evoke far more raptures than the fragment of an inscription which might turn out to be a building-block in the writing of history.

It was by no means easy to get a licence to dig at Tell el Amarna, and Petrie had not been at all sure of getting one, for Amarna was regarded by the authorities as the most fruitful region, as an area which was still largely unexplored and which might still harbour secret treasures. Amarna, a desert plain bounded in the east by rock walls and in the west by the Nile, was for a short time, only a few years, the capital city of the Egyptian Empire, the city in which Nefertiti and Akhenaten had ruled. And yet, although only short-lived, this city, to which now only a few lines and mounds in the landscape bore witness, gave its name to a whole epoch.

The Egyptian Department of Antiquities, traditionally occupied since the time of Maspero by a Frenchman, was anxious to dig under its own management at places that promised special discoveries. But it had finally proved possible to wring the digging-licence for Amarna out of the new Director-General, Eugène Grébaut, well known for his obstinacy and lack of imagination – with one restriction: the tombs were to remain taboo. There were twenty-six of them in the rocks of Amarna, of incalculable value for the documentation of the period.

Flinders Petrie received the concession, and he recalls, 'I then fetched five of my old workers from Illahun and reached Tell el Amarna on 17th November, 1891. A few days were occupied in building huts and looking over the ground, and on the 23rd November I began work.'

The remains of Amarna presented themselves at that time as foundation walls across which the desert wind had blown for thousands of years. Early in the morning and late in the afternoon, when the sun's rays were oblique, the outlines of buildings and streets could be clearly discerned. Here and there excavators had already tried their hand, and time and again made interesting discoveries. Above all, the so-called Amarna archive, the correspondence of the pharaohs with the Middle Eastern kings, recorded on hundreds of clay tablets, which had been found by chance by a peasant woman four years previously, promised even greater discoveries.

Petrie, with the help of the remains of buildings, could already distinguish streets and the lay-out of the palace and the temple, and he went to work systematically, the first to do so. He cut trial trenches in the palace and after only three days came upon a magnificent painted pavement, with water-fowl in reeds, and exotic, highly-coloured flowers. The government observer, who never left Petrie's side, reported the find at once to Cairo, and within a fortnight the government began to erect a protective house over the floor which was more than 3,000 years old – a house which, incidentally, was paid for, as Petrie expressly recorded, by the British. Later Petrie found a second palace floor, which made it necessary to extend the house.

With his two assistants, J. Hawarth and M. Kennard, who had both joined the expedition at their own expense, Petrie excavated the palace of Amarna; Howard Carter, who had made finds at the Great Temple after only a few days, went on digging there, and even had the means to treat himself to a few labourers.

The digger's luck, however, which had favoured Howard

immediately on his arrival, appeared to desert him after those first days. He slaved away with his men as if possessed; he tried to compensate for unproductive days with extra shifts; he cut trial trenches and uncovered foundations, but after weeks' of work he had found little more than three blocks of stone from what was obviously a large memorial tablet. On one of these bits of stone the head of Akhenaten could be recognised; the others bore script-signs. Petrie thought they might be parts of a stele, a memorial stone, of which there were a whole series in and around Amarna.

But although he made no spectacular discoveries, Carter's excavations were of great scientific importance. That, however, meant nothing to the young hothead. For him archaeology was still some sort of digging for treasure; without valuable finds to lay on his lordship's writing-table, the work was, in his eyes, of no avail. Flinders Petrie found it difficult to explain to the seventeen-year-old that the uncovered foundations of one of the greatest temples in the world were more important for history and the understanding of history than a few bits of gold and precious stones. That was a conviction that Carter was only gradually able to make his own.

While his workers dug on at the Great Temple, he, disappointed, set himself to draw scale plans of the edifice. Petrie suggested that it might be greatly to his credit if he were to integrate the plan of the temple into a plan of the city of Amarna, which so far didn't exist. That was something Howard Carter, the trained draughtsman, didn't need to be told twice. Every day he tramped thirty, forty, often fifty kilometres across the endless wide plain, taking measurements, making sketches, and within a few weeks he had drawn up the first plan of the city of Tell el Amarna, the ancient capital, Akhetaten.

The plan of the city was so perfect that Petrie suggested that Carter should send it to the Department of Antiquities in Cairo, so that he might earn archaeological laurels among the great. Carter did as he was told and took the plans to the post at Minia, after which they disappeared. They never arrived in Cairo; the hard work of weeks had been in vain. For him, the adventure called archaeology had in truth not begun very auspiciously.

Flinders Petrie, on the other hand, thirty-eight and at the peak of his archaeological activity, always broached the earth with visionary certainty wherever the past seemed to present its relics richly and without obstacles. 132 boxes of finds, some of them invaluable, were the outcome of *his* work between November and June; it took two months just to pack them.

But Carter was young, too young to give up.

He followed with amazement the work of his master, who seemed to have dug himself into the 'palace'. Although it might have been identified as any one of three large sites, Petrie was convinced that only the site he was working on could be the palace, because that building alone was palace-like in ground plan, with several sets of apartments, and in that alone were fragments of pottery found of a type not used in temples, for instance. In this palace, Petrie located three different sorts of find: parts of brick buildings, pillar-bases of sand-stone, and the foundations of stone walls. In the south of the palace a large hall came to light, 140 metres wide and 77 metres long; it contained the remains of 542 pillars. In the south-east of this hall, Petrie dug up a large number of wine and oil jars. Most of them bore the year-number 'two', which probably referred to the second year of Akhenaten's reign. North-east of the hall were several store-rooms; here, amongst other things, fragments of blue vessels appeared with the name-signs of Akhenaten and Nefertiti. The most interesting part of the building, however, was visible outside, on the long side of the palace. Petrie speaks in his excavation report of 'a great pylon or gateway, of un-Egyptian form, across the main road; it had two footways, and a wider chariot-way, between them, like a Roman triumphal arch'.

He soon found an explanation for the unusual building. It was a connecting structure between the palace, lying to the west of the royal highway, and the private residence of the royal pair, which had lain to the east of the road. Over this high bridge, Nefertiti and Akhenaten could get from one building to the other without having to set foot on the road running between.

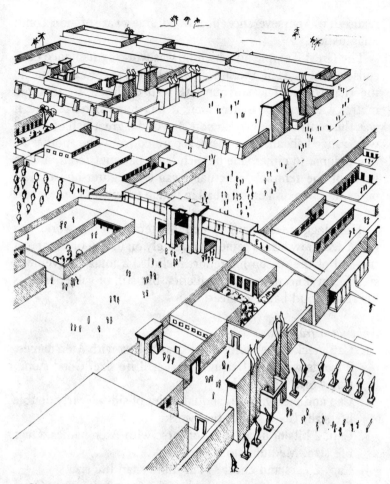

City centre of Tell el Amarna (Akhetaten). From the government palace (right) the king could reach the royal residence (left) over a roofed bridge. Note in the middle the king's window for public appearances. (Reconstruction according to Pendlebury.)

The royal private apartments were grouped round an inner courtyard. Petrie located a large bedroom with doors off it leading to a dressing-room, bathroom and separate lavatory, and a pavilion-like nursery with quarters for the governesses.

The primary virtue of an excavator, as Carter had long since realised, was perseverance; he now became aware of the second: imagination.

The Great Temple on which he was working had once been consecrated to Aten, the sun. It was aligned to the east, open to the rising sun. The surrounding wall enclosed an area 275 metres wide and 800 metres long; it was more than a temple; it was the centre of a new religion. Beyond a great hall of pillars were ranged six antechambers, separated from one another by five pylons; to either side of each lay a banquet room, and in front of the temple's sanctuary was a slaughter-house. The outer wall was broken by a hall in which tributes were received by the king.

The doggedness with which Carter went to work was rewarded; now he too came increasingly on useful finds, and at the end of the season his report included a total of seventeen significant objects – only fragments, but still of value. Here is his first proud balance-sheet:

Akhenaten fragments
1. Cap, neck and shoulders, pieces of chest with Aten names, 2 hands with an offering slab, leg. Life size. Good stone, fine work, dry finish.
2. Cap and pier, mouth, shoulder, bit of side. Nearly double life size. Good stone, fine work.
3. Cap, 2 bits of head, most of torso with Aten names. Over life size. Medium stone and work.
4. Cap, 2 ears and cheek. Half more than life size.
5. Cap, mouth, nose, ear and neck. Over? life size. Good stone and work.
6. Cap and most of head, neck. Over? life size. Good stone, fair work.
7. Cap and most of head, scrap of mouth. Life size. Good stone, fair work.
8. Smooth wig, top front of head, bits of beard and chest. Over? life size. Medium stone and work.
9. Smooth wig, most of the head, chest with Aten names. Under life size. Medium stone and work.

10. Ribbed head-dress, half head, bit of chest with Aten names. Life size. Good stone, fair work.
11. Ribbed head-dress. Piece of lappet, and tail of cloth, one shoulder. Small size. Bad stone, fair work.
12. Ribbed head-dress, and ear, scraps. About life size. Medium stone, scanty work.

Nefertiti fragments
13. Short wig. Bits of head, torso. Nearly life size. Medium stone and work.
14. Plain wig, inscription on back.
15. Plain wig, inscription on back, mouth and nose. Finest stone and work.
16. Lappet wig, two bits, shoulder, breast.
17. Torso. With back pier, nose, feet, throne. Nearly life size. Finest stone and work.

From the excavations of 1891–2 at Tell el Amarna, certain historical events could be deduced, on which Flinders Petrie wrote a penetrating book. And it is astonishing what a high degree of knowledge this work already shows. Here one must remember that such world-famous archaeologists as Ludwig Borchardt, Thomas Eric Peet and John D. S. Pendlebury were not excavating at Amarna until decades *after* Petrie. The famous Berlin bust of Nefertiti was not found until twenty years after the British excavations at Amarna.

Petrie was the first to record the Amarna style as an epoch of its own. In his day, historians were still exercised by the question whether Amenophis IV and Akhenaten really had been one and the same person. Today we know fairly certainly that Amenophis IV, in the fifth year of his reign, on the 19th day of the 3rd winter month, in 1359 B.C., changed his birth-name Amenophis, which was pronounced at that time as Amanhatpa, to Akhenaten – Akhanyati, as the ancient Egyptians called it. But towards the end of the last century even serious scholars were of the opinion that Amenophis IV had died after a short reign and that Akhenaten, a man (some even said a woman), had seized the throne with the help of a palace intrigue, adopted his throne-name, and introduced the Amarna style, which in the Egyptian environment was completely new.

Petrie recalls, 'It has been proposed that the new ruler was a woman, masquerading with a wife and suppositious children; such a notion resting on the effeminate plumpness of Akhenaten, and the alleged prevalence of feminine courtiers. It has also been proposed that he was a eunuch.' Among those who took Akhenaten to be a woman was at that time also his assistant Carter, who had found in his excavation-area torsos of typically feminine appearance with Akhenaten's name-cartouche.

The rays of the Aten fill Akhenaten with life-force as he rewards courtiers with presents.

With the help of the finds and excavations of the British expedition, Flinders Petrie was eventually able to present solid grounds for the following historical facts:

Amenophis IV had been married to Nefertiti. This was shown by inscriptions on two blocks of stone and an alabaster vessel. Nefertiti, however, was also Akhenaten's wife. That is recorded often enough on the boundary tablets set up around the city or cut into the rock. On some of these tablets the couple have a daughter, on others two, and even three on a further tablet – on which the third, as can easily be seen, had been added later. From this Petrie reached the logical conclusion that in the course of the years at least two daughters had come out of the marriage. As he wrote:

> The question of identity may then be summed up thus. Amenophis IV and Akhenaten both worshipped the Aten alike, they both had a wife of the same name, they both had two daughters, they both had the same features, they both had the same throne name, they both specially honoured Maat or truth and the reign of one ends in the fifth while the other begins in the sixth year. If such points are not sufficient to satisfy any one, it would be difficult to prove the continuity of the history of any king.

The question whether Akhenaten had been a woman or a eunuch Petrie was unable to establish anatomically, as the royal tomb, a little way from Amarna, had been found empty. He believed, however, that although the numerous representations of Akhenaten give him a very plump appearance, his anatomy in them still presents a clear contrast to that of his wife Nefertiti. And, Petrie asks, 'Is it credible that the most uxorious king of Egypt, who appears with his wife on every monument, who rides side by side with her in a chariot, and kisses her in public, who dances her on his knee, who has a steadily increasing family – that this king was either a woman in masquerade or an eunuch?' So the supposed death-mask of Akhenaten, a plaster cast which Petrie found in Amarna, does not show the face of a

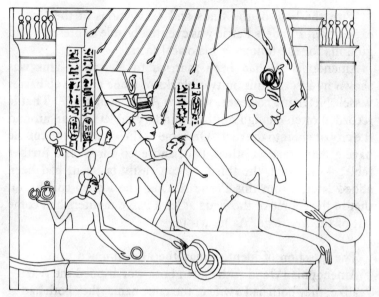

Akhenaten and Queen Nefertiti bestow golden collars on deserving court officials. Between her parents is Princess Ankhesenpaaten, who later married Tutankhamun. Two other daughters are on the left behind the queen.

woman either, but the features of a man, albeit a strange one.

Young Howard Carter was amazed: so that was how history was reconstructed.

Night after night he sat with the great archaeologist; he listened, discussed, made deductions, theorised, until the paraffin in the soot-blackened lamp was all gone. And when he crawled into the blankets of his camp-bed, often long after midnight, when the howling of the dogs echoed back from the bordering hills of Tell el Amarna, when he shivered in the cold that descended on the valley at night, after the heat of the day, then he felt at times like an explorer on the tracks of past millenniums. And the next day, when he walked through the ruins of this ghost town of Akhetaten, with sketch-pad and tape-measure, it seemed to him as though the walls, the stumps of columns, the rooms, were speaking; as though he heard voices, snatches of conversation. Figures took on life before him, disappeared, cropped up again in another light, watched him; and Carter, the seventeen-year-old, knew that all his life he would never again be free of them.

Was there anything finer than to grub about in this sandy, dusty, stony past, to make it speak, to turn it into history? Was there anything more exciting than to raise a find from the earth, a jar that no hand had held for 3,000 years, an inscription unseen by any eye for 3,000 years? If at first, in the service of his noble patron, he had looked only for decorative relics of the past, this past itself was now beginning to fascinate him.

Flinders Petrie sensed the fire that burned in his protégé and, remembering his own development, greeted young Carter's zeal with a grin: archaeology had acquired a new disciple.

History, the life of Nefertiti and Akhenaten in their new capital Akhetaten, would not leave Howard alone. Petrie and he set to work to draw up a time-scale of the Amarna epoch. And here it is quite astonishing to see how close this chronology came to present-day findings. Today, more than seventy-five years after it was drawn up, scholars can put forward only minor corrections. It really takes some imagining: at the time when Petrie and Carter drew up their time-scale, the Hittite people had not even been discovered, to say nothing of Hittitology.

In the following chronology of the Amarna period, events according to Petrie and Carter are on the left; on the right are the findings of modern research (in the middle are the probable dates B.C.).

Here were two men at work who were literally making history, the history of a period that had not previously existed – or rather, the epoch had not been known. Carter's endless questions as to how this epoch could be integrated into the history of Egypt, Petrie was unable to answer very satisfactorily. He knew about the preceding history of Amarna; it was established that Akhenaten had succeeded his father Amenophis III on the throne, but as to what came after him there were only suppositions.

Age	Year of reign	Petrie/Carter	Date	Modern Research	Year of reign	Age
12	1	Akhenaten ascends throne; Tiye sole ruler; building begun at Amarna.	1364	Akhenaten's accession, August 1364; Tiye conducts government affairs	0	12
13			1363	Marriage to Nefertiti	1	13
14			1362	Birth of first daughter, Meritaten	2	14
15			1361	Birth of second daughter, Meketaten	3	15
16	4	Marriage to Nefertiti; conversion to Aten worship; birth of first daughter, Meritaten	1360	Birth of third daughter, Ankhesenpaaten; putsch by priests of Amun (?); decision to found Akhetaten	4	16

17	5	Latest document with the name Amenophis IV; change of name to Akhenaten	1359	5	Latest document with the name Amenophis IV; change of name to Akhenaten	17
18	6	Steles at Tell el Amarna with one daughter; birth of second daughter Meketaten; changes in Akhenaten's facial expression	1358	6	Eleven new boundary steles in Amarna; removal to Akhetaten; birth of fourth daughter, Neferneferuaten Tashery	18
19			1357			19
20	8	Steles with two daughters; birth of third daughter, Ankhesenpaaten	1356			20
21			1355	9	Akhetaten finished; birth of fifth daughter, Neferneferure	21

Age	Year of reign	Petrie/Carter	Date	Modern Research	Year of reign	Age
22	10	Birth of fourth daughter, Neferneferuaten Tashery	1354			22
23			1353	Birth of sixth daughter, Setepenre	11	23
24	12	Birth of fifth daughter, Neferneferuaten (Neferneferure was meant)	1352	Last representation of Akhenaten and Nefertiti together; death of their daughter Meketaten	12	24
25			1351	Marriage of Meritaten and Smenkhare; liaison between Akhenaten and Smenkhare	13	25

26	14	Birth of sixth daughter, Setepenre	1350	Meritaten becomes main royal consort; Nefertiti has to step down; Smenkare co-regent	14	26
27			1349			27
28	16	Birth of seventh daughter, Baketaten (a mistake!)	1348	Akhenaten marries his third daughter, Ankhesenpaaten, later the wife of Tutankhamun.	16	28
29	17	Association with Smenkhare; last dated find	1347	Death of Smenkhare and, shortly after, death of Akhenaten	17	29
30	18	Death of Akhenaten				

If one could believe the list of kings in the temple of Abydos (drawn up by Sethos I) of all his predecessors on the throne of the two lands, then Akhenaten did not exist, and there was also no question of a successor to him. A 'historical gap' of thirty years had simply been tacked on, by Sethos I, to the reign of the soldier-pharaoh Horemheb. Documents show, however, that Horemheb reigned for only twenty-eight years, and that he was no longer the youngest of men when he took office. So if a reign of fifty-eight years is attributed to him in the list of kings, there must be either a mistake or a deliberate falsification. Historians call it historical bias, and it is as old as the history of mankind.

Akhenaten had left so much evidence behind him in Tell el Amarna and Thebes that his existence was beyond question. For a good ten years, however, the records showed no pharaoh at all. Yet there must have been one, for without a king the empire would have collapsed; the king was its political and religious head. Was it possible that the records had forgotten a pharaoh? Or *wanted* to forget him?

Carter made up his mind there and then to look for this forgotten pharaoh; but that, of course, was the fanciful resolve of a seventeen-year-old. One can't look for a pharaoh, Petrie pointed out; one can only find him, by chance, or because there are particular indications on a particular terrain.

And indeed, Howard very quickly forgot his intention. Then one evening, at the usual display of the day's yield, Petrie showed his young assistant a ring, a seal-ring with the name-cartouche of a king.

'Do you know what that means?' he asked Howard, who looked at him questioningly. 'Tut-ank-Amun – absolute in life is Amun!'

It was the name of the forgotten pharaoh; *he* must have been Akhenaten's successor.

Tutankhamun had been flitting about the archaeological scene for some years. Scholars had found his name, or allusions to it, here and there, but they had not known quite what to do with it. Petrie was the first to concern himself systematically with the chronological integration of this forgotten pharaoh.

Before the excavations of the British team at Tell el Amarna, historians had allotted to Akhenaten a reign of only eight years, for none of the monuments of his reign known up to that time bore a higher year-number. Here we must remember that the ancient Egyptians did not reckon time continuously by years; for that they lacked a point of reference, a Year 0, such as we have in the birth of Christ. So they measured time in each case from the accession of a king. When the old pharaoh died and a new one ascended the throne, they started again with the Year 1.

In the excavations in Amarna, however, Flinders Petrie found numerous labelled storage jars on which year-numbers were noted going beyond Year 8, though none of them bore a year-number higher than 17. So Petrie concluded from this — and has so far not been refuted – that Akhenaten had reigned for seventeen years. This conflicted with official historiography, which was based mainly on Manetho and Josephus.

Manetho, from Sebennytus in the Nile delta, was a priest who, in about 280 B.C., at the instance of Ptolemy II, set down a history of Egypt. In so doing, he fell back on the traditional lists of kings, though only parts of his work have been preserved, mostly excerpts and quotations, which were taken over by later writers of antiquity. The title of his history of Egypt, written in Greek, was *Aigyptiaka*.

Parts of this *Aigyptiaka* are to be found in the Jewish historian Josephus (A.D. 37/38–100), who in turn had taken them over from earlier Jewish scholars. By descent, Josephus was closely related to the Sadducees, but at the age of nineteen he joined the Pharisees. It is little wonder that in him the dates of Egyptian history got shifted about; all the Jewish historians, after all, were concerned to bring Joseph's stay in Egypt and the exodus of the sons of Israel (and hence the Old Testament) into line with history.

Manetho and Josephus assigned Akhenaten a reign of thirty-seven years. But this Petrie believed, probably referred to the period of Aten worship; it included the reigns of Smenkhare and his successor Tutankhamun. The death-mask which Petrie found at Amarna reflected the features, not of an old man, but those of a thirty-year-old, roughly the age Akhenaten must have been when he died.

There used to be archaeologists who placed Tutankhamun chronologically between Amenophis III and Akhenaten. They based this on the fact that none of the evidence on Tutankhamun shows the least influence of the very typical, unmistakable Amarna style. Petrie insisted, however, that the finds relating to Tutankhamun were to be placed between Akhenaten and Horemheb; for – so he argued – on the one hand there was no chronological gap between the reigns of Amenophis III and Akhenaten, and on the other the evidence from the time of Tutankhamun was by no means obliged to show stylistic features of the Amarna period: the works from the time of Horemheb and Sethos I, which arose only a few years after Tutankhamun, also showed no Amarnan influence whatever. The name of Tutankhamun's wife was further proof; she too had to change her name, just like her husband. Tutankhaten became Tutankhamun; Ankhesenpaaten became Ankhesenamun.

Petrie also found at Tell el Amarna seal-rings with the names Akhenaten, Nefertiti, Smenkhare and Tutankhamun, but not one bore the name of a later pharaoh. 'And therefore,' wrote Petrie, 'it appears that the town was mainly deserted in his reign, and the factories moved elsewhere. As rings of Ay and Horemheb are found at Memphis, it seems likely that the industry moved to that centre. Of the reign of Ay there is no trace at Tell el Amarna, but the unfinished tomb there was probably made by him when he was a high courtier of Akhenaten.'

As extensive later excavations have revealed, with the end of King Tutankhamun every trace of life disappears from Akhetaten. And not only that: Akhetaten, which for a generation had been the fabulously beautiful centre of the Egyptian empire, was razed to the ground.

Horemheb, the new strong man on the throne of the pharaohs, had the city reduced to rubble; he had the valuable building-materials of the public edifices taken to Memphis and Heliopolis, where they were used for his own monuments. Statues that had been executed not too typically in the style of the Amarna period, with elongated limbs, were reworked. Ignoble practices became widespread: Horemheb took possession of statues and reliefs of Tutankhamun by having *his* name placed over that of his predecessor. In the temple of Luxor he appropriated whole reliefs. Statues that had been intended for Tutankhamun's funerary temple, and which had already been requisitioned by the old king Ay, were worked over by Horemheb a second time. 'All the new ideals,' lamented Petrie, 'the "living in the truth", the veneration of the rays, the naturalism in art, the ethical views, all melted away, without leaving perceptible trace on the minds and ways of the Egyptians.'

This is confirmed also by a list of finds which the excavators drew up at the end of the 1891–2 season. The table includes all the pieces found to which some name could be assigned. Among these was also that of the sun-god Aten, whose name, like that of a king, was written in a name-cartouche.

	Objects	Moulds	Total
Akhenaten	72	54	126
Aten	22	36	58
Nefertiti	9	35	44
Ankhesenpaaten	10	–	10
Smenkhare	43	4	47
Meritaten	5	–	5
Tutankhaten	15	11	26
Tutankhamun	12	3	15

Flinders Petrie used this table for a statistical exercise hitherto unknown in archaeology, which – with certain reservations – is still employed today by some excavators. He believed, that is to say, that the pharaoh who had reigned longest would also have left behind him the most finds. With regard to Tutankhaten, who at some time changed his name to Tutankhamun, Petrie wrote, 'From that I suggested that 6 years were on the Aten system, and the remaining 3 on the Amun system.'

With the beginning of the hot season the excavators had to suspend their work. Petrie wanted to return to London, where a chair of Egyptology had been created for him; Carter was sent by the Egypt Exploration Fund a few hundred kilometres up the Nile to Luxor, where fresh tasks awaited him, and where he would be closer to the forgotten pharaoh than he could suspect.

2 Gold rush: the battle for the past

> *If, among other peoples, history consists of a series of events, then it is so with the Egyptians, who achieved just such a mighty realm of deeds in works of art, whose ruins demonstrate their indestructibility and which are greater and more astonishing than all the works of other ancient and modern times.*
>
> Georg Wilhelm Friedrich Hegel
> (*Philosophy of History*)

They came from everywhere, from England and France, from Germany and Italy; they even made the journey from America. Some were rich, even rolling in money, others desperately poor, so poor that the journey alone devoured all their savings. Yet all were united by a passion, a fever, a kind of gold rush; all wanted one thing: to make a discovery.

These men – there were also some women among them – who descended on the land of the Nile towards the end of the nineteenth century came, however, only in very rare cases with the idea of making a profit out of their enterprise. For one or two it was a matter of trophies, of amazing objects to show their friends back home, but most were intent on bringing to life a piece of the past. To this end they brought with them a doctorate or some successful research, or simply unbounded enthusiasm.

Amongst those in the last category was Howard Carter, now barely twenty. He went to Luxor and presented himself to Edouard Naville, saying that he had sent by the 'Fund'. Naville knew all about it. He was chief excavator for the Egypt Exploration Fund; he came from Geneva and had studied with Richard Lepsius, the father of Egyptology. He had lived in Egypt for nearly thirty years and could boast of three doctorates, in philosophy, literature and theology. No wonder Carter was dismayed when Naville asked him what *he* had to show, and he had to reply 'Nothing!'

Naville already had two assistants, D. G. Hogarth and Somers Clarke, but Carter's abilities as a draughtsman were extremely welcome to him. Only he ought, Naville suggested, to learn how to prepare photographic material.

It was a hard job that the twenty-year-old was taking on. Naville was quite different from Petrie, the very opposite of a comrade. Not only was he better dressed, had better manners and prepared himself better for his work; he was also far more authoritarian than Petrie; what he said went. He wouldn't tolerate contradiction and very seldom gave explanations. Edouard Naville was accustomed to express himself in writing.

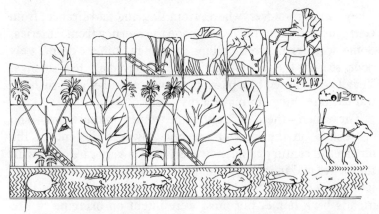

A village in the land of Punt (wall painting from the temple of Deir el Bahari).

Howard Carter worked with Naville for nearly six years and in that time the foundation was laid for his later, independent work. What Carter learned, above all, was to work with scientific precision. His prentice-piece on the edge of the desert, the terraced temple of Queen Hatshepsut, was a marvel.

When Carter first saw the massive scree slope under which a temple was supposed to be concealed, he would have believed anything possible, except that this temple could ever be laid bare. But if there is a science without prospect, then it is archaeology. Carter soon realised what perseverance and conviction can do: for years, hundreds of workmen shifted thousands of tons of stone. Carter drew, constructed, photographed, documented and, in so doing, witnessed a rebirth. A temple, buried and forgotten, rose again; its history came to life.

The rock-temple of Deir el Bahari had been a puzzle to archaeological research for nearly a hundred years. 'It is,' said Auguste Mariette, 'an exception and an accident in the architecture of Egypt.' For the temple, which today presents itself to millions of visitors to Egypt as a modern-looking terrace-building, was, until the middle of the last century, just a quarry, fed for thousands of years by the rocks that close the Valley of the Kings in the east. Jollois and Devilliers, two scholars in the Napoleonic expedition, were the first to give a report, in 1798, of a temple in this area.

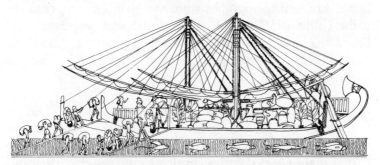

Relief in the temple of Deir el Bahari: two ships of the Eyptian fleet in the land of Punt are being loaded with myrrh trees, elephant tusks, timber and live baboons.

The attention of Napoleon's two companions was in the first place only drawn to the buried structure by a sphinx-avenue, 400 metres long and 13 metres wide, that led straight into the scree slope. The plan which the two scholars drew up at that time, of the ruins standing out from the masses of stone, already gave indications of the storeyed nature of the monument. It proved to be helpful for later excavations, because – as was to appear — only half a century later the temple had become even more submerged.

There was one obvious reason why the unusual structure at Deir el Bahari had long been of no interest to excavators: the granite portal of the first terrace, the most striking part of the building, which projected from the stony slope, had been polished and painted with the figures of saints. So treasure-hunters and grave-robbers believed they were confronted with the remains of an early Christian church and didn't bother to look further. Copts had, in fact, made use of the temple remains, and after a short time abandoned them to decay; even the natives had nothing to say about the significance of the ruins. The English traveller Richard Pococke, who was in the area sixty years before the French, learned also that under the ruins a passage led into the next valley – a fabrication.

Then came Jean-François Champollion, in order – as he wrote — 'to establish the age of the unknown building and its original purpose'. Under the early Christian saints, Champollion discovered hieroglyphs from the New Empire, read the name Tuthmosis III on the granite portal, and even then established that this king's name had been a later addition. He probed further, and detected the underlying name; he read it as Amenenthe.

I was well and truly surprised, [he said] when I saw here, and also at other places in the temple, the well-known Moeris [Tuthmosis III had been known as Moeris since the time of the Greeks], attired in all the royal insignia. He had supplanted that Amenenthe for whom we look in vain in the lists of kings. I was still more amazed to find that all the inscriptions to do with this bearded king, attired in the familiar costume of the pharaohs, contained feminine nouns and pronouns, as though it were a matter of a queen. . .

The combinations that Champollion employed at that time already came astonishingly close to the truth. He believed that the unknown queen had been the sister of Tuthmosis II, and that after the death of her first husband she had married another, who looked after the business of government for her.

The first to conduct precise scientific researches at Deir el Bahari was the Berliner Richard Lepsius. He discovered a mysterious connection between the terrace temple and the lay-out of Karnak on the opposite bank of the Nile: an extension of the main axis of the temple of Deir el Bahari ended straight in the Amun temple of Karnak. The solution to the riddle: the terrace temple was also dedicated to Amun, and there was a religious connection between the two sanctuaries. It was Lepsius also who finally deciphered the name of the mysterious queen: Hatshepsut.

If Carter had learnt to excavate under Petrie, under Naville he learnt to research. Here it was not a matter of bringing to light as many finds as possible in the shortest possible time, but rather of recognising, restoring, reconstructing and conserving

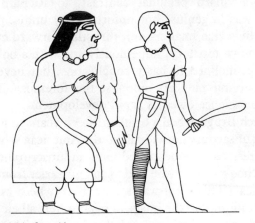

Perehu and his fat wife.

what was on hand. The purpose of the the enterprise lay not in discovery but in preservation.

This was a decidedly modern idea, a view which Carter also adopted as his own and which is regarded today as self-evident. At that time, however, it was by no means so. Under the cloak of archaeology, pillagers were roving through Egypt who today would be taken to court. But where there is no prosecutor there is also no judge. The authority that should have been responsible was filled with corrupt officials, right up to the highest level. A little baksheesh – and all was forgotten. Even excavators who today wear the halo of worthy researchers conducted themselves at that time like vandals. The first whom Carter encountered were two Germans, the brothers Brugsch.

Heinrich Brugsch had been selected by Ali Pasha Mubarek, *Ministre de l'Instruction Publique*, to be the director of a small, exclusive school located in a Mameluke palace in the suburb of Bulak. Here, there were bats in the rooms and rats and mice in the kitchen and cellar, but from the roof, with its projections like a Chinese parasol, Brugsch was the daily witness of fabulous sunsets. Here he instructed the offspring of the Egyptian bureaucracy in French, German, English, Abyssinian and hieroglyphs.

The German archaeologist Kurt Sethe once called Heinrich Brugsch a 'sharp personal contrast' to Richard Lepsius. Brugsch was 'a genius, but unfortunately undisciplined and inspired by a rich imagination, thrusting forward everywhere into unknown territory, impetuously and with a bold spirit of adventure, inclined to hasty conclusions, but nevertheless a most deserving pioneer, amongst the foremost of those to whom our science owes its rapid development'.

Heinrich Brugsch had a brother fifteen years younger called Emil, 'an unsavoury individual', as the American scholar James Henry Breasted once described him, an 'unscrupulous adventurer', a 'book-keeper who fled as an embezzler from Germany to America'. This Emil was known everywhere as 'the little Brugsch', for he was the image of his brother, albeit a bad one. He already had several careers behind him, which must, however, have been rather more modest than his usual description of them, or he would hardly have given them up. He had had a business training in Berlin and then emigrated to South America, where he had served as an actor and later a photographer, an artist of life, à la Belzoni.

After that he had lived for a year in California and finally come to Egypt, because he hoped to benefit from the personal relations which his brother Heinrich cultivated with the Khedive Ismail Pasha. In Cairo the younger Brugsch married a woman from Ismail's harem and was given a job in the state Department of Antiquities. Breasted, who was not exactly a friend of his, said, 'As everyone is very certain, [he] is now industriously stealing from the museum of which he is in charge.'

Emil Brugsch was well known as an intriguer, and had good contacts in the underworld, especially with receivers, with whom he had dealings both as speculative buyer and as seller of antique finds. In 1881, as a result of these shady contacts, he managed to find out about the mummy-cave of Deir el Bahari. There, the ancient Egyptian priests had hidden from the clutches of the grave-robbers the mummified bodies of more than thirty pharaohs.

In underworld circles, this hiding-place had been known for ten years; papyri, statuettes and decorative objects with the names of various kings, whose tombs had been found empty, cropped up at irregular intervals on the antiquities market – each time without any indication of provenance. On the basis of his dubious contacts, Emil Brugsch followed up the tracks of these finds. They ended in Luxor, with a peasant from El Qurna and the British vice-consul. Both of them were known to have illegal dealings in antique finds, but nothing could be proved. The consul enjoyed diplomatic immunity, the peasant the trust – for a price – of the authorities; even the village elders declared that he was the most upright and unselfish man in those parts, that he had never dug up anything, and never would; that he wouldn't think of laying hands on even the most insignificant find – let alone the tomb of a king. What the worthy citizen did for a living, however, nobody was able to say; he had long since given up tilling the soil.

His source of income lay in a rock-wall in Deir el Bahari, 60 metres above the rock-temple of Hatshepsut: a shaft 2 metres in diameter and 11.5 metres deep; then a corridor 1.4 metres wide and 80 centimetres high, straight for 7.4 metres; and after that a bend and a further 60 metres into the cliff: here the man had found the mummies of Egypt's greatest pharaohs, Rameses II, Sethos I and Tuthmosis III. The last grave-goods left to them in their mummiform coffins became income for our grave-robber from El Qurna.

In the end the brother of this millionaire peasant betrayed the hiding-place to Brugsch, and, since Gaston Maspero had just left for Paris, his German assistant was left to deal with the matter. The brother received £500 sterling as reward for the tip-off, and on 14th July, 1881, a boat brought the mummies to Cairo.

Emil Brugsch's machinations as assistant curator were criminal. But it must be pointed out that Egypt at the end of the nineteenth century was not the Egypt of today, neither did archaeology and museum work hold anything like the place they now have.

Heinrich, Emil's respectable elder brother, often related, for instance, how the museum director at that time, Auguste Mariette, helped him out of financial difficulties. Mariette gave Brugsch an antique gold statuette from the museum for him to turn into money – which he duly did. Heinrich Brugsch didn't mind talking about it; to him it was not a criminal offence, but evidence rather of the great archaeologist's readiness to help.

So brother Heinrich was less disturbed by the shady dealings of his office-holding brother than by his way of life. How many wives he acknowledged no one quite knew, but one of them was in fact his undoing. He had, God knows why, registered his house in Cairo in his wife's name and never dreamt that this wife might one day throw him out of the house and keep his money.

When and wherever the Brugsch brothers cropped up

together there was scandal in the air. So too in 1881, when Auguste Mariette, sick and confined to bed, sent the pair to Saqqara. There, two sheikhs, who had excavated the Serapeum with the French, had discovered the entrances to three small pyramids. Heinrich and Emil boarded a train, travelled to the next station, Bedreshein, and with two donkeys reached the little pyramids, where the sheikhs were awaiting them. The four men climbed into the westernmost pyramid and came to a chamber in which stood a sarcophagus of red granite. 'Next to the stone coffin,' reported Heinrich Brugsch, 'on the floor of the burial chamber, lay the well-preserved mummy of the pharaoh Methesuphis, as he is called in Manetho's list of kings, a fairly accurate transcription of his true Egyptian name, Mehtemsuf. From its external appearance and bodily development, the corpse could only be that of someone who had died young.'

Grave-robbers had torn the wrappings from the mummy's body; the shreds lay scattered all over the chamber. Perhaps, thought Heinrich, we could give the dying Mariette one last pleasure, if we could bring to his sick-bed the mummy of one of the oldest kings of Egypt. So he got the others to fetch a plain wooden coffin, of which dozens had come to light through other excavations in the neighbourhood, packed the pharaoh into it and laid the box across the back of his brother's donkey.

A few minutes before the train was due to leave, the two arrived at the railway station. When the guard saw what the Brugsch brothers were carrying in their box, he turned them out of the first-class carriage and told them, since they didn't want to be parted from their treasure, to find a place in the luggage compartment. Which they did.

A few kilometres short of their destination, the train came to a standstill on an open stretch. This was not a rare occurrence, since the rails became distorted from time to time in the midday heat. The repair, it seemed, would take a little while. The elder brother recorded with pride, 'We brothers took hold of the wooden coffin by its two ends to carry it to the station. The sun went down, the sweat poured off our brows and the dead pharaoh seemed to get heavier every minute. To lighten our load we got rid of the coffin and grasped his dead majesty by the head and feet. At that, the pharaoh broke in two, so each of us tucked half under his arm.'

By means of a horse-drawn cab the two Germans finally reached the Kasr en-Nil bridge. A policeman stopped them.

'What's that?' he asked, pointing to the two halves of the king.

'Salt meat,' replied Heinrich.

'Move along!' said the policeman.

Late that evening the Brugsch brothers arrived at Mariette's sick-bed. Decorously each placed his half-pharaoh in front of the dying man. Mariette did not survive the sight. He died on 19th January, 1881.

As has been said, Auguste Mariette and Heinrich and Emil Brugsch are regarded today as respectable archaeologists. The point needs to be made in order to understand Carter's precipitous career. The Brugsch brothers were not even great exceptions. When Wallis Budge, a keeper in the British Museum in London, arrived by boat in Alexandria, a red alert went out in the Cairo Department of Antiquities, for Budge was known to have excellent connections with receivers, grafters and black marketeers. A man like Howard Carter, on the other hand, disinterested, conscious of his duty, serious and full also of zeal for research, was found far more rarely. Carter was the ideal official.

So, at least, thought Gaston Maspero, the all-powerful director of the Egyptian Department of Antiquities. In the first place he tried to steer the business of excavation into orderly channels by dividing the administrative chaos into two halves, an inspectorate for Lower Egypt and one for Upper Egypt. So, at twenty-five, Howard Carter became Inspector of Antiquities for Upper Egypt and Nubia, with his headquarters at Luxor. Karnak, Thebes, Edfu, Philae, Abu Simbel, the great temples and sanctuaries now belonged to him; at least, they were under his control. He thereby became the second most important man in Upper Egypt – after Maspero.

Maspero, successor to the legendary Auguste Mariette, was actually of Italian descent. His parents had been forced to leave their home-town of Milan for political reasons and had found refuge in Paris. There Gaston was born. He attended the Lycée Louis-le-Grand and gained his professorship in Egyptology at the Ecole des Hautes Etudes.

Egyptian antiquity had cast its spell over him right from the age of fourteen, when the great Mariette showed him two newly-discovered hieroglyphic texts. In 1880 Maspero went to Egypt for the first time and embarked on an enterprise which had not occurred to anyone before: he organised a written record of all the excavations and discoveries that had been made on Egyptian soil, especially in the Valley of the Kings. He opened various smaller pyramids and worked on the funerary texts found there. And he was the first to take in hand the seemingly hopeless task of cataloguing and recording the excavated objects, finds and explanatory material in the Egyptian Museum in Cairo, which even then were virtually without number. Today Dr. Ali Hassan still produces with awe the dusty handwritten folios in which Maspero noted down every single piece.

As an Inspector of the Antiquities Department, Carter undoubtedly had authority, but what he lacked was money. Excavations at that time, towards the end of the last century, were not a question of how or why or scientific qualifications, but quite simply a matter of money. Anyone who wanted to gain renown for a great discovery had no need of academic studies; he needed a sizeable bank account. The cases in which by chance the two were united in the one person could be counted on one hand. Thus it came about that the most important discoveries were linked, not to the names of archaeologists, but to those of financiers.

These patrons cultivated excavation as a hobby, in the hope of being able to bring home an original collection. In those days a man of the world didn't display his stamp collection, but his antiquities. To come into possession of these illustrious and valuable objects one hired an archaeologist. A suitable young professor then cost about £150 – per year; workmen carried baskets full of debris all day long for a piastre, a penny, and children received half. Yet the archaeologist Henry Sayce, who between 1879 and 1908 spent most winters in Egypt, complained about the constantly rising prices: 'Where I had bought twenty fresh eggs for a piastre or a turkey for fourteen piastres, I now had to give ten or fifteen for the one and sixty or eighty piastres for the other.'

The distinguished gentlemen who had a rendezvous on the Nile in those days could hardly be said, therefore, to be forcing themselves into bankruptcy. One wouldn't want to belittle their (financial) achievements, but the most costly part of excavating was usually the expensive journeys, for the gentlemen naturally didn't hang about the site for the whole of the laborious campaign. They went home to England or America and were summoned whenever the archaeologists made a discovery, in order to supply the last touches.

There was the shady American Edwin Smith, who in the last century was one of the first to scent Big Business behind the digging. Mr. Smith, from Connecticut, lived in Egypt from 1858 to 1876, mainly in Luxor, where he established himself as a money-lender for archaeologists and antiquity dealers. His channels were murky. In 1872 he sold to the German Egyptologist Georg Ebers the medical papyrus that was later to bear Ebers's name. The surgical papyrus named after himself Smith retained in his private possession during his lifetime; then, in 1906, his daughter handed it over to the New York Historical Society.

Carter's backer, William Amherst Tyssen-Amherst, first Baron Amherst of Hackney, an ardent collector of antiquities and manuscripts, also appeared on the scene as the promoter of various excavations. William Berend, a New York banker and one-time fellow-student of Gaston Maspero in Paris, only withdrew from archaeological field work after he had lost four million francs in speculation. The American businessman Eckley B. Coxe Jr. financed excavations in Nubia and in Egypt, and in the 1890s the Marquis of Northampton conducted excavations, as a financier, in the Valley of the Kings, followed by the British industrialist Sir Robert Mond. Sir Robert supported the excavations in the Theban necropolis for almost three decades, and it was his great pride to show visitors from all over the world 'his' tombs.

The Germans, too, had their Maecenases. Among them was the rich Egyptologist Friedrich Wilhelm Freiherr von Bissing, who financed his own, but also British, excavations and was well known as a ready buyer of antiquities; or the Berlin financier and collector James Simon, who was responsible for Ludwig Borchardt's Amarna excavations; or E. V. Sieglin of Stuttgart and Wilhelm Pelizäus of Hildersheim.

It was far easier, however, for the French, English and Americans to organise excavations and buy up expensive finds: France regarded herself as the birthplace of Egyptology, and all the scientific offices were filled by Frenchmen; Britain – especially after the occupation of Egypt – could draw on her historical power status; while America, finally, threw her financial resources into the battle for Egyptian culture. As a result, the Germans had to confine themselves for decades on end to working over the published material on the finds. This earned them a reputation as theoreticians; the 'desk archaeology' of the Berlin school was regarded, among archaeologists like Edouard Naville, almost as a term of abuse.

They were all outdone, however, by Theodore M. Davis, an American copper tycoon from Newport, Rhode Island. When he first visited Egypt in 1899, Carter had just become an official inspector. Davis arrived at Luxor on the boat of the Revd. Henry Sayce. Sayce was actually an Assyriologist, but for ten years he had spent every winter in Egypt, and for that purpose kept a sailing boat with the name *Istar*. On board the *Istar* was a library of 2,000 volumes.

Sayce introduced Howard Carter to the rich American. Together they sailed along the Nile, Carter showing his visitor 'his' realm. It would give him quite a kick, said Davis, if he too could have a go at digging there, and he wouldn't mind spending some money on it. Inspector Carter said that he would see what he could do.

Naturally Carter would have much preferred digging to checking cash accounts, paying the watchmen's wages, and engaging workmen. One of his first tasks required a whole host of labourers. On 3rd October, 1899, eleven of the 134 vast columns of the great temple at Karnak had collapsed. The foundations of one of the sixty-foot-high colossi had given way; the columns had leaned to one side and carried away the others like a row of dominoes. Now it was a matter of re-erecting the columns.

Carter was also head of an armed troop, which kept watch day and night in the Valley of the Kings over the pharaohs' tombs that were known at the time, especially the well-preserved tombs of Sethos I and Amenophis II. At that time the tomb of the latter still contained the pharaoh's mummy.

The French archaeologist and student of Maspero, Victor Loret, had discovered the tomb in 1898 and in it had found a further nine royal mummies. Since Amenophis II still lay in his original sarcophagus, Loret decided to leave the body where it was and not to transport it to Cairo with the others.

On the morning of 24th November, 1901, one of the night-watchmen came rushing to Luxor, where he reported to Howard Carter in great excitement that he and his men had been attacked by bandits the previous night; they had been tied up and the Amenophis tomb robbed. The Inspector of Antiquities hurried to the scene of the crime. There he found the mummy of Amenophis II lying by the sarcophagus. As Carter wrote in his official report:

The bandages had been ripped open, but the body not broken. This had evidently been done by an expert, as only the places where objects are usually found had been touched. The boat in the antechamber had been stolen, the mummy that was upon it was lying on the floor and had been smashed to pieces. I carefully examined the wrappings of the royal mummy to see if there were any signs of their having contained jewellery, but could find no traces. . .

Oddly enough, the great padlocks to the tomb seemed to be intact, yet they appeared so only at first sight. After a close examination, Carter discovered that they had been broken open and subsequently 'stuck' together again with 'little pieces of lead paper'. From this Carter concluded that his guards had been bribed, and that in all probability hardly anyone had been at his post that night. When the watchmen realised the next morning what criminal use had been made of their absence, they were overcome with fear and pretended that they had been attacked. Carter was beginning to be a detective. He sent for a tracker, secured and measured the footprints by the tomb, and was finally able to follow the trail to El Qurna. It led to the house of the Abd-el-Rasul brothers, well known in this connection. Though Carter could show that Mohammed Abd-el-Rasul's shoes exactly fitted the footprints he had secured by the tomb, this was still far from being proof, especially as Mohammed allowed his house to be searched quite freely. And Carter naturally found no jewellery.

The Valley of the Kings had always been an uncanny place, watched over by the inhabitants of El Qurna. The British adventurer and traveller Richard Pococke, who travelled through Egypt in the middle of the eighteenth century and published an account of his journey in two thick volumes, was able to report of his visit to the Valley of the Kings:

Having viewed these extraordinary sepulchres of the Kings of Thebes with the utmost pleasure by the help of wax-lights we bought, and being much fatigued, we thought to sit down and take some refreshments we bought. . . but unfortunately we had forgot to bring water; the Sheikh also was in haste to go, being afraid, as I imagined, lest the people should have opportunity to gather together if we stayed too long. From Gournou to this place there is a very difficult foot-way over the mountains, by which the people of Gournou might have paid us a very unwelcome visit. . . the people had come rudely to the boat when I was absent, and said they would see whether this stranger would dare come out another day, having taken great umbrage at my copying the inscriptions; and they dropped some expressions as if they would assault the boat by night if I stayed. . . for they seemed strongly desirous that I should leave the place, being possessed of a notion of a power the Europeans have of finding treasures, and conveying them away by magic art. . .

Anyone who has seen the Valley of the Kings is overwhelmed. It is one of the most fascinating landscapes in the world. Superficially it is a desert region, stony, dusty, hemmed in by a range of red-brown hills which at midday turn the hollow of the valley into a merciless incubator, which is never – although the Nile is not far away – visited by a cool breath of air. Here the air is as still as the brittle rock millions of years old. As Howard Carter describes it:

From now on we are to imagine a deserted valley, spirit-haunted doubtless to the Egyptians, its cavernous galleries plundered and empty, the entrances of many of them open, to become the home of fox, desert owl, or colonies of bats. Yet, plundered, deserted and desolate as were its tombs, the romance of it was not yet wholly gone. It still remained the sacred Valley of the Kings, and crowds of the sentimental and the curious must still have gone to visit it. Some of its tombs, indeed, were actually re-used in the time of Osorkon I (about 900 B.C.) for the burial of priest-esses.

Today one can reach the Valley by taxi, albeit in a vehicle that would fetch a high price on any European veteran-car market; but it gets there, all the same, and on a narrow asphalt road at that, in fifteen minutes from the landing-stage of the Nile ferry. I find this a pity. In Carter's day there was only *one* means of transport here, the donkey, and the Valley had to be conquered each time on its humble back. People who still choose this means of transport today know why not only all one's bones are shaken up, but also one's brains.

Every time Howard Carter made a ride of inspection into the Valley of the Kings it became more and more clear to him that he was not the right man for the job. He was both a man of action and a man of ideas, whenever he was confronted with a site. History was not reconstructed in official bureaux, with documents and maps, but on the edge of the desert, in dust and dirt, with pick and shovel.

Carter met Theodore M. Davis, mentioned earlier, who in the meantime had been coming to Luxor every winter. Luxor was then, before the turn of the century, a fashionable resort where the aristocracy of money, but also of blood, used to spend the winter. Even today there are at most only one or two more hotels than there were then. So the difference lies not in the number but in the kind of visitors. Today almost anyone can afford a package tour to Luxor, but then only the best people went there, or those who, by reason of their purse, thought they were the best. Archaeologists were sought-after exotics in that exclusive company.

Anyone who thought anything of himself, like Theodore Davis, stayed at the fashionable Winter Palace Hotel on the Nile promenade. One could also stay at the Luxor Hotel, a stone's throw away; both were, as they are today, booked up for years ahead, and radiated, inside, the morbid charm of comparable establishments of plush and plumes in Vienna or Carlsbad. Bohemian head-waiters like the beloved 'Herr Franz', who operated in Carlsbad during the summer and in winter at Luxor, could feel at home, especially as the guests were largely the same in both places. There they sat, then, the gentlemen in elegant riding-habits, the ladies in bright clothes with wide-brimmed hats under sunshades, on the terrace of the hotel, and made polite conversation about whether, for instance, the American family-name of Ramsey was to be derived from Rameses.

Davis and Carter were soon agreed: they decided to dig together. Davis would provide the money, Carter the

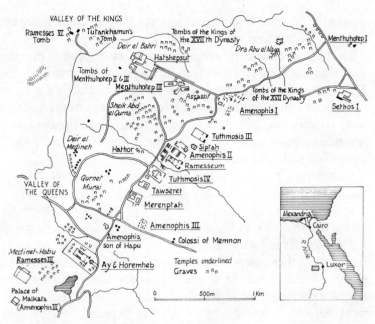

The Theban necropolis.

experience. On behalf of the rich American, Carter applied for a concession in the Valley of the Kings. Maspero gave his consent against his will. For one thing, he thought that Carter's official duties might suffer from the excavations; for another, he believed that the Valley of the Kings was not the place where archaeological results could still be achieved. Victor Loret, with his discovery of the tombs of Tuthmosis I, Tuthmosis III and Amenophis II, had supposedly brought things to an end.

Carter remained adamant. If the tombs of Amenophis II and Amenophis III had been found in the Valley of the Kings, then the tomb of Tuthmosis IV, who had reigned between them, must also be there to find. The probability that he too had been buried in the Valley of the Kings was at any rate very high. Maspero finally gave the enterprise his blessing and, early in January 1902, Carter began excavations in the Valley of the Kings, the first under his own management.

He considered first the south-east wall of the basin. The area was hard of access, but Carter still couldn't understand why no one had tried to dig there before. After three days he made finds: stone steps, the entrance to a tomb, a corridor, a burial chamber, ransacked except for some furniture and a chariot: it was the tomb of Tuthmosis IV.

Carter's first discovery of his own, as he was to realise all too soon, was pure chance, luck. For him and for Davis, however, it was an encouragement without which they would probably never have taken on the unbelievable labour of exploring the tomb of Hatshepsut.

In excavating the tomb of Tuthmosis IV, Howard Carter had found a little alabaster and a small blue scarab with the name of the queen. Then on 2nd February, 1903, about 60 metres north of the Tuthmosis tomb, right in front of the entrance to a tomb on which Napoleon and Lepsius had already tried their hands in vain, he found a stone with Hatshepsut's cartouche, and he knew that the tomb could only be that of the eccentric queen. It was a challenge.

As Theodore Davis noted, 'Subsequently I undertook the exploration of this corridor for the benefit of the Cairo Museum, under the direction of Mr. Howard Carter, the Inspector-General of the Service des Antiquités, who most kindly undertook the management of the work, for which I am under great obligations.'

The opening of the rock-tomb of Queen Hatshepsut was, from the technical point of view, one of the most complicated undertakings ever to face an archaeological exploration, for the tomb, 213 metres long and ending 97 metres below the entrance, was filled with debris throughout its length. And how long the passage was remained, at first, of course, unknown. Napoleon, who visited the Valley of the Kings in 1799, had already found the entrance to Hatshepsut's tomb, and on the map he had made of the Valley he described it as *commencement de grotte taillé circulairement dans le rocher* ('the beginning of a cave cut circularly into the rock'). He had 26 metres of the passage, which curved to the right, cleared of rubble, but then gave up; the project seemed hopeless. Even Giovanni Belzoni, for whom no grave was too deep, no stone too heavy and no colossus too large, if the payment was right, left this tomb unregarded. It fell to the German Richard Lepsius, in 1844, to take up the work again where Napoleon had left off. Lepsius managed a further 20 metres, thus clearing 46 metres in all, but then he too gave in; he found the work too expensive and unpromising.

The walls were unadorned; they bore no inscriptions, and at first there was simply no telling where the approach was leading. In addition, the debris with which the tomb was filled had become as hard as concrete, through the effects of pressure and rain-water, and could only be hacked out with pick-axes. At the same time, the piled-up rubble and the soft natural rock were often hard to distinguish, so that the excavators no longer knew whether they were on the right path.

The poor state of the rock, however, was also the reason why Queen Hatshepsut had caused such an 'impossible" approach to her tomb to be built. Hatshepsut, like most of the other pharaohs, had doubtless wanted to have an approach of 80–100

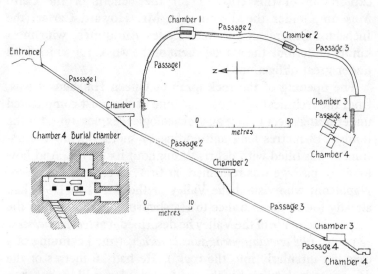

The tomb of Hatshepsut. Bottom left: the burial chamber. Upper right: the general lay-out.

metres hewn into the rock. But after 50 metres the stone was already proving to be soft, friable and useless for reliefs and inscriptions. The work of years could not be wasted, however; so she had her architect change the direction of the passage, in the hope of coming upon better rock.

For the first 50 metres, the job of clearing was not particularly hard. Richard Lepsius had done some good preliminary work. Carter came on a chamber filled with debris, which had fallen from the walls and ceiling, and was still falling. As Davis described it:

> We decided that it could not be the burial chamber, and we also were satisfied that there must be somewhere in the chamber, a corridor leading below, and the question was, where to find it without clearing the entire chamber – the work of weeks and our time limited. There being no certain solution of this situation, we agreed to toss a penny, with the understanding that if 'heads' came up, we were to make for the right-hand corner. Fortunately it came 'heads', and when we had tunneled through the *debris* to the designated corner we found the mouth of the descending corridor.

15th April, 1903. Carter notes: 'It was here that one of the difficulties of the work began, for the latter stratum of rock [marl, instead of limestone] was so bad that there was fear of it falling at any moment.' But Carter had the walls and ceiling cleaned down and went on. The air, 100 metres deep in the rock, become ever fouler, the heat ever more unbearable. The candles, the only illumination, began to melt; the men grumbled about the inadequate light. 'At this point,' wrote Carter, 'I was obliged to stop the work on account of the heat and the exhaustion of the air, owing to the great numbers of workmen required to carry out the excavation.'

During the summer break, electric cables were laid in the passage, and also an air-tube, through which a suction pump at the entrance to the tomb was to pump fresh air.

15th October, 1903. Work resumed. Carter had come upon a second chamber. He dug on in a clockwise direction, as in the first chamber, and found a corridor. The electric light made the work easier, but the supply of fresh air was insufficient and the men, and especially the children employed as carriers, had to give up, and fell over one after the other. The excrement of bats, thousands of years old, disintegrated into black dust at the slightest movement. The noses and mouths of the workmen were gummed up. Carter could risk a descent into the tomb only two or three times a week. 60 metres after the second chamber came a third, 10 by 9 metres in size, and 4.40 metres high.

26th January, 1904. Carter became convinced that this chamber, too, although larger than the two preceding ones, was still not the burial chamber. He dug a trial trench straight across the room, and in the right-hand corner came upon some stone steps, which led on downwards. This passage, however, was far narrower than the previous corridors; grave-gifts and fragments of stone vases with the names of Ahmes-Nofretaris, Tuthmosis I and Hatshepsut indicated that the actual burial chamber could no longer be far away. They also showed that at some time the tomb must have been robbed.

12th February, 1904. After the removal of a collapse in the wall, it became certain that the excavators had found the burial chamber. Three pillars supported the ceiling of the room. Large parts of the vault, 3 metres high, had fallen in. The debris lay so deep in the room (11 metres by 5.5) that in some places one could only crawl. In the middle stood the queen's sarcophagus, empty. The lid lay on the ground. Next to it, on its side, was a second sarcophagus, also empty; this bore the name of Tuthmosis I. Davis relates:

When the tomb of Tuthmosis I was discovered, in 1899, it contained his sarcophagus; we found in Hatshepsut's tomb not only her sarcophagus, but one which she had made for her father Tuthmosis I, as is told by an inscription thereon. Doubtless she had his body transferred from his tomb to hers, and placed in the new sarcophagus, where it probably remained until about 900 B.C., when, during some great crisis in the affairs of Thebes, the priests, thinking it wise to remove the bodies of many of the kings from their tombs in the valley, and to hide them in a safer repository, moved the contents of Hatshepsut's tomb to the tomb sometimes called the 'cachette', near her temple at Deir el Bahari. The great find made by the Museum Authorities in 1881 of the Royal Mummies which had been deposited in the 'cachette', included the body of Tuthmosis I, an ornamented wooden box bearing the names and titles of Hatshepsut, and containing a mummified liver, and also two female bodies stripped of all covering and without coffins or inscriptions.

Therefore, with some timidity, I trespass in the field of Egyptology to the extent of expressing my convictions that Hatshepsut's body was moved with that of Tuthmosis from her tomb to the 'cachette', and that the logic of the situation justifies the conclusion that one of the two unidentified female bodies is that of the great Queen Hatshepsut.

Sic transit gloria mundi.

Right to the end, Carter believed that there was a further passage leading downward. To prove this, he had to remove all the debris, a laborious task that lasted till the end of March. In the course of it he came upon fifteen limestone tablets, which were inscribed in red and black ink and contained several chapters from the Book of the Dead. Clearly, the tablets were intended to serve as texts for the artistic adornment of the burial chamber. But the decorations were omitted, since the rock-walls proved to be so soft that work on them was out of the question. From under the masses of stone there appeared also vases, bowls and jars of diorite, alabaster and crystalline limestone; the head and feet of a large wooden statue covered in pitch; charred pieces of wooden coffins and caskets; and bits of inlaid work.

Carter's entry for 25th March, 1904: 'I then started the removal of the canopic box and the two sarcophagi, in order to send them to the Cairo Museum.'

It was to be Carter's last excavation report for several long years. How this came about can only be understood in the light of his character and the prevailing social climate.

Although Carter had found the Hatshepsut tomb ransacked, unadorned and without inscriptions, it still brought him fame; after all he had succeeded where Napoleon and Lepsius had failed. So Howard Carter, the discoverer, was all at once a person of interest, someone who would be invited to tea or to receptions. Luxor was the playground of an illustrious society of four classes. It consisted of a small upper layer of rich or newly-rich business people and public officials; an inexhaustible stream of substantial tourists and *bon vivants*; and the broad mass of the native population, one half of whom pursued a regular activity, while the other thought up ways of extracting money from the pockets of the tourists and the upper layer. Archaeologists, with a few exceptions, not being exactly well endowed with worldly goods, were bright birds of paradise, tossed by chance into one group or the other.

Carter, the simple man of modest origins, never felt the attraction of high society. Introverted and withdrawn, he offered himself only unwillingly as an object of display, to be passed round at the numerous evening receptions. If he had been a party lion, his career would undoubtedly have taken a different course. As it was, the ever-correct, incorruptible Englishman living in seclusion made himself increasingly unpopular. His tough action after the raid on the tomb of Amenophis II had made him many enemies, especially among those in so-called higher circles, who had obviously been pulling the strings in that enterprise. Carter was transferred; he became Inspector of Antiquities for Lower and Middle Egypt, with headquarters at Saqqara. Maspero tried to present the measure as a promotion, but Carter never thought of it as anything but what it was, a forced transfer.

3 Saqqara: the end of a career

> *Just as the sky in Egypt is different
> from anywhere else, and the river
> has a different character from that
> of other rivers, so too do the
> Egyptians, in their manners and
> customs, reveal for the most part
> the opposite of what is found
> amongst the rest of mankind.*
>
> Herodotus

The greatest tourist attraction at Saqqara, before the gates of
Cairo, is the Serapeum, the underground labyrinth of sacred
Apis bulls, discovered by Auguste Mariette. The passages, 340
metres long, and the twenty-four sarcophagi for bulls, each
weighing from sixty-five to seventy tons, dimly lit by feeble
lamps, make a visit to the place an impressive experience. It was
one which, at the end of 1905, a group of drunken Frenchmen
didn't want to miss. Reeling and shouting and without entrance
tickets, these cultural tourists tried to push their way past the
attendant at the gate. But he refused to let them in.

This trifling incident, which at first had nothing whatever to
do with Howard Carter, developed into a matter of grave consequence. Carter himself never said a word about the affair;
only his closest friends had an inkling of what really took place.

Percy Newberry describes the incident thus:

One afternoon his *reis* of the guards of the necropolis came
to Carter's office to report that a party of Frenchmen, very
much the worse for liquor, demanded admittance to the
Serapeum although they did not possess the necessary
tickets. One of the visitors struck a guard, and this led to a
free fight. Carter, on his arrival at the scene, remonstrated
and was answered by insults. He then ordered the guards
to protect themselves and one of the Frenchmen was
knocked down. On their return to Cairo the visitors lodged
a formal complaint against Carter and the French
Consul-General demanded an apology. Carter refused to
give it, saying that he had only done his duty, and as a
result of his refusal he had to resign his post.

Gaston Maspero begged his Inspector to apologise, so that the
matter could be settled, but Carter preferred to resign. Maspero, who knew the quality of his Inspector, got friends to
intervene as mediators. They implored him to think again, but
Carter remained adamant.

Overnight a great archaeological career was at an end. At
thirty-one, Howard Carter was out of work. What should he
do?

Saqqara, Memphis, Lower Egypt had never appealed to him
as much as Upper Egypt, Luxor, Thebes and, above all, 'his'
Valley. So he sailed up the Nile to Luxor, not to the worldly east
bank of the tourists – but to the west bank, where there was not
a single hotel, only native villages opposite the Valley of the
Kings; that was his world. On the way there he met Ahmed
Gurgar, his old foreman, who greeted him with delight, but
Carter gave a dejected wave and told him of his misfortune: that
he had no roof over his head, no job, no money. So Ahmed took
Carter home with him, and Carter considered his position.

He remembered his professional training, got hold of paste-
board and paints and began to do water-colour landscapes for
the tourists. He didn't find it easy to peddle his wares to
tourists, like a native, but he had to live. Business was slow, but
he was finally able to repay Ahmed the money he had lent him

for the first few weeks. He made painting after painting of the Valley of the Kings, the strange craggy cliffs at whose base lay the approaches to tombs. At first he painted from nature, but then only from memory; after all, he knew almost every square yard.

Theodore Davis, meanwhile, still had his licence to dig in the Valley, and the Department of Antiquities had provided him with a new excavation leader, Edward Ayrton.

Ayrton, like Howard Carter, was no academic; he was a man of action and earnest in character. 'Ted', as he was called by his friends, had been born in China, where his father, William, was in the British colonial service, but his schooling took place in London; on that his father had been adamant. Despite good results at St. Paul's School, he couldn't raise much enthusiasm for a prolonged course of study; he was drawn to the East. So in 1902, when he was barely twenty, he went to Egypt for the Egypt Exploration Fund, as assistant to Flinders Petrie. He dug with him at Abydos for two winters, and when the Professor transferred his activities to Sinai, Ayrton was sent by the Fund to Deir el Bahari, where he took over the position, made vacant by Carter's departure, as assistant to Edouard Naville.

Edward Ayrton and Howard Carter were much alike. Both were incapable of a joke; both lived by the motto 'Be more than you seem', and so both were popular with the natives. In contrast to Carter, however, Ayrton always had an eye for his career, and in contrast to Carter, who covered every mile on his donkey, Ayrton was an ardent walker. No one who knew him could remember ever having seen him on a donkey, let alone in a car. Instead, he was always accompanied by two dogs, both Theban mongrels, who went with him everywhere, on his journeys to England, and later also to India. The amazing thing about them was their obedience to their master's every word; among the astonished natives this actually gave him a reputation for magical practices.

Theodore Davis began to dig on with Ayrton where he had left off with Carter. This was at the site of the nameless Tomb No. 12 from the 20th Dynasty. When, after days of burrowing, no trace of any earlier working appeared, the excavators applied their spades to the east of the Valley, south of the tomb of Tuthmosis IV. But there too they failed to make any finds.

Now and then, Carter would turn up. He had become in the meantime a pitiable spectacle as he walked up the narrow mule-track to the Valley of the Kings in the early morning, a drawing-block under his left arm, and in his right hand a carpet-bag with painting equipment. Formerly, as Chief Inspector, he had had a service donkey; now he went on foot. 'Hello Meesterrr!' called the workmen from afar. The natives liked him, although he had always been strict with them —strict, but fair. To them it was quite inexplicable that the Boss should all at once be only an onlooker.

There he sat to one side, his straw hat tipped over his eyes, and made little sketches for Cook's tourists. In the autumn and the early part of the year, during the main travelling season, his takings were just enough to live on, but in the summer, when the tourists were no longer there. . . Then Howard Carter paid more visits than usual to one or other of his former workmen; in the course of these he always came by something to eat.

Carter's post as Inspector of Antiquities had been filled in the meantime by another Englishman, James Edward Quibell. Quibell and Carter had known each other for years; they had both learned their trade with Flinders Petrie. As Chief Inspector of Thebes, Quibell also supervised excavations in the Valley of the Kings.

Theodore Davis was not untouched by the sight of Carter to whom he owed such great achievements as the opening of the tomb of Queen Hatshepsut and that of the pharaoh Tuthmosis IV. One day he spoke to him. How were things going? Carter told him frankly how he was placed: that he had barely enough to live on, but didn't want to go back to England; here, his state was easier to bear.

If he couldn't dig for him, would he draw? asked Davis; for payment of course. In the next digging season, Carter could draw all the finds and copy the inscriptions. The unemployed archaeologist had no choice; he had to agree, although it was humiliating work.

The first weeks of his new job were frustrating. Davis, who could dig more or less wherever he liked in the Valley of the Kings, had transferred his men to a side valley. From 1st November to 20th December, 1904, he had vast masses of sand and stone removed, but the result was always negative. Carter received not a single find to draw. After a short pause for Christmas and the New Year, Davis marked out with Chief Inspector Quibell a relatively small area at the entrance to the Valley of the Kings. The spot lay between the tomb of Rameses III (1184–1153) and that of Rameses XI (1099–1070). The latter was still attributed at that time to 'Rameses XII', who, as it later turned out, had never existed.

'What do you think, Carter?' asked Davis.

Carter shrugged his shoulders. 'It's not up to me to have an opinion, but if you really want to know what I think, a great many people have dug over this patch of ground for a great many years; I can't believe there can be another tomb just there, in the narrow space between the entries to these two tombs.'

As an original proposition, [Davis wrote later] I would not have explored it, and certainly no Egyptologist, exploring with another person's money, would have thought of risking the time and expense. But I knew every yard of the lateral valley, except the space described, and I decided that good exploration justified its investigation, and that it would be a satisfaction to know the entire valley, even if it yielded nothing.'

January went by without any occasion for Carter to go into action. It seemed he had been right. Why should there be a further tomb right there, between two others? Davis came over from Luxor once a day, stared morosely into the sand-pit, growing ever bigger, and, disappointed, rode back to the Nile ferry. At the beginning of February Quibell was replaced as

Chief Inspector by Arthur Weigall who, like Quibell and Carter, had been a student of Petrie's; he was twenty-five.

During these days, the head of the Cairo Department of Antiquities, Gaston Maspero, announced that he would be visiting Luxor. Remembering that he was the man who had fired Carter, Theodore Davis told the Englishman to keep away from the Valley for the next few days; there must on no account be a confrontation. Perhaps also, however, Maspero was not supposed to know that Carter was drawing for him, Davis.

On 6th February, 1905, as Theodore Davis was riding to the Valley of the Kings, his foreman came running towards him shouting from afar, 'A step, a step!' At the bottom of the pit the workmen had exposed a clearly recognisable stone step – at that depth an unmistakable sign of a tomb entrance.

Davis now supervised the progress of the work from morning to night. On 11th February, when twilight was already falling over the Valley of the Kings, the upper part of a stone doorway came into sight. As was to appear next day, it was 1.35 metres wide and 4.02 metres high. From now on the tomb-entrance was guarded. The watchmen were supervised in their turn by police from Luxor.

A narrow layer of Nile-mud bricks at the upper edge of the stone walling in the doorway indicated that this tomb, also, had already been opened at some time. The soft bricks were easily knocked out of the wall. The stone was another matter. Weigall and Davis chiselled away by torchlight half the night, until the hole was large enough to look through. The torches made the scene even more spectral. Near the entrance, in the corridor, which led downwards in a series of steps, lay a club; Davis could discern nothing further.

'Is one of the boys brave enough to climb through the opening?' he asked his foreman. He didn't have long to wait. In the hope of good baksheesh, several small boys came running up at once. Davis chose the smallest, and Weigall lifted him up to the break in the wall, where he disappeared in a flash.

Davis and Weigall had to take care not to singe their hair. To see anything inside the corridor they had to hold their torches right up to the hole. The boy took only a few steps, lifted something up (the club), bent down again and again, came back and passed through the opening the club, a staff, a yoke and a large stone scarab; then he himself came through.

Next morning, Gaston Maspero, with the usual train of officials, appeared in the Valley. He had arrived at Luxor in his sailing-boat and had with him the Oxford professor, Archibald Henry Sayce. Maspero seemed impressed by the discovery, but asked for the opening to be postponed for a day, as the arrival of His Royal Highness the Duke of Connaught was expected the following afternoon.

Carter observed events from a distance and found out in the evening what had happened during the day. For him it was anything but pleasant. What concerned him above all was the question: whose grave had Davis discovered? For Carter, as for all the other experts, it could only be the tomb of a pharaoh. It lay, after all, in the Valley of the Kings, between the approaches to two royal tombs. But the experts were to be mistaken.

Next morning Davis was at the entrance to the tomb at crack of dawn. He had the foreman take out the stones from the break in the wall one by one, and he examined each for seals or script-signs. But he found nothing. After about an hour, having been joined meanwhile by Maspero and his distinguished guest, Davis had torches lit. An electric cable had in fact been laid and a lamp placed at the entrance to the tomb, but for the first reconnaissance of the grave Theodore Davis rejected electric light. It would have involved the presence of an electrician, and the American didn't want that. Not even the Duke of Connaught was permitted to set foot in the 'virgin' tomb, and the archaeologist, Arthur Weigall, who was leading the excavation, had to consider himself highly honoured that Davis, as he said, 'invited' him to go with him.

Davis, Maspero and Weigall set out along the passage. It led steeply downwards, hewn out of the rock, 1.75 metres wide and 2.05 metres high, and interrupted by stone steps, which made the descent even more hazardous. After about 9 metres, a wall from floor to ceiling barred the way. The wall had been daubed with Nile mud, and seals of some kind had been pressed into the soft plaster. Like the wall across the entrance, this blocking wall, too, had a hole up by the ceiling. It might have been big enough for an agile grave-robber to squeeze through, but for plump Monsieur Maspero it was far too small. So Davis's original plan, of leaving the dividing wall standing, had to be abandoned and, as they had no tools with them, the three began to tear out the bricks with their bare hands. When the wall had been pulled down to breast-height, furniture shimmering with gold could be seen within.

Neither exhortation nor threats of possible consequences could now persuade Theodore Davis to take down the rest of the wall. He thrust his torch into Weigall's hand and with a mighty leap that did credit to his sixty-eight years, swung himself over the barrier. He then had his torch passed over to him. On the other side it was muggy, almost hot, and there was a sweet smell, as though sugar-beet was being cooked. Maspero's desperate efforts to get over the wall were supported by Weigall from behind, by pushing, and by Davis from in front, by pulling. Despite his considerable bulk, the manoeuvre succeeded.

Blinded by the light of their own torches, the men groped about aimlessly in the room. The numerous effects could hardly be discerned, but their attention was caught above all by a mummiform coffin, in the middle of the chamber, covered in a black mass of something like pitch. Maspero handed Davis his torch and asked him to throw more light on the coffin. He himself kneeled down and looked for script-signs on the parts not covered in black, which gleamed with gold. Suddenly he said: 'Yuya!'

Davis stared in self-forgetfulness at the disfigured mummiform coffin. A tap on his arm made him start. 'Be careful!' cried Maspero at the same time. The fire from one of the torches had already licked at the pitch-covered sarcophagus. A moment more, and the coffin would have been in flames. As Davis wrote later, 'As the entire contents of the tomb were inflammable, and directly opposite the coffin was a corridor leading to the open air and making a draught, we undoubtedly should have lost our lives, as the only escape was by the corridor, which would have necessitated climbing over the stone wall barring the doorway. This would have retarded our exit for at least ten minutes.'

After this incident, the three ascended to the outside. Workmen had first to demolish the rest of the wall, and finally even the electricians were allowed in to lay cables into the tomb. That same day the three went down to the burial chamber once more, this time with electric lights, which they held above their heads, to avoid being blinded.

Only now could they take in the multifarious nature of the contents of the burial chamber. In one corner stood a chariot; the shaft had obviously been broken off later by a grave-robber. On the chariot lay two alabaster vases. Out of one of them hung mummy bandages, with which the vase had originally been closed. Grave-robbers had torn out the stopping, probably in the hope of finding something valuable inside; but contents were still there. 'Honey!' said Davis on seeing the glutinous substance. Maspero corrected him: 'Natron!'

Finally, amongst all manner of equipment, they found a second coffin. It too bore a name: Thuya.

The mummies of Yuya and Thuya, the parents of Queen Tiye and hence Akhenaten's grandparents, are the best preserved that have been found in Egypt. Both lay in triple coffins, one inside the other, the lids of which had been broken open. In their hurry, however, the grave-robbers had left behind them, or lost, a satisfactory quantity of grave-goods, above all a gold plate as big as the palm of the hand; this covered the incision through which the embalmers had removed the heart of the 'Divine Father', Yuya, in order to subject it to a special process of preservation. On the mummy of Thuya, the gold plate was missing.

Theodore Davis described his feelings thus:

When I first saw the mummy of Thuya she was lying in her coffin, covered from her chin to her feet with very fine mummy-cloth arranged with care. Why this was done no one can positively state, but I am disposed to think that the robber was impressed by the dignity of the dead woman whose body he had desecrated. I had occasion to sit by her in the tomb for nearly an hour, and having nothing else to do or see, I studied her face and indulged in speculations germane to the situation, until her dignity and character so impressed me that I almost found it necessary to apologise for my presence.

Hardly had Gaston Maspero and his guest disappeared, together with their followers, when Howard Carter came along, to examine what till then he knew only from hearsay. He drew and sketched the finds for a work which Davis published, in 1907, with Archibald Constable & Co. of London. These drawings were of great importance, for the Yuya-Thuya tomb was, to date, the only one that had been found with its original contents.

Impressed by the sensational discovery, Gaston Maspero invited Davis to choose one or two articles for himself. The agreement between the Egyptian Department of Antiquities and the American provided that *all* finds were to be handed over. 'I confess,' wrote Davis, 'that it was a most attractive offer, but, on consideration, I could not bring myself to break up the collection which I felt ought to be exhibited intact in the Cairo Museum, where it could be seen and studied by probably the greatest number of appreciative visitors.' An honourable way of thinking, with which few would have credited the American businessman, and Carter, too, was impressed by Davis's decision. Seventeen years later, when he himself made the greatest of all Egyptological discoveries, this decision was to play an important part.

Yuya and Thuya made Theodore Davis, literally overnight, the most popular excavator in the early years of the twentieth century. Newspaper reporters came from all over the world and asked the American question after question. How did the discovery come about? Why had he dug precisely at that spot?

Why had precisely this tomb not been ransacked? Davis had to find an answer to all the questions.

Perhaps the most interesting was this: Davis regarded the breaching of the tomb as the work of an individual.

When the robber found the outer doorway barred by a wall, he took off enough of it to enable him to crawl through; and when he reached the second and last doorway, he found a corresponding wall, which he treated in the same manner. He seems to have had either a very dim light or none at all, for when he was in the burial chamber he selected a large stone scarab, the neck-yoke of the chariot, and a wooden staff of office, all of which were covered with thick gold foil, which evidently he thought to be solid gold: he carried them up the corridor until he came to a gleam of daylight, when he discovered his error and left them on the floor of the corridor, where I found them.

The discovery of the Yuya-Thuya tomb showed up certain principles of archaeological field work which are typical and still apply today:

1. The greatest discoveries of archaeologists depend largely on chance.
2. No spot can ever be so improbable that it could not be good for a discovery.
3. The fame of a great discovery makes more demands than all the foregoing work.
4. A discovery of historical significance should not belong to a collector or the scholars of an institute, but to the whole of mankind.

Next, Davis had long trial trenches dug in front of the tomb of Yuya and Thuya, but without result: no other tomb-entrance was to be found there. Disappointed, he turned to the tomb of Rameses IV. In front of the entrance, the desert floor seemed to be untouched. He had two trenches dug. Vast quantities of debris appeared, perhaps the chippings from a pharaoh's tomb, probably from more than one, for there were potsherds with several names, including that of Amenophis I and Rameses II. Somewhat further north, twenty roughly-worked funerary statuettes of Rameses IV came to light, a result that by no means justified the expense. As Davis admitted, 'Results here were not satisfactory.'

Next day an unannounced visitor appeared in the Valley of the Kings, a self-willed American who, with his wife and child, had come to Egypt to fit out a scientific expedition: James Henry Breasted. He was to be one of the few people to gain Carter's confidence. The two met for the first time in the Valley of the Kings. Carter was standing next to Ayrton and Davis, who smoked one cigarette after another. Carter seemed calm and poised. Davis, on the other hand, was visibly nervous; he stared restlessly into the entry-shaft of a tomb, from which the workmen were bringing out a mass of debris. The arrival of the American family of excavators filled Davis with delight. There, in that godforsaken solitude, a visitor from home gave more pleasure than anywhere else in the world.

Davis first introduced his scientific excavation leader, Edward Ayrton, then Howard Carter, who was, as Charles Breasted recalls, 'a black-haired, black-eyed young English artist of medium stature who was one day to achieve unparalleled world renown'.

The Breasteds had had to pinch and scrape for a journey such as this; they had lived in wretched hotels and guest-houses, in furnished rooms and apartments, in tents and on house-boats, in trains and on board ships.

For years [the son Charles recalls] they habitually ordered only two portions of food at the back-street restaurants we frequented, gave one portion to me and divided the other between themselves. We crossed and recrossed the Atlantic – seven times before I was five – and our only home was under the roof currently sheltering our trunks and my father's travel-scarred box of scientific books and the grey canvas-covered telescopic case filled with his growing manuscripts. We belonged to a nomadic host of scholars and little academic families of every creed and description from every civilised corner of the world. . .

'I very much hope,' said Theodore Davis to his American visitors, 'that this will prove to be the first tomb of a king, intact and untouched by ancient robbers, ever to be found in Egypt by an authorised modern excavator.'

Breasted was fascinated. For hours on end he stared into the ever-growing hole in the ground being dug by the noisy workmen. With tropical suddenness twilight descended over the Valley, but the work went on. Davis had his foreman fetch a lantern; he spread a cloth over the ground and laid on it all the finds that he had wrested from the earth at that spot. Breasted picked up the pieces one by one and examined them for scriptsigns. On the alabaster statuette he found the name Siptah; Davis's excitement grew.

Late that evening work was suspended. With their American guests, the excavators rode down to the Nile on donkeys. Charles Breasted was to describe that ride by night many years later:

We made our way by starlight out of the Valley, and from the crest of the ridge saw the distant lights of Luxor. As we descended toward the river plain, I remember the warmth which rose from the sunbaked limestone cliffs through the chill of the desert night; then the familiar rich fragrance of irrigated fields, the odours of musk and aromatic smoke drifting from groups of shapeless figures gathered about small fires before wattle huts as they guarded their crops; the sounds and smells of farm animals munching, off in the dark; the muffled clatter from our donkeys' feet, whose dust was constantly in our nostrils; and overhead, stars beyond anything I had ever known.

Next morning, Breasted and his family travelled on upstream

to Aswan, while Davis, Ayrton and Carter resumed their work in the Valley of the Kings. It was not until the following day, however, that it became clear that all they had found was the insignificant vault of an insignificant king, the plundered grave of Siptah, a child-king like Tutankhamun, who had reigned from 1194 to 1188.

Davis had his men go on digging. On a stifling hot day in February they came once more upon a stone step. The Boss was called. He poked about round the step with his stick, knocked a few stones aside and nodded to the diggers. 'Go on!' A day later they had exposed a steep stairway leading downwards. Edward Ayrton crawled into the tomb on all fours. Davis and his men waited expectantly for any sound from within. Nothing. Minutes went by. When Davis stuck his head into the opening, he was met by a fusty atmosphere. Then all at once, from deep inside the rock, came the sound of stones knocking against each other; it became louder, drew nearer, and Ayrton, panting, crawled out. Struggling for breath, he blurted out: 'Horemheb, it's Horemheb!'

'This was a surprise,' Davis related, 'as we had always thought that Horemheb was buried at Memphis, or at some place in Lower Egypt.' Davis was not so very wrong in his

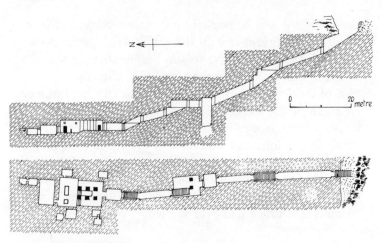

The tomb of Horemheb.

belief, for Horemheb had two graves. He had never expected, that is to say, that one day he would be Pharaoh of the Two Lands. So in his capacity as supreme commander of the armed forces he first had a resting-place built for himself at Saqqara; this must presumably have been during the Amarna period, for the Amarna style is unmistakable in the wall-reliefs. Later, when he promoted himself to Pharaoh, he was naturally entitled to a tomb in the Valley of the Kings, and that, indeed, is where he was probably buried.

The tomb led almost 90 metres deep into the rock. When he first went in, Ayrton got less than halfway; but he recognised the name Horemheb on the walls. Three days after Ayrton's bold solo effort, he and Davis and three other men, equipped with carbide lamps, set out down the awkward passage into the depths. Davis describes the passage thus:

It was necessary to drag ourselves over the stones and sand which blocked the way, with our heads unpleasantly near the rough roof; there was little air, except that which came from the mouth of the tomb 130 feet above, and the heat was stifling. The sand over which we had passed had evidently been put there for the protection of the body of Horemheb. Beyond the sand, we came to an open well or pit, cut vertically in the rock; this was for the purpose of receiving any water which might find its way from the mouth of the tomb, and to aid the discharge of the water a smaller room had been cut in the rock next to the well.

This theory advanced by Davis has been disputed. The shaft, which, incidentally, is to be found in the tombs of many pharaohs, was probably only a trap for grave-robbers. But the crooks were able to overcome even this obstacle. In the tomb of Tuthmosis IV a rope was found, tied to a pillar. The robbers had used it to lower themselves into the shaft. Another man had tried in the meantime to find a hold on the opposite side of the shaft, using the noose of a second rope.

Davis and his men crossed the shaft, some ten metres deep,

with the help of a ladder, which they had dragged laboriously behind them. On one side, the reliefs on the wall of the shaft were interrupted; so here too grave-robbers had found the bricked-up entry to the actual tomb. On the walls of the passage to the burial chamber, the men saw paintings of the king conversing with various divinities; some were unfinished.

Two further inclined passages led into several antechambers, and in the last, the largest room, stood the red granite sarcophagus of Horemheb. Only now could they take a good look round the burial chamber: the grave-robbers had done their job thoroughly; apart from three skulls, the chamber had been cleared. So Davis and his men approached the sarcophagus with no hope of making even the smallest discovery. But they were wrong.

Davis and Ayrton could hardly believe their eyes: in the sarcophagus lay a human skeleton. But their first joy of discovery was soon followed by disillusionment. Ayrton's objection that the skeleton could not be the mortal remains of Horemheb, because there was no sign whatever of mummification, could not be denied. In a room adjoining the burial chamber, which they called the Osiris room, because of its wall decoration, more human bones were lying about. The anatomist Dr. Elliot Smith, who assembled the bones a little later, was able to show that they came from two women. The skulls in the burial chamber and the skeleton in the sarcophagus were from others again. No mummification had been carried out on any of these people. It will probably always remain a mystery as to who was involved here; perhaps the human bones bear witness to a grave-robbing drama.

In the winter of 1906, Theodore Davis's attention was caught by a large rock tilted to one side. 'For some mysterious reason,' he wrote, 'I felt interested in it, and on being carefully examined and dug about by my assistant, Mr. Ayrton, with the hands. . . [a] beautiful blue cup. . . was found. This bore the cartouche of Tutankhamun.'

A year later, Davis was digging north of Horemheb's tomb, only a few steps from the place where the cup was found, when

E. Harold Jones, one of his assistants, found a vault at a depth of about 8 metres, which at some time in the course of the millenniums must have lain under water; it was filled to the top with dried mud. In the belief that they had discovered a new royal tomb, the excavators shovelled, scratched and brushed the mud away laboriously, and after a few days the first find did in fact appear: a broken casket, which contained several thin pieces of gold-leaf. These fragments of gold bore name-cartouches. Ayrton read one as 'Tutankhamun'; on another was 'Ankhesenamun', and a third was stamped with the names of Ay and his wife Tey.

Davis was puzzled at first. Naturally the Tutankhamun cartouche suggested that he had found the tomb of that king. But would his tomb really have been so lacking in ornament, so meagre? Would it really have been so thoroughly plundered by robbers?

Then a new find, only a few days later, banished his doubts. A few metres from the vault he came upon a pit, filled with large earthenware jars, in which there seemed to be nothing more than debris such as might arise from the furnishing of a pharaoh's tomb: dried wreaths, flowers and foliage, and little bags containing a mysterious powder that was later analysed by chemists as natron. The jars were closed with lids, except for one, the lid of which was cracked. It was wrapped in a cloth, and on the cloth Theodore Davis recognised the cartouche of Tutankhamun and a date, 'Year 6'.

To Davis it was now beyond doubt that the vault they had first uncovered must have been the tomb of the forgotten pharaoh and that ancient bandits had plundered the grave and left all the useless things behind in the neighbouring pit. 'I fear that the Valley of the Tombs is now exhausted,' wrote Davis, and brought his work to an end.

This resigned decision was the most momentous in the eventful life of Theodore M. Davis. Worn out by his years of excavation in West Thebes, emaciated by the merciless sun, often struggling for breath in the shimmering dust, seeking shelter and coolness in vain in the muggy, sickly-smelling shafts of tombs, Davis had come to the end of his strength. The copper tycoon from Newport was not to know the glory of making the greatest discovery in archaeology.

For six years, from 1903 to 1909, Davis had searched through the Valley of the Kings with unbelievable *élan*; he had begun where another had already given up. Seven tombs with inscriptions, and nine without any marking, had been found by this enthusiastic American, and each of the discoveries had been like the proverbial search for a needle in a haystack, each find a triumph, each negative dig a personal defeat. Who could blame him if he now no longer wanted to go on, could not go on? What in the world was he supposed to discover still, in this godammed Valley of the Kings?

4　The Earl of Carnarvon: a lord and his lackey

He and Howard Carter owed their success not to a stroke of good luck but to the patient following-out of a logical theory.

Leonard Woolley

George Edward Stanhope Molyneux Herbert, born on 26th June, 1866, the son of a British statesman, Henry Howard Molyneux Herbert, and his wife Evelyn, the only daughter of the Right Honourable Earl of Chesterfield, loved two things above all: horses and cars. With his horses, this aristocrat, who became Earl of Carnarvon on the death of his father, never had any trouble; but with cars. . . The British law dating from 1865, which set a speed limit of 6 m.p.h. and prescribed that a man with a red flag had to walk in front of a self-propelled vehicle, so annoyed him that he maintained two of his cars in France. Only later did he apply for a motor licence at home; his was the third in the United Kingdom.

It was the motor-car, too, which turned Lord Carnarvon into a disciple of archaeology, in a rather gruesome manner. In 1901, his wife, Lady Almina, was taking the cure at the German spa of Bad Schwalbach. Lord Carnarvon, with his chauffeur Edward Trotman, set out on the journey to fetch her. He himself was driving when, in trying to avoid an ox-cart, he left the road and overturned. The chauffeur was thrown out, but Carnarvon was trapped under the car. He suffered severe concussion and burns on the legs; one wrist was broken, his jaw and palate were injured, and for a time he lost his sight.

For the rest of his life, Lord Carnarvon never fully recovered from this accident, which entailed several follow-up operations. He was troubled above all by difficulties in breathing, and his doctors advised him to avoid the dampness of an English winter. In 1903 Carnarvon spent the year's end for the first time in Egypt, and in doing so met that species of man that had interested him ever since his college days: those scientifically-trained moles that burrow in the ground for relics of the past – men who indeed 'make' history. As he wrote at the time, 'It had always been my wish and intention even as far back as 1889 to start excavating, but for one reason or another I had never been able to begin.'

This had been one of the many whims which the rich lord had entertained. From earliest childhood he had been accustomed to do unusual things. While his father was alive, he bore the title Lord Porchester, and grew up on the vast family property of Highclere, near Newbury, in the midst of broad acres, shielded from the rest of the world. He could ride even before he went to school; that is to say, Lord Porchester didn't go to school; the teacher came to him. After he had done his work, he would gallop his pony through the woodlands or fish in the ancient ponds for pike, and perhaps gather water-lilies. Up to the age of nine, 'Porchy' spent a dreamily carefree childhood. Then his mother died in giving birth to her third daughter.

Two aunts, Lady Gwendolen Herbert and Lady Portsmouth, took charge of the children – which entailed all sorts of complications, because Lady Gwendolen, good-natured and indulgent, allowed almost everything, and Lady Portsmouth, unyielding and strict, forbade almost everything. Aunt Gwendolen would give Porchy a saw; Lady Portsmouth would take it away from him, tie it up in blue ribbon and hang it on the wall as a terrible warning.

Porchy escaped from this endless conflict when his father

sent him to public school, to Eton, where every British aristo-crat had to spend a few years of his life. There he learnt Latin, Greek and German. French he knew anyway: he had been brought up on it by his mother and teachers. But he didn't like Eton, and so his father had him return to Highclere, where the young lord had a private tutor at his disposal.

At nineteen, he entered Trinity College, Cambridge, and here Porchy's future course in life gradually suggested itself. It became evident that the free and easy ways of his early child-hood had appealed to him, and that he was probably not pre-pared ever again to give them up completely. He was fond of every form of sport, especially those to do with horses and water, and it gave him the greatest pleasure to look for things, to collect and to explore. He scoured all the antique shops within reach for old cups, engravings and drawings, and he put in a request to the college administration for the wood panelling in his room to be cleaned of its disfiguring layers of paint.

In the meantime, Porchy's father had built a villa in Porto Fino, on the Italian Riviera. Here the undergraduate spent his summer vacations, and here he became a reckless yachtsman. No squall was too fierce, no waves too high, to prevent him from putting to sea. His sister, Lady Burghclere, tells of a sailing adventure that befell him off the coast of Sicily. Porchy hired a boat, rowed by two fishermen, to take him out to his ship, anchored at sea. Exactly half-way between ship and shore, the fishermen dropped their oars, became threatening and demanded money; otherwise they would throw him into the water. Carnarvon kept calm, and indicated to the fishermen that they should pass him his dressing-case. This they did, expecting him to produce money; instead, the two men found themselves looking down the barrel of a revolver.

'Either you row me ashore or you'll be shot,' said Carnarvon very calmly, in his fine English way. No lord was ever rowed ashore so fast! As his sister wrote later: 'The chuckle with which he recalled what was to him an eminently delectable episode still remains with his hearer.'

That was the kind of adventure he was looking for; that was how he could show his mettle. So it was hardly surprising that, at the end of his college days in 1887, he took it into his head to go round the world in a sailing boat. With a skipper, crew, cook and ship's doctor, Porchy set sail from Porto Fino to Vigo, in the Spanish province of Pontevedra; from there he laid course for the Cape Verde Islands, off the west coast of Africa, and after a six-week crossing the *Aphrodite* reached the West Indies. Porchy sailed on southwards – there was as yet no Panama Canal – and landed at the Brazilian city of Recife, where he allowed himself and the crew a rest of two weeks. From Rio de Janeiro the *Aphrodite* made for the Argentinian capital of Buenos Aires.

There, the appearance of the British adventurer caused such a stir that Porchester had to give a reception on board for the Argentinian president. The season was already far advanced, and Carnarvon's captain thought it would be suicide to round Tierra del Fuego and the tip of South America at that time of year – and, moreover, in a sailing-boat. Lord Porchester may have been reckless but he was not stupid, and so he hoisted the Blue Peter for home. The other side of the globe, Australia and Japan, he saw in the following years. He had just got back from Japan when his father died. Porchy was now the fifth Earl of Carnarvon.

Lord Carnarvon's passion for archaeology was encouraged by an influential friend, Sir William Garstin. Sir William was at that time adviser to the Cairo Ministry of Public Works, which was responsible for the Department of Antiquities. That was how far things had gone in 1906.

I may say that at this period [wrote Lord Carnarvon] I knew nothing whatever about excavating, so I suppose with the idea of keeping me out of mischief, as well as keeping me employed, I was allotted a site at the top of Sheik Abdel Gurna. I had scarcely been operating for 24 hours when we suddenly struck what seemed to be an untouched burial pit. This gave rise to much excitement in the Antiquities Department, which soon simmered down when the pit was found to be unfinished. There, for six weeks, enveloped in clouds of dust, I stuck to it day in and day out. Beyond finding a large mummified cat in its case, which now graces the Cairo Museum, nothing whatsoever rewarded my strenuous and very dusty endeavours. This utter failure, however, instead of disheartening me had the effect of making me keener than ever.

Lord Carnarvon very soon realised that no amount of zeal could make up for a modicum of expert knowledge. After weeks and months of vain effort in the sand of El Qurna, the impetuous Englishman sent his workmen home, went to Cairo and consulted the head of the Department of Antiquities. He grumbled that he had been allotted nothing but a long-since worked-out area, which was incapable of yielding anything but stones. Maspero replied that the chances of making a find were almost as great everywhere; it just needed certain preconditions, and for that, expert knowledge and experience would not come amiss. Carnarvon understood: the highly-placed men who seemed to have a monopoly of Egyptian antiquity were not so keen on excavators who brought with them only money and nothing else.

'Whom would you recommend to me?' asked his lordship in his excellent French.

Maspero, it seemed, was ready for the question. He knew an Englishman there who was at the moment virtually unemployed; he kept his head above water by painting. Archaeologically, he was a most talented man called Carter, a pupil of Flinders Petrie, and he had previously been an inspector in the Department of Antiquities. Unfortunate circumstances had forced him to resign the post; now he was painting pictures for tourists.

Carnarvon was not exactly enthusiastic about this suggestion. Naturally, he would much rather have worked with one of the great archaeologists, with Flinders Petrie, Wallis Budge or James Henry Breasted. But Maspero's advice was not to be mistaken, and he alone could decide the success or failure of such an enterprise.

Once a year the government Commission for Antiquities met and issued digging-licences; Maspero was its chairman. Excavation areas were allocated, on condition that half of all finds were to be handed over. Even if an excavator discovered, after only a few days, that he had drawn a blank with his claim, nothing was of any avail; he had to wait for a year before he could receive a new digging-licence for a different spot. In any case, the most fruitful spots were allotted to natives. In Luxor these were mostly dealers in antiquities who, because of their knowledge, were at an advantage.

Maspero wanted to give Carter a chance. His resignation had been made under political pressure; Maspero knew the young Englishman's abilities and at the time had tried everything to keep him; he had implored Carter in vain to apologise.

Carnarvon didn't need long to reflect. 'Good,' he said, 'Where is this Mr. Carter? We'll give it a try!'

When the two met for the first time, it was anything but love at first sight. But for the next sixteen years, for better or for worse, these two men, so alike superficially and yet so completely different, were to be in each other's hands — Carnarvon, then forty-one, immensely rich, light-hearted, who regarded archaeology as a fascinating pastime and an opportunity to build up a collection; Carter, thirty-three, impecunious, resigned, wrapped up in himself, a failure whose life had been robbed of its content. It was from the beginning a kind of love-hate relationship; each had need of the other. Carter received one British pound per day, rounded up to £400 a year; for that he had to dig and keep his mouth shut.

What Carter thought of Carnarvon he wrote in 1923, in his book *The Tomb of Tut-ankh-Amen*, and anyone aware of Carter's usual reserve will know that what he wrote there came from the soul. He was inveighing against the widespread notion that archaeology was not really work, but some kind of amusement. Without naming Carnarvon, he wrote:

Excavation is [thought to be] a sort of super-tourist
amusement, carried out with the excavator's own money if
he is rich enough, or with other people's money if he can
persuade them to subscribe it, and all he has to do is to
enjoy life in a beautiful winter climate and pay a gang of
natives to find things for him. It is the dilettante
archaeologist, the man who rarely does any work with his
own hands, but as often as not is absent when the actual
discovery is made, who is largely responsible for this opinion. The serious excavator's life is frequently monotonous
and. . . quite as hard-working as that of any other member
of society.

Although his lordship's name is not mentioned, there is no
doubt that it was he whom Carter had in mind: *he* spent the
winter in the pleasant climate of Luxor; *he* was not in Egypt
when Carter discovered the tomb of Tutankhamun; *he* was rich
enough to carry out excavations with his own money. These few
lines are a clear indication of the love-hate that bound Carter to
Carnarvon. He hated him, his view of life, his nature, his
money, but he was dependent on him if he wanted to work.
In the concession for the spring of 1907, Maspero had allocated the two Englishmen an area that lay north-west of the spot
where Carnarvon had until then been digging under his own
management, in Deir el Bahari. From the very first day he
made it clear who was the boss; he was in command; Carter had
only to serve as adviser. His lordship chose the *reises*, the
foremen, who in turn recruited the army of workmen. These
offered themselves in large numbers, for there was no work in
El Qurna and the neighbouring villages. Between 75 and 275
men and children worked for the Englishmen's team, led by
Mansur Mohammed el-Hashash, Mohammed Abd el-Ghaffer
and Ali Hussein.
Carnarvon, whose chief concern was the largest possible
yield of finds for his Egyptian collection, lived in constant fear
of being cheated by his workmen. So he gave orders that as soon
as a tomb was found, as few workmen as possible were to come

in contact with it. At every little discovery, work had to stop at once, until he or Carter was present. Carnarvon not only organised the timetable; he also laid down where digging was to take place. Full of pride he kept a diary of the excavation. In it can be read:

> After perhaps 10 days work at Deir el Bahari in 1907, we came upon what proved to be an untouched tomb. I shall never forget the first sight of it. There was something extaordinarily modern about it. Several coffins were in the tomb, but the first that arrested our attention was a white brilliantly painted coffin with a pall loosely thrown over it, and a bouquet of flowers lying just at its foot. There these coffins had remained untouched and forgotten for 2,500 years. The reason for the sepulchre being inviolate was soon apparent. There was no funerary furniture, and evidently the owners of the coffins were poor people, and they or their relations had put all the funeral money they were able to spend into the ornamental coffins that contained their bodies.

A few weeks later, the heat at Deir el Bahari had become almost unbearable; a further entry in Carnarvon's diary runs:

> The results of this season were very poor, still one day we thought that we had at last found something which had every appearance of an untouched tomb some 400 yards from the Temple of Deir el Bahari. In the morning, I rode out, and no sooner did I see Carter's face than I knew something unpleasant and unforseen had occurred. Alas! What looked promising the day before turned out to be merely a walled-up sort of stable where the ancient Egyptian foreman had tethered his donkey and kept his accounts.

The manifest failure of the first digging campaign made Carnarvon realise that the experienced Carter should at least select the spots at which they should set their spades. Leadership of the enterprise, however, was to remain in his lordship's hands; Carter agreed – what else could he do?

For the following year's work he selected three sites that seemed to him promising. These were: 1. a spot a few metres north of the village mosque, where, according to statements by the natives, there was supposed to be a tomb; 2. a place further north between the hills of the village of Drah Abu el Nagga and the fertile land; 3. an area on the north side of Deir el Bahari. Carnarvon was anxious.

Work was begun at Site 1. The first week went by without even the smallest find, which gratified Carnarvon. When the second week remained equally unproductive, his lordship called his private archaeologist to account. Did he still expect anything from his excavations? Would it not be better to start somewhere else? No, replied Carter; his lordship must be patient. Carter was fairly sure of what he was doing. If the natives, especially the inhabitants of El Qurna, spoke of a tomb that they had heard of, then this tomb existed, although they would long since have cleared it of anything that was not nailed down, and sold it on the black market. So he went on digging.

At the beginning of the third week he came upon the tomb, between vast heaps of rubble. It was indeed almost empty, but

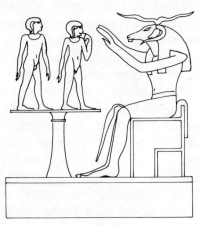

Khnum at the potter's wheel creating men.

it dated from the beginning of the 18th Dynasty and was significant on account of its excellently preserved inscriptions and reliefs. These identified it as the last resting-place of a king's son called Teta-Ky, and the tomb contained, amongst numerous scenes, a full-length relief of Queen Ahmes-Nofretari, mother of the pharaoh Amenophis I, one of the few queens to be worshipped as a divinity during her lifetime. A whole pile of wooden funeral statues and little wooden coffins, which the grave-robbers had obviously considered worthless, also gladdened the heart of the collector Carnarvon; he had made finds as an excavator for the first time.

His lordship was pressing. Once he had acquired the taste he wanted to make a new discovery every day if possible. Carter had hardly recorded the tomb of Teta-Ky, i.e. sketched the reliefs, inscriptions and ground plan, when work was transferred to Site 2.

For three days Carter and his men dug at a spot some 150 metres north-east of the approach to the valley of Deir el Bahari; then once more he made a find: this time it was a tomb of the 17th Dynasty. Since the name of its one-time inhabitant could not be discovered, and because it was the ninth tomb in the vicinity, Carter called it Tomb No. 9. They had to remove unbelievable masses of debris and potsherds before the entrance could be freed. First to come to light were a couple of naked mummies that had been laid to eternal rest there at some later period, and subsequently plundered.

On the threshold to the antechamber lay two wooden tablets, which claimed Carter's close attention. Both were coated with gesso and painted with hieratic script-signs. Carter sought help from the Oxford Egyptologist Francis Llewellyn Griffith, one of the most brilliant linguists at the time. The Professor examined the find and became wide-eyed. 'Carter', he said, 'I congratulate you. You've made a historical find of extraordinary importance!' Carter looked at him doubtfully. The Professor held out the tablet to him. 'This is the history of General Kamose, who freed Egypt from Hyksos rule, an important document, you lucky devil!'

Carnarvon was not unduly enthusiastic about the find; it was not an object for a collector of antiquities – it was only of historical interest.

A horde of Asiatic horsemen – until then Egypt had never seen a man on horseback – had pressed into the land of the Nile in about 1650 B.C., settled in the Nile delta and even founded their own capital, Avaris. The Hyksos, 'Princes of the Foreign Lands', ruled over Egypt for a hundred years, until Sekenenre, a Theban city-prince, took the field against the Hyksos king Apopi in the delta. Sekenenre was killed, but he had two sons. The elder was Kamose, the Kamose who was the subject of the wooden tablet. Kamose avenged his father's death and drove the Hyksos out of their capital. His younger brother, Ahmose pursued the foreign invaders right into south Palestine and, on the death of Kamose, he became the first king of the 18th Dynasty.

At the end of the digging-season in April 1908, Tomb No. 9 was filled in again. Carter, who had got no further than examining the antechamber, believed the main chamber might conceal even greater treasures, and he was afraid that in the absence of the excavators during the summer it might be robbed.

But in 1909 [wrote Howard Carter] owing to the depth and sliding nature of the rubbish, a more extensive excavation had to be made to open the main chambers. Little more was found here than further examples of pots, a child's coffin too decayed for preservation, and a reed burial of a poorer and much later man. The tomb consisted of a court formed by low stone and mortar walls, with a cutting in the centre leading to the entrance: this entrance or doorway gave access to a passage, cut in the rock, some six metres in length, which led to a rectangular chamber that apparently formed one of the sepulchural repositories. Cut in the floor of the chamber, on the west side, was a shaft nearly three metres deep, giving ingress to two other chambers, one above the other.

It hardly seems credible that such a mass of pottery as was found in the rubbish outside could have all come from so small a tomb, and one is inclined to think that the greater part must have come from some neighbouring and perhaps larger tomb.

Carter was to be proved right. A few days later his workmen came upon a well-preserved stone wall only a few centimetres below ground level. Carter dug along the wall; 10 metres, 20 metres, finally 40 metres of stonework were laid bare. The excavator asked Carnarvon for more workmen; his lordship engaged a few children. For a couple of piastres they carried rush-baskets of debris from early morning to mid-day.

The wall, 2.60 metres wide, became ever longer; finally it made a turn, and indicated the extent of a building. In the north an approach came to light. On the inner side, worked blocks of stone indicated that they had originally belonged to an older structure and had been put to new use in this project. Lord Carnarvon noticed that 'the size of the blocks and their chiselling were similar to the masonry of the Mentuhotep temple at Deir el Bahari'.

The laying bare of the vast edifice that Carter had come upon, and which posed endless questions, took up the whole of the 1909 season. Archaeologists from all over the world, who inspected the outlines of the walling, were unable to explain its significance and purpose.

About 800 metres away to the south-west lay the terrace temple of Hatshepsut and the funerary temple of Mentuhotep, from the 11th Dynasty, though not much of this building was to be seen. An inclined ramp once led up to the Mentuhotep temple, which rested on 140 octagonal pillars. In the middle of the terrace was a small pyramid, and under it a false tomb, in which lay a mummified royal statue. The real tomb had been hewn 150 metres deep into the rock behind the temple. Mentuhotep's funerary temple was not so close under the steep rock-wall of Deir el Bahari as the neighbouring Hatshepsut temple, which had been covered by stones and scree that had been crumbling away for thousands of years. Both temples had been excavated. Now Carter had come upon a third building.

Was it a monument, a temple? From what period did the remains derive? Who had erected the building?

A first answer to these questions was provided by a couple of blocks of stone that were drawn out of the sand a few days after the start of excavations in the autumn of 1910. Carter noticed inscriptions: the names of Queen Hatshepsut, Maat-ka-ra, and the architect and 'Second Priest of Amun', Ipuemre. Soon afterwards, a few similar blocks became visible, built into the stonework. His lordship was full of enthusiasm. 'These, together with a single block bearing the name of the great queen's famous architect, Senmut, clearly proved that the wall which we had found must have belonged to some building of Hatshepsut's reign.'

The terrace temple of Queen Hatshepsut must have been linked in some way with the building discovered by Carter. This was suggested by the road that led from one to the other in a straight line. Carter remembered the buildings of Giza and Abusir, and suddenly the significance and purpose of this building became clear to him. It was a so-called valley temple, the entrance-building to the main temple. From there, along a sphinx avenue – the statues all bore the head of Hatshepsut — the visitor reached the entrance to the actual temple, a pylon, which today has disappeared. What Carter didn't know at the time was that a line between the terrace temple of Hatshepsut and the valley temple, if produced, ended exactly in the axis of the Amun temple at Karnak. Why it does so remains a mystery to this day.

Under the foundations of the valley temple Carter came upon several simple tombs that had been hewn out of the solid rock. Not one had escaped plundering; some had obviously been ransacked twice, for the excavators found traces from the Middle Kingdom and relics from the reign of Queen Hatshepsut. Fragments of one and the same memorial plaque were discovered in two different tombs (No. 27 and No. 31).

In the tomb designated No. 25 stood an unopened coffin, but it was unadorned, and the mummy gave no indication of the name and lifetime of the dead person; only a bronze mirror with ivory handle and a necklace with gold and semi-precious stones excited the particular interest of Lord Carnarvon. Howard Carter, on the other hand, occupied himself with some 200 fragments of wood, little panels and splinters of cedar, ebony and ivory. His experience told him that they were pieces of a jewel casket, and such caskets usually bore inscriptions that gave information about the owner. While Carnarvon supervised the excavations, Carter withdrew for a few days and assembled this thousand-year-old puzzle. He succeeded, and what he suspected proved true. The casket, embellished with delicate ornaments, bore the name Amenophis IV, a largely unknown pharaoh of the 12th Dynasty, and the name of the 'Keeper of the department of Food', Kemen. On the lid of the casket Sebek was invoked, the 'Lord of Hent', a place in the Faiyum where the kings of the 12th Dynasty were particularly active.

By 1911 the British excavating team had dug over an area of 1,100 square metres to a depth of 8 metres; sand, debris and scree had been piled up elsewhere with the help of 275 workmen from the village of El Qurna, a good half of them children. Measured against the expense, the yield in finds was modest – at least for a collector like Lord Carnarvon. The costs were unexpectedly high, and he was undoubtedly dissatisfied with the result. Even their last hope, that they had made a really big discovery, proved to be delusive. A gigantic tomb, No. 37, did indeed contain sixty-five coffins, but they were without decoration or adornment, and had been plundered into the bargain. Some bandits had obviously used the tomb as a store-room.

A close friend of his lordship, Wallis Budge, described Carnarvon and his passion for collecting thus:

The dry bones of Egyptian philology left him cold, and when Egyptologists squabbled over dates and chronology in his presence his chuckle was a delightful thing to hear. But he was fired by the exquisite beauty of form and colour which he found in the antiquities of Egypt, and his collection of small Egyptian antiquities at Highclere Castle is, for its size, probably the most perfect known. He only cared for the best, and nothing but the best would satisfy him, and having obtained the best he persisted in believing that there must be somewhere something better than the best!

He could be regarded as a snob, and he certainly was in some respects; the unique, the distinctive, exerted a magnetic influence over him. When it was a matter of antiquities money played no part; then he agreed with the British Assyriologist, Sir Henry Rawlinson, that 'it is easier to get money than antiques'.

Although he was so rich – perhaps precisely because he was – Lord Carnarvon had a very special attitude to money; at any rate he didn't like to spend it in vain. The thought that he might have made a bad investment, as now in these excavations, seemed to him almost unbearable. Sir Leonard Woolley, the discoverer of the royal tombs at Ur, who dug in Egypt for the University of Pennsylvania, relates an episode that was typical of the excavating lord from Highclere.

One day a man called on Carnarvon at his hotel in Cairo and said, 'You collect antiquities?'

'Yes,' said Carnarvon.

'Well,' said the man, 'I've got something wonderful. Wonderful!'

'What is it?' asked Carnarvon. 'Show me.'

'Oh,' said the man, 'I can't show you here. It's in my house.'

'Well,' said Carnarvon, 'if it is as good as all that I'd like to see it.'

'Yes,' said the man, 'you can come and see it, but on my terms.'

'Oh, what are those?'

'You have got to come at night, and you have got to submit to being blindfolded and I shall take you to my house, because I don't want you to know where it is. And,' he added, 'you have got to bring with you £300 in gold.'

Strange conditions! Who in the Egypt of those days would have gone, with bound eyes and £300 in gold coins in his pocket, to see an unknown man? But when it was a question of antiquities, Lord Carnarvon knew no fear. 'Oh certainly, I will do that,' he said, and added, 'is that the price you're asking?'

'Yes,' said the man. 'It's £300, and I'm not taking a penny less, but for £300 you can have the things if you like.'

That night after dinner three men arrived. They took Carnarvon outside, bound his eyes, put him into a carriage, drove a little way, got out and led him into a house. There they removed the blindfold.

'Where are the antiquities?' asked Lord Carnarvon.

They showed him two objects. The first was a vase of polished stone with a gold cover, and on the cover was the cartouche of a pharaoh of the 1st Dynasty, a wonderful piece. The second was even more important: a magnificent flint knife with a gold handle incised with animal figures, a pre-dynastic antiquity.

Carnarvon didn't reflect for long: 'All right, I'll buy them.' He paid the £300, which was dirt cheap, his eyes were bound once more, and he was taken back to his hotel.

In his suite he examined the pieces more closely, and the more he looked at them the more his suspicion grew that he had seen them somewhere before. His first thought was that they might be copies, and so the next day he went to the museum. In the glass case containing some of the oldest and most valuable finds, laid out on red velvet, Carnarvon saw a patch of velvet darker than the rest, which had faded in the sun. He noticed a second, longish patch, which corresponded to the size of his flint knife, and it became clear to him: his latest acquisitions had been stolen from the museum. His lordship was sitting on stolen property.

Eventually he went to Gaston Maspero, the director of the museum. 'Professor Maspero,' he said, 'I want to ask you, have you had any valuable things stolen from the museum of late?'

'Good heavens!' said Maspero. 'What makes you say that?'

'Well,' he said, 'I've got a suspicion about it. It is really true?'

'Yes,' sighed Maspero, 'it is. We have lost two great treasures.'

'Have you taken any steps to recover them?'

'No,' said Maspero, 'I daren't.'

'I've got these objects,' said Carnarvon. 'I got them from a man whom I couldn't possibly trace – he was very careful about that; I paid £300 for them. Would you like to buy them back? If so, pay me the £300 and you shall have them, because they are not mine.'

'That is more than generous of you,' said Maspero, 'Please bring them along.'

So Carnarvon took the two objects to Maspero's office and asked for a cheque. The museum director wrote it out and said 'Now of course you will give me an official receipt.'

'Give you a receipt?' said Carnarvon, 'Not on your life. I'm not going to give you a receipt for stolen goods.'

'Without a receipt I cannot give the cheque,' said Maspero.

'Without the money I'm not going to hand over the objects,' replied Carnarvon. 'Either you give me a cheque without a receipt or I walk away with the two things.'

Maspero thought for a while. Finally he sent for an attendant and said, 'Here is a form; I want a signature to it. Go out into the bazaar and get hold of the first man you like; give him sixpence and get him to sign his name to this.'

The attendant came back, and cheque and finds changed hands; the finds are still to be seen today in Cairo Museum. It is also known today who was behind this ominous art robbery: it was none other than our old friend Emil Brugsch.

A quite different episode shows that mixture of shrewdness and whimsicality so typical of Carnarvon. He went to California to fish, and on the way made a stop in New York, where he sought an interview with a well-known financial magnate. His lordship wanted his advice as to whether he should buy certain shares. The answer was No, a clear, definite no. Carnarvon looked at his interlocutor for a moment, then expressed his thanks and went straight to a telegraph office, where he sent a wire to London: 'Buy shares at all costs!' After which he happily boarded his train for California.

When he came back to New York six weeks later, his adviser

was in a fine state; he had heard about the fantastic gains the Englishman had made by not following his advice, and was naturally awaiting with mixed feelings the announcement of a visit from his lordship. But when Carnarvon arrived, he was full of praise for the American; his generous bit of advice had not only paid for the wickedly expensive holiday in California, but had also significantly increased his capital.

The financier was puzzled. 'But Lord Carnarvon, I advised you *against* buying,' he said uncertainly.

'Oh, yes,' replied Carnarvon, 'I know you said that, but of course I saw that you wished me to understand the reverse.'

There was a moment of thoughtful silence, then the great financier broke into roars of laughter. He held out his hand and said, 'Pray consider this house your home whenever you return to America.'

Anyone who asked his lordship whether this financier was the most interesting person he had met on his American trip would receive a characteristic answer. 'Oh, dear no! The most interesting man by far was the brakesman on the railway cars to California. I spent hours talking with him.'

As his sister, Lady Burghclere, wrote of him:

> Carnarvon had indeed an indefinable charm, which, when he chose to exert it, attracted the confidence of all sorts and conditions of men and women, whether brakesmen or millionaires, archaeologists, generals or peasants. Gifted with a fine memory and the scholarly instinct of thoroughness in any work or recreation he undertook, he had touched life at so many points that he could readily establish contacts with a great variety of folk, and a certain whimsical wit entirely his own gave savour and pungency to his talk.

In spite of his odd passions, Lord Carnarvon was an affable man. He formed contacts even with little people; fellahin were among his friends as much as highly-placed government officials. His ready wit, his sense of humour, were well known. His mentality was thus in sharp contrast to that of the eccentric, quiet, self-contained excavator Howard Carter, who could have lived for a year or more on what the peer, with his mania for collecting, often spent in a day.

In 1912, after five years' work in Thebes, Carnarvon was convinced of the fruitlessness of the excavations in the Valley of the Kings and applied abruptly for a new licence somewhere in Lower Egypt, preferably in the Nile delta. The Department of Antiquities assigned him the ancient Xois, near the mouth of the Nile. Reluctantly, Carter accompanied his patron to Lower Egypt, but the venture lasted only two weeks. It seemed as though the gods had sent a sign: hundreds of poisonous cobras defended the ancient Xois; every thrust of the spade became a danger to life, and in addition an unbearable heat lay over the delta. Carnarvon gave up.

For his lordship the question now arose whether it was worth applying for a new digging licence at all. The attractive places, such as Saqqara, Amarna or Thebes, were firmly in the hands of the French, Germans or Americans. The Valley, Carter suggested, was still good for a discovery. But Carnarvon brushed that aside. Carter persisted and eventually wrung from his boss permission for a new, final attempt. Carnarvon applied once more for a digging-licence for the Valley of the Kings. Then came the outbreak of the First World War.

Hathor of Thebes was represented as a woman with a cow's head.

5 First World War: the King's Messenger

Would that we had died by the hand of the Lord in the land of Egypt, when we sat by the fleshpots, when we did eat bread to the full.

Exodus 16.3

The Germans attacked Verdun, the Emperor Franz Joseph died in Vienna, the United States of America entered the war – and a man with rope and pick tramped through the Valley of the Kings, solitary and self-forgetting: Howard Carter.

Even Carter didn't escape the First World War entirely, but of all the archaeologists he undoubtedly drew the best lot. As a King's Messenger, as a diplomatic courier, with the Middle East as his field of operations, he was based at G.H.Q. in Cairo, and since the Middle East was in any case occupied by enemies, i.e. Turks, the courier Howard Carter was not exactly over-worked. Most of his 'diplomatic missions' took him to the Valley of the Kings, to generals and potentates who had laid down their batons and sceptres more than 3,000 years before. There he tapped rock after rock, stone after stone, in the hope of coming upon a hollow space, on loose rock. The war was far away.

The solitary walks in the Valley of the Kings were certainly

unnerving. Anyone who saw Carter must have thought a mad-
man was at work. Centimetre by centimetre he tapped on the
walls, and listened, as though he were expecting an answer from
within. But no answer ever came – not there, at any rate.

Eventually, with a couple of fellahin, he wandered out of the
area to a gorge in the Libyan desert two kilometres away, with
the unpronounceable name of Wadi e Taqa e Zaide. Winding
paths to the summits of the cliffs, the remains of ancient stone
huts, and hieratic inscriptions on the rocks gave Carter reason
to suspect that officials and workmen of the Theban necropolis
had once been active there.

My preliminary investigations [Carter noted in his
report] consisted of a cursory examination of the site,
commencing at the south-east end and working along to
the north-west, each valley being taken in turn. With the
help of a small staff of men, soundings were made in places
thought to contain tombs such as could be easily plundered
by the native tomb-robbers who have been systematically
working this site. Beside the inscriptions on the rocks I
have marked H.C. 1916, so that any future investigator
will know that some attempt at least has been made to note
or copy them.

Carter discovered various rock-tombs in the side valleys, and
numerous inscriptions, but these were, all told, of minor significance. He hadn't in fact placed great hopes on the enterprise; the wadi was too remote, too 'barren'. Kings were buried
in the Valley of the Kings, queens in the Valley of the Queens,
and the nobility and the rich lay in the Deir el Medineh or at El
Qurna. What was there for him to discover here?

All the same again and again he searched with his eyes the
sheer rock-walls in the Wadi e Taqa e Zaide. But nothing,
absolutely nothing, showed any trace of artificial working: only
rock, eternal rock. Carter himself didn't know what drove him
to climb the rock-wall, over a hundred metres high, from the
back. When he had reached the top and was looking down into

the narrow gorge, stones rattled and crashed into the depths. Their great leaps could be heard for several seconds. One stopped after only a short flight; its path had not been half as long as that of the others. Carter looked down; he had to crane right forward, to the edge of the perpendicular rock-wall. From there he could see where the stone had lodged: it was a small projection in the rock. But then he saw something else: a stone step – there was no doubt about it: the uppermost step of a flight that led into the rock. 70 metres above the valley bottom and 40 metres below the top of the cliff, a stairway went into the mountain. Who had hidden themselves so inaccessibly and impregnably from the world?

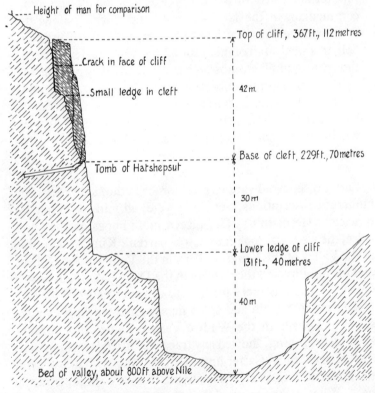

Section of cliff at the valley-head.

Howard Carter lowered himself on a rope down the almost perpendicular rock-wall, to a ledge some 20 metres below, barely 5 metres wide. From there he climbed down a crevice until he stood by the stone step. The hope of finding himself in the next moment before a treasure chamber glinting with gold was, however, frustrated. The passage at the bottom of the steps, which seemed to lead horizontally into the rock, was filled from floor to ceiling with debris. Below the ceiling of the blocked passage, 2.20 metres high, human moles had burrowed a tunnel just big enough to crawl through on their stomachs.

Carter didn't stop long to think: the passage must lead some-where; it must have fulfilled some purpose. Pushing a carbide lamp in front of him, he crawled into the mysterious fox-hole. The operation was the most dangerous, the most precarious, he had ever undertaken. He had no idea where the passage might lead, or whether the rock above and below him was firm. A single careless movement and he would have found his own grave. He crawled on, pushing the lamp in front, on and on. The passage became longer and longer, turned corners and went up and down. It was undoubtedly a trial tunnel dug by grave-robbers. 'A dangerous performance,' Carter reported, 'but one which I myself had to imitate, though with better tackle. . .' If the lamp went out, as Carter knew, it would mean the end of the oxygen; his life then would no longer be worth a rap.

The lamp didn't go out. When Carter had crawled 29 metres, the passage ended abruptly; the grave-robbers had given up. The risk he had taken only dawned to the full on Carter when he again felt the rays of the low October sun on his face. But the adventure was not yet over. The rope by which he had lowered himself from the top was now useless. How could he climb over 40 metres up an almost vertical rock-wall with that? He looked into the abyss 70 metres below, and asked his men above to untie the rope and throw it down to him. He himself tied the lower end to a projection of rock. To shin down the rope was far easier than climbing vertically to the top; of that Carter was sure, and so he tried to reach the valley bottom, and eventually succeeded.

With the certain feeling that he was on the track of an important discovery, Howard Carter decided to clear the debris from the passage. The available men would be sufficient. Long trails for carrying away the stone would not be necessary; it could simply be tipped over the side of the rock-platform. The problem was how to get himself and his men to the scene of operations without danger to life and limb. He solved the problem in a complicated technical manner. Beams of wood were brought to the cliff-top on pack animals. From there he lowered them by rope to the projection of rock at the entrance to the passage and knocked up a precarious arrangement of timber whose vital element was a projecting arm, with block and tackle. With this, *one* man at a time could pull himself up from the valley bottom and rope himself down again. Since there was never room for more than two or three men at the airy work-place, Carter laboured day and night in relays for three weeks.

Five stone steps led down to a doorway, beyond which a corridor 17 metres long ran at a slight incline into the mountain. It ended in an antechamber, exactly 9 square metres in size; on the right, a short inclined passage led into a burial chamber 5.40 metres by 5.30, and 3 metres high. In the middle of this chamber, after removing vast masses of debris, Carter came upon a sarcophagus of yellow sandstone. It was empty; the lid rested against the short side. Numerous hieroglyphs gave information about the creator of this remote labyrinth. Carter read, 'The hereditary Princess, great in favour and grace, mistress of all lands, king's daughter, king's sister, wife of the god, the great wife of the king, lady of the two lands, Hatshepsut.'

Hatshepsut! Carter was bewildered. Had he not, after immense labours, dug out the tomb of this mysterious queen thirteen years earlier in the Valley of the Kings? The more thoroughly he investigated the burial chamber the closer Carter came to the solution of the riddle. 'There were no traces that the tomb had ever contained a burial,' he wrote, 'the only objects that were found besides the sarcophagus and its lid being two

Tutankhamun's gold mask: pure gold and precious lapis lazuli symbolise union with the sun-god Re.

The Valley of the Kings after a water-colour by Howard Carter. Carter originally went to Egypt as a draughtsman and became an excavator by chance.

The entrance to the tomb of Tutankhamun (A) was covered over during the construction of the tomb of Rameses VI (B), and so became forgotten. Photograph from 1923.

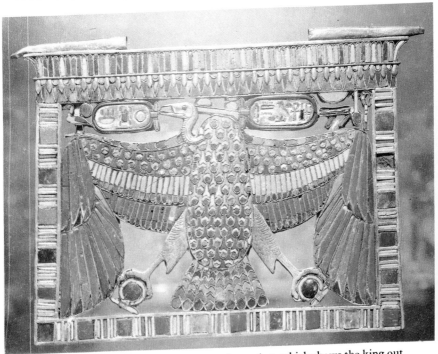

Above: Carter found this painted wooden casket, which shows the king out hunting, in the north-eastern corner of the antechamber to the tomb.
Below: A pendant from the Treasury, worked in gold and coloured glass, showing Nut, the goddess of the sky, as a vulture.

Above: Howard Carter (*in front*) accompanied every find under police protection as it was taken from the royal tomb to the near-by laboratory.

Below: Tutankhamun's dismantled chariots in the antechamber to the tomb.

After clearing the antechamber, Lord Carnarvon and Howard Carter (*right*), in the presence of numerous guests of honour, break open the sealed wall to the burial chamber. Through the narrow opening in the wall his lordship saw a vast gilded shrine.

The excavating team: (*from l-r*) Arthur Mace, Carter's secretary Richard Bethell, his assistant A. R. Callender, Carnarvon's daughter Evelyn and Howard Carter, Lord Carnarvon, Alfred Lucas and the photographer Harry Burton.

An exciting moment: Howard Carter (*kneeling*) and his assistant Callender at the opening of the fourth and last shrine.

The golden throne of the forgotten pharaoh. On the back-rest is an intimate scene of Tutankhamun and his wife Ankhesenamun. The Amarna style is unmistakable.

Wall painting in the burial chamber of the tomb: Ay, Tutankhamun's successor (*right*), dressed as a priest, performs the ceremony of 'opening the mouth' on the king, who has now become Osiris.

Carter (*second from left*) and Callender (*right*) remove part of the roof of the first shrine. The excavators could only dismantle this precious work of art after they had discovered the ancient method of construction.

A great day for Howard Carter: with a ceremonial stick from the treasure of the forgotten pharaoh, the archaeologist marks the re-opening of the tomb.

Lid of a chest inlaid with ebony and ivory. The king and his wife, represented in the style of the Amarna period, stroll in the garden.

The king as the god Horus harpooning hippopotami, into which the wicked god Seth and his companions have transformed themselves. The gilded wooden statue symbolises good in general.

This portrait head of Tutankhamun emerging from a lotus flower shows the pharaoh in his early years. The earlobes are pierced: earrings were then much in fashion.

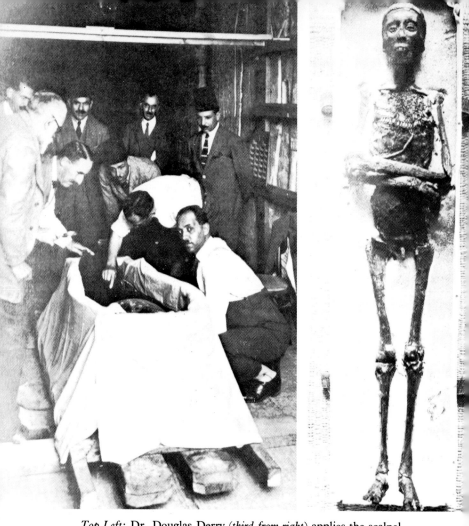

Top Left: Dr. Douglas Derry (*third from right*) applies the scalpel.
Top Right: The bare mummy of Tutankhamun.
Below: The forgotten pharaoh in his gold coffin.

Above: Two of the numerous alabaster vessels that were among the king's grave-gifts.

Left: What Carter saw after removing the shroud.

Relief from the small gilded shrine. Tutankhamun pours perfume on to the
outstretched hand of his wife Ankhesenamun.

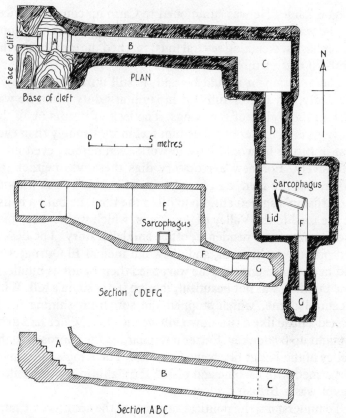

Plan of the tomb of Hatshepsut.

broken necks of pottery jars such as were used by workmen. Indeed, the state of the tomb tended in every way to show that it had been abandoned when in preparatory stage.'

Yes, that was the solution: Hatshepsut had had this secluded tomb constructed when she had still been married to her step-brother Tuthmosis II. Later, after his death on 30th April, 1490 B.C., when she herself was conducting the pharaoh's affairs, she had laid claim to a tomb in the Valley of the Kings. So she stopped work on her first tomb and began digging her tomb in Biban el Moluk.

In January 1917, Howard Carter ended the work in Wadi e

Taqa e Zaide. He was summoned to Cairo on courier service. But he was exercised by a further question: how had the stone sarcophagus, weighing several tons, reached the entrance to the tomb 70 metres up?

The question, it should be said, is still unresolved today.

Hardly had Carter fulfilled his military duty when he was back in the Valley of the Kings. The lack of results in all the previous efforts merely made him feel more strongly than ever that in future he would have to work even harder, even more intensively. For new exploratory digs there was neither the money nor the men, and in any case he couldn't start without his lordship's agreement. So to fill in the time, he built a house on the road to the Valley of the Kings, which was to serve him and Carnarvon as residence, office and laboratory. The design and plans were his own, and a few old men of El Qurna, who had been found unfit for the war, tried their hands as builders. The building was not beautiful, though it did sit on a hill. With a central dome, which stopped the sun from shining in, it looked a little like a run-down village mosque. Water had to be brought up by donkey. Carter now guarded the approach to the Valley of the Kings like some Cerberus. The King's Messenger was armed with carbine and pistol; the rights of war prevailed; Egypt was a British protectorate.

To understand the political situation of the country, we must take a look at its recent history. For hundreds of years Egypt had been under the sovereignty of the Ottomans. In the last century Mohammed Ali, an officer of Albanian origin, managed to organise a modern state. This system was extended by Abbas I and Said, who reformed taxation, abolished slavery, and built railways and the Suez Canal. To the industrial installations, Ismail Pasha added a postal and communications network. Under his regime the Suez Canal was opened and Egypt obtained greater independence from Turkey. But reforms cost money; the state was on the verge of bankruptcy. The French and British saw their chance, and each put a minister in the Egyptian cabinet.

A rising under Ahmed Pasha Arabi, formerly a doorkeeper at

a warehouse, brought the British on to the scene. They occupied the country, and Egypt became a condominium. Arabi Pasha had to board a British ship, on 26th December, 1882, and go into exile in Ceylon, where he lived for nineteen years. In 1901, impoverished and forgotten, he was allowed to return. He died ten years later in a little house in Heluan on the edge of the desert.

The British crown contemplated granting Egypt greater freedom and sovereignty, but this idea was dismissed in a report which Lord Dufferin was commissioned to make, and which he sent to London in October 1882. In it he declared that, in his view, 'European assistance in the various departments of Egyptian administration would be absolutely necessary for some time to come.' And he went on, '. . . it is frightful to contemplate the misery and misfortune which would be entailed on the population were these departments to be left unorganised by a few high-minded European officials.'

So Her Majesty's government retained an army of occupation in Egypt, and despatched officials and a consul-general, to whom in the last analysis the whole Egyptian state was subordinate. Officially, Egypt was still a Turkish province and had to pay the Sultan an annual tribute of £682,000 sterling. Political discussions could be held only with the authorisation of the Turkish foreign office; a declaration of war was no more permitted than a conclusion of peace. The Egyptian army was limited to 18,000 men. Outwardly, Turkish sovereignty could hardly be felt; the sultans in Constantinople continued in residence, but their rule was slackening.

On a visit to the Bosphorus, Lord Carnarvon badly wanted to exchange a few friendly words with Sultan Abdul Hamid II, nicknamed 'the Damned'. Sultan Abdul was one of the last exotic Ottoman rulers, a story-book figure, small, slim and sallow. He bathed every morning in milk, kept a harem of a hundred and, in light opera tradition, had a loved one outside the heavily guarded harem walls – a little blonde seller of gloves. She was called Flora Cordier and came from Belgium. One day her shop was shut. She was said to have gone home.

At all events, Abdul the Damned interested his lordship. But on the day when Carnarvon was preparing for the audience, with extra brass buttons sewn on his yachting jacket, a messenger informed him that the Sultan would be unable to receive him.

'Perhaps another day?'

'No, the Sultan feared no other day was available, but as a slight token of his esteem, he begged Lord Carnarvon's acceptance of the accompanying high order.'

It was quite a while before Carnarvon discovered the reason for this obvious rebuff. It lay many years back. His father had once been chairman of the Society for the Protection of the Armenians, one of the minorities persecuted by the Turks, and Abdul Hamid II, who lived in constant fear of assassination, thought, when he heard the name Lord Carnarvon, that the protector of the Armenians was standing at his palace gates and wanted to kill him. The news that the fourth Earl of Carnarvon had been dead for nearly ten years had not yet reached the Bosphorus.

In Egypt, especially in cultural matters, French influence was making itself increasingly felt. In better circles it was the fashion to speak French, and French was the official language at the court of the Khedive, and in government offices and the banks. The administration of the Suez Canal was French, in the same way as the administration of Egyptian antiquities; so with this language barrier, it was no wonder that the British occupation, which understandably enough was in any case unpopular, had an even harder time. This could account for many administrative difficulties in the field of archaeology.

The secret ruler of Egypt in the days of the great archaeological discoveries of Davis and Petrie was the Earl of Cromer; he had been in the Indian colonial service since 1872, and in 1883 took office as British consul-general in Cairo. On the Egyptian side the ruler was Tewfik Pasha, no great politician, no expert in European culture, no forceful character. Lord Cromer had an easy hand to play, but, as he said later, 'he [Tewfik] should be remembered with gratitude as "the Khedive who *allowed* Egypt to be reformed in spite of the Egyptians".'

The government and administration of the Egyptians, towards the end of the last century, was played out in the complacent splendour of musical comedy, and the reforms proudly announced by Lord Cromer were not exactly revolutionary. As he himself said:

> I had at one time to do nothing inconsistent with a speedy return to Egyptian self-government, or, at all events, a return to government by the hybrid coterie of Cairo, which flaunts before the world as the personification of Egyptian autonomy; whilst, at the same time, I was well aware that, for a long time to come, European guidance will be essential if the administration is to be conducted on sound principles.

The Khedive Tewfik, with whom Cromer had a thoroughly friendly relationship, died in 1892 and was succeeded by his son Hilmi, as Abbas II. In the same year, Sir Herbert Kitchener was appointed sirdar, or commander-in-chief of the Egyptian army. The British field-marshal, as he was later to become, had already served for ten years in the Egyptian army. He won back the Sudan and became its governor-general, chief of staff of the British army in the Boer War, commander-in-chief of the British forces in India, and later, in 1911, consul-general in Egypt. Lord Cromer retired in 1907 on health grounds. His successor, in a difficult situation, was in the first place Sir Eldon Gorst.

A nationalist movement was gaining ground and wanted the British out of the country; attacks on British soldiers, Christians and Europeans were increasing; the country was again going through a financial crisis; Europeans stopped investing. Sir Vincent Corbet, financial adviser to the Egyptian government, resigned his post; Sir William Garstin, adviser to the Minister of Public Works, was about to do the same, and so was Major Mitchell, adviser to the Minister of the Interior. Rumours were rife: Lord Cromer, when he left the country, was supposed to have carried away several million pounds from the Egyptian treasury.

Sir Eldon Gorst was the exact opposite of his predecessor. Lord Cromer had not spoken a word of Arabic; he had always dressed as an English gentleman, and had only sparse contacts with the people. Sir Eldon, on the other hand, appeared on the streets of Cairo dressed in Arab style and rode a pony to go shopping, or drove a motor-car from which he shouted 'Look out!' in best Arabic.

It was not very adroit of him, however, to appoint a Copt, i.e. an Egyptian Christian, as prime minister. The nationalists, most of them Mohammedans, were shocked, and their followers divided; in February 1910 the Christian Prime Minister was murdered by a Mohammedan nationalist. Now there were four parties in the country: the British and their sympathisers, the Khedive (viceroy by the grace of the Turkish Sultan) and his followers; the Copts; and the nationalists. The times were difficult and demanded a strong man.

This strong man was Lord Kitchener; the ennobled general from Ireland was a figure of authority. When he took office, the Cairo newspaper *Al Ahram*, which was anything but friendly towards the British, wrote, 'If we are to be ruled, let us be ruled by a manly man. Lord Kitchener's appointment should be welcome, since he is so well known to us. His justice in the army is proverbial, and Egypt is hungry for justice.'

The outbreak of the First World War prevented that Egyptian hunger for justice from being appeased. Lord Kitchener took over as minister of war at home, organised a volunteer army to begin with, and eventually put through general conscription. Egypt became a British protectorate; the viceroy was deposed, and the rights of war prevailed.

Archaeology and scientific exploration were now out of the question for some time. No sound of pick or spade, nor even the monotonous sing-song of the workmen, echoed back from the bleak rock walls in the Valley of the Kings. Even Carter had to limit his surveys; he wandered through the Valley now and then with a large-scale grid-map, inspecting every corner and ticking off every square metre that had already been turned over by excavators. It looked very important, and the old men and women left over from the war supposed it was something to do with defence.

The war not only made it impossible to dig, it also created in itself invisible trenches between archaeologists of different nationalities; it erected barriers and opened irreparable wounds.

Edouard Naville, Carter's teacher at Deir el Bahari, was a captain in the Swiss army and as president of the International Committee of the Red Cross he inspected prisoner-of-war camps in England, where Germans were interned. Naville had studied in Germany, and at Deir el Bahari he had worked alongside Germans for years, but all at once he became an anti-German and wrote savage tirades against the research methods of the 'Berlin' school. On the other side, the Berlin historian Eduard Meyer informed the American James Henry Breasted that he had nothing against him personally, but he could no longer have any relations with an American – and that was in 1922. Eduard Meyer lost two· sons in the war; the Frenchman Gaston Maspero mourned the death of a son, and so did the German excavator Adolf Erman.

While Howard Carter held the fort in his house on the road to the Valley of the Kings, Lord Carnarvon tried in his own way to come to terms with the war. Because of his poor state of health, he was unfit for military service. Anticipating a food shortage, he made preparations for the provisioning of the 253 souls of Highclere. At the outbreak of war, a hospital was established there, with which Lady Almina concerned herself. But in order to ensure better medical care, the hospital was soon transferred to London, and Lady Almina went with it. One of the first patients to be admitted to the new hospital in Bryanston Square was – Lord Carnarvon, with a perforated appendix. Three quarters of an hour later, said his surgeon, Sir Berkeley Moynihan, and it would have been all up with him. Carnarvon bore the whole business with British humour. He maintained that his sufferings were too acute to allow him to die.

From Egypt Carter sent accounts of the situation – not war reports, but reports of the discovery of the second Hatshepsut tomb, of his soundings in the Valley of the Kings, new thoughts, old theories. He was, he wrote, on the track of a really big discovery.

Although it was wartime and sea voyages were suicidal, Lord Carnarvon tried more than once to get to Egypt. The fascination, the adventure that archaeology spelt there, and the man who supplied him freely with this adventure, had him in their spell. Once, there was no way to go; another time his health would not allow him to travel, which proved lucky, as he would have arrived in Cairo on the very day the Turks made their attack on the Suez Canal. Eventually, in 1919, berths were obtained. It was a risky crossing, owing to the floating mines; a French vessel had recently been sunk by one. Equally dangerous, however, were the unhygienic conditions on board. The boat had been a troop-ship during the war and was badly in need of disinfecting; instead, it was packed with returning soldiers and invalids; a few died on the way.

In Cairo, Lord Carnarvon at once met Carter. 'Where shall we carry on?' was his sole concern. Carter pulled a folded map out of his jacket pocket; it was a plan drawing of the Valley of the Kings. Without a word he pointed to a cross marked on the plan. Then he said tersely, as was his way, 'Here!'

His lordship was doubtful, disappointed – annoyed in fact. Hadn't this man Carter given up the Valley of the Kings even now? All the archaeologists in the world knew by now that there was nothing more to be had there. Only Carter knew differently. He booked two berths on a Nile steamer to Luxor. Here he gathered his old excavating team around him. Where he had formerly paid the men and children ten piastres for their work, they now did it for a fraction of that; times were wretched, although the war had turned out well for Egypt. The Turks had been defeated and Sultan Fuad I now ruled on the Nile; England found herself forced to abandon her protectorate control over Egypt and to recognise Fuad as king. British troops, however, continued to be stationed in the country.

Carter began excavating near the spot where he had stopped four years previously, but after digging for only a few days the men from El Qurna got down to bed-rock; here, indeed, there was nothing more to be had. 'We're going back to Cairo on the next boat,' said his lordship. For Carter it was a slap in the face. The Earl of Carnarvon no longer saw his future as an excavator in the Valley of the Kings. The Faiyum, the vast oasis on the edge of the Libyan desert, with a better climate and communications, would undoubtedly be more fruitful than this dried-up valley of tombs dug over by countless excavators.

Observing his companion's lack of enthusiasm, Carnarvon himself took in hand the preparations for the Faiyum expedition. Baggage and equipment stood ready to go, the day and hour of departure were appointed, when a revolt broke out in the Faiyum; the country found itself in a state of anarchy. For Europeans there was only one place in which one could be more or less safe, Cairo.

Carnarvon had to postpone his Faiyum plans; for Carter this was not untimely. His lordship waited upon events for a few weeks in Cairo, but when it became clear that a start on excavating was no longer to be thought of that winter, he went back to London. Carter's great moment had now arrived.

6 The discovery: the pharaoh's last secret

*The announcement. . . of the
discovery of the tomb of
Tutankhamun. . . sent a thrill of
wonder and expectation through all
the civilized peoples on the earth.*

Wallis Budge

5th November, 1922. In the fashionable West End of London
the philologist Alan Gardiner and his wife Hedwig were sitting
at dinner. The two spoke in German; Hedwig, née Rosen, was
Viennese, and Alan, son of a rich businessman from Eltham,
had spent ten years in Berlin. They had been married for over
twenty years and led a restless life, for Gardiner, Professor of
Oriental Languages, Hebrew and Arabic, was much in
demand. He was secretary of the Egypt Exploration Society and
was currently working on an Egyptian grammar.

The telephone rang. At the other end was Lord Carnarvon,
whom Gardiner had come to know seven years previously in
Egypt.

'Listen to this,' said Lord Carnarvon. 'I've had a telegram
from Carter. It reads: "At last have made wonderful discovery
in Valley – stop – a magnificent tomb with seals intact – stop –
re-covered same for your arrival – stop – congratulations – stop
– Carter".'

It took Alan Gardiner a moment to grasp the brief words of the telegram.

'Do you think this could be the tomb of Tutankhamun?' asked his lordship impatiently.

Gardiner made a cautious reply. 'I've no detailed knowledge of the close of the 18th Dynasty, but it does seem probable.'

'Well, this is all most exciting,' said Carnarvon. 'I'm arranging to go out to Egypt with Evelyn as soon as possible. Will you come out with me? There are almost certain to be inscriptions for you to study.'

Alan Gardiner expressed his regrets. He couldn't go until the New Year, as he wished to spend Christmas at home with his children, but he would try to get out to Luxor early in the next year. His lordship said good-bye and hoped he would see Gardiner soon in Egypt. The Professor put down the receiver and remarked to his wife with a smile, 'Carnarvon's discovered Tutankhamun's tomb again.'

The episode is vouched for, and it is typical. There was not a single archaeologist-professor in the whole world who still thought the eccentric peer and his obsessed excavator had the slightest chance in their enterprise. And that was hardly surprising, for it was six years since the two had last made a find. Since then there had been nothing but expenses. The Valley of the Kings, all the experts knew, had been ploughed up, metres deep, to the last stone. What on earth was this man Carter supposed to have found?

The event had its pre-history. Howard Carter had spent the summer of 1922 at home in London, as he did every year. His spirits had been at rock bottom. Carnarvon's remarks during the previous digging-season had made it fairly clear that his lordship was not prepared to spend more money on excavations in the Valley of the Kings. Then came a letter from Highclere, summoning Carter for an interview. He suspected what was about to befall. Since receiving the digging concession in 1914, he had rooted his way through the Valley of the Kings, opening up and refilling – always in search of that forgotten pharaoh. All the professors had emphasised again and again that there was nothing more to be had there. Yet Lord Carnarvon, in spite of his growing scepticism, had been impressed again and again by the determination of his private archaeologist. Year after year he had financed the expensive excavations, without seeing the least result. Carter's journey to Highclere was a trip to Canossa.

His lordship expressed his appreciation of Carter's work in previous years. 'But,' he declared, without beating about the bush, 'in view of the economic stringency of the post-war period, I find it impossible to support further this obviously barren enterprise.'

Finished. It was the end of the archaeologist Howard Carter. Without mercy Carnarvon had spoken what Carter had feared. Had he any idea what he was doing to this man?

'My lord,' replied Carter vehemently, 'our consistent failure to find anything has not weakened in the slightest my conviction that the Valley contains at least one more royal tomb, that of Tutankhamun.'

'I believe you,' said Carnarvon, 'but. . .'

'You know the circumstances that point to it,' Carter interrupted. 'Well, even this tomb may have been robbed in antiquity – but there is always the possibility that it has not.'

Carter pulled out a map. Lord Carnarvon recognised it. After every digging season Carter had recorded all the surveys and excavations on the map, and ticked off every square metre of ground he had dug. At first glance it really did seem as though every square inch of the Valley had been ransacked. 'But' – Carter pointed to a little triangle – 'below the entrance to the tomb of Rameses VI are the remains of the foundations of ancient stone huts, presumably built by grave-workers. I should like to remove these foundations in order to investigate the ground beneath them. Only when this triangle has been cleared will I feel that my work in the Valley is ended.'

To his lordship it seemed pointless to finance a further digging season for this. Carnarvon declined.

Would he at least give him permission to dig for one more season at his own expense, asked Carter; he only needed the concession, the workmen and the equipment. 'If by the end of this last season I've found nothing, I will agree with a clear conscience to abandon the Valley. But if I should make a discovery, it will belong to you, as the concession prescribes.'

The proposal moved Carnarvon. But to let Carter dig at his own expense – his lordship couldn't have that. Carnarvon shook Carter's hand. 'All right! One last digging-season – but at *my* expense.'

Carter was happy. He had hardly hoped any more to be able to wring a last season from his lordship. He was in fine fettle, according to his friend James Henry Breasted, and for the first time in his life even expressed dissatisfaction with his bachelor existence. He was a typical bachelor, and in that too he was in clear contrast to Carnarvon. His lordship was accompanied on almost all his journeys by his wife Almina. The pair had been married in 1895, on Carnarvon's twenty-ninth birthday, at St. Margaret's, Westminster. They had a son, Henry, and a daughter, Evelyn.

Breasted, who was in Oxford at the time to receive an honorary doctorate, was puzzled by the complaints of his friend Carter: he was sick and tired of working alone in Egypt all the time; he had been doing it now for thirty years. 'Well, well,' thought Breasted, 'Carter wants to get married.' But Carter didn't go to the altar – he went to a pet shop and bought a canary bird.

The true and only love of his life was Evelyn, Lord Carnarvon's good-looking daughter. Carter called her Eve. When he was digging in Egypt and Eve was staying with her parents in England, the two wrote tender letters to each other, often every other day. 'If you could only be here,' she sighed in one of them. But the couple knew that convention was against them, that a jumped-up excavator couldn't pay court to the daughter of a peer. The relationship remained platonic, and Carter remained a bachelor all his life.

With his canary in his luggage, the odd-man-out went back to Egypt; he hung the bird up in the portico of his house on the road to the Valley of the Kings, much to the delight of the natives, to whom singing birds were completely unknown. Only croaking vultures and jackdaws circled over the Valley.

'The bird will bring good fortune,' said Carter's workmen of the fabulous creature, and they were right; that same year Carter came upon the tomb of Tutankhamun. The natives called it 'the Tomb of the Bird', and that yellow bird was to play a further quite remarkable part in the discovery of the tomb.

Carter realised that the present digging-season was bound to be his last: either he found that forgotten pharaoh or the enterprise came to nothing; then he would be finished as an excavator: a failure, out of work, as he had been twenty years before.

After arriving in Luxor on 28th October, 1922, he engaged his old digging team. On 1st November work began. Below the entry to the tomb of Rameses VI, projecting from the debris, were the foundations of some huts which had obviously been built 3,000 years before by grave-workers. Carter had the foundations removed. His workmen shook their heads. By 3rd November the foundations were cleared. The next morning, as he approached the digging-site, work was at a standstill. Carter knew at once that something had happened. The foreman led him to a spot where a foundation wall had still been standing the day before, and pointed to a step cut into the rock.

Years of failure had made the excavator sceptical. 'I almost dared to hope,' he wrote, 'that we had found our tomb at last.' Almost. It was not until the afternoon of the following day that, after feverish work, twelve stone steps were laid bare and the upper part of a walled-up doorway became visible. Carter couldn't grasp it: he had been digging in that country for thirty years and discovered numerous tombs, but never one whose doorway was sealed. Yet here in the plaster, thousands of years old, were the seals, clearly visible. Carter recognised the necropolis seal, the jackal and nine captives. A second seal, visible in several places, puzzled him at first; he interpreted it as that of Rameses IX.

The tension was hardly bearable. Was he to succeed in discovering an untouched royal tomb, something that no man had been privileged to see for thousands of years?

For Carter the work was going far too slowly. He who was usually calmness itself stood feverishly alongside the workmen; he seized a spade and carried out baskets of debris. Finally he thrust the workmen aside, took hammer and chisel and knocked a hole in the wall big enough for an arm, just below the beam of wood that closed the doorway at the top. He inserted an electric torch, and with his hand over his eyes blinked through.

What he saw was both disappointing and encouraging: the passage that opened up behind the blocked doorway was filled from top to bottom with rubbish. Didn't that show that the tomb had escaped the hands of the robbers? During the New Empire it was customary, after bringing in the mummy, to fill up all the passages in the tomb with building debris as a protection against grave-robbers. Although Carter still didn't know whose tomb he had found, it cost him, as he later admitted, all his self-control not to break open the entrance at once. But standing invisible behind him was the Earl of Carnarvon: it was *his* money that was being shovelled away here; *his* money had been supporting Carter for fifteen years.

Meanwhile, dusk had fallen. Carter got his men to fill in the exposed stairway. The danger of a nocturnal break-in was too great. He didn't leave the site until he had arranged a guard; then he got on his donkey and in the moonlight rode down the stony road to his house, alone with his thoughts.

Next morning in Luxor he sent off the telegram to Lord Carnarvon quoted at the start of the chapter. The answer came by return: 'Possibly come soon.' And a day later: 'Propose arrive Alexandria 20th (November).'

Carter used the time for preparations. He reinforced the guard. He had naturally imposed a strict silence on all his workmen, but a discovery could not be kept secret in Luxor for more than two days. On 18th November he travelled by train to Cairo. He had to report his discovery to the Department of Antiquities; in addition he needed tools and packing materials.

His hope of meeting Lord Carnarvon in Cairo was disappointed. The boat was late. So Carter went back to Luxor, and two days later Carnarvon and his daughter Evelyn also arrived. That was on 23rd November, 1922.

Work on clearing the stairway was begun at once, more carefully and more thoroughly than the first time. Carter could proudly present to his patron sixteen steps: sixteen insignificant stone steps, but for him they were sixteen steps to bliss.

Now that the blocked doorway was completely exposed, he noticed further seals right at the bottom. He had overlooked them because at the first effort he had cleared only twelve steps. Now, however, half a metre deeper, cartouches with the sun-sign and the scarab had come into sight. There was no doubt about it: Tutankhamun! Peer and excavator threw their arms about each other. For one brief moment, the greatest in the lives of the two men, social barriers, money and appearances were forgotten. Tutankhamun!

The exuberance of their joy, however, was suddenly damped. Only a few moments later Carter pointed in dismay at the wall blocking the entry. Without a word he just pointed to a patch in the upper right-hand side of the doorway. Now Carnarvon saw it too. Clearly discernible in the oblique rays of the sun was a hole in the wall, half a metre in diameter, which had later been replastered, perhaps even twice.

Carnarvon was close to saying, 'Was it for this you brought me out from England? To witness yet another shameful failure?'

No one can say what went on at that moment inside the head of the unfortunate excavator. Triumph and disaster lay so close together. Carter was even more in despair than his lordship, for Carnarvon hadn't yet noticed something else: in clearing the last step, fragments and scarab had come to light, bearing the names of Tuthmosis III, Amenophis III, and Akhenaten. Didn't that point to a cache of grave-goods made by robbers?

On 25th November, 1922, the walled-up doorway was broken open. The suspicion that the tomb might have been entered before was confirmed. There were clear differences in the colour of the debris that filled the passage, which led downwards at an incline. In the upper left-hand corner of the vault, which was about two metres high, the robbers had made a hole to crawl through. But, as Carter pointed out, large objects could not have been removed through such a small tunnel.

At about three o'clock on the following day, after the mass of debris had been cleared, a second sealed door became visible, 8.5 metres from the entrance. This opening, too, bore traces of a hole subsequently replastered, but the hole appeared to be so small that a man would have had the greatest difficulty in squeezing through. When Carter noticed seals with Tutankhamun's cartouche he took heart again. Perhaps Tutankhamun's tomb had not been plundered after all.

Carnarvon saw Carter's hands trembling, as he cautiously applied his chisel to the upper left-hand corner of the sealed door. Everything that took place in the next seconds, minutes and hours went by for Carter like a dream; it was 'the day of days, the most wonderful that I have ever lived through, and certainly one whose like I can never hope to see again'.

At first he saw nothing. Then he took an iron rod and poked about through the hole in the wall. He came on nothing. So the space behind the wall was not filled with debris. Carter lighted a candle and held it up to the little opening in the wall; the light flickered in the hot air escaping from within. His fear that poisonous gases might extinguish the flame proved unfounded. In order to insert the candle, he had to enlarge the breach in the wall. This took a long time, much too long. Finally it was done. Carnarvon and his daughter Evelyn stared spellbound at the hole through which the excavator's left arm disappeared with the candle. Carefully he put his head in, as far as it would go. Slowly and gently, as though behind a veil, fabulous objects emerged from the darkness: strange animals stared at him, life-sized human figures armed with staves seemed to step towards him, and in between stood sumptuous chests and vessels of lustrous alabaster; chariots waited to be hitched, and elegant couches with animal heads and legs invited rest.

'Can you see anything?' asked Lord Carnarvon impatiently.

'Yes,' replied Carter, 'wonderful things.'

He let his lordship have a brief look, and then enlarged the hole, so that they could both look in comfort. Like children they stood there, and in the glimmer of an electric torch, procured in the meantime, they gazed into a fairyland, into a life that had been extinguished 3,260 years previously.

Carnarvon was not the man to keep the sensation to himself. He asked *The Times* correspondent, Arthur Merton, to come to Luxor; and on 30th November, 1922, *The Times* reported on the 'Egyptian treasure', extolling Carnarvon as the great discoverer. The next day, his lordship wrote the following letter to Wallis Budge, keeper of the Egyptian section of the British Museum in London:

One line just to tell you that we have found the most remarkable 'find' that has ever been made, I expect, in Egypt or elsewhere. I have only so far got into two chambers, but there is enough in them to fill most of your rooms at the B.M. (upstairs) [the British Museum]; and there is a sealed door where goodness knows what there is. It is not only the quantity of the objects, but their exceptional beauty, finish and originality, which makes this such an extraordinary discovery. There is a throne, or chair, there, more beautiful than any object that has been found in Egypt; alabaster vases of the most marvellous work, and quite unknown except as represented in the tombs; couches of state, chairs, beds, wonderful beadwork, four chariots encrusted with precious stones, lifesize bitumenised figures of the king in solid gold sandals and covered with insignia, boxes innumerable, the king's clothes, a shawabti about 3 feet high, sticks of state. I have not opened the boxes, and don't know what is in them; but there are some papyrus letters, faience, jewellery, bouquets, candles on ankh candle-sticks. All this is in [the] front chamber, besides lots of stuff you can't see. There is then another room which you can't get into owing to the chaos of furniture, etc., alabaster statues, etc., piled up 4 or 5 feet high. Then we come to the sealed door behind which, I am sure, is the king and God knows what. Some of the stuff is in excellent condition, some is poor, but the whole thing is marvellous; and then there is that sealed door!! Even Lacau was touched by the sight. . . It is going to cost me something awful, but I am going to try to do it all myself. I think it will take Carter and three assistants nearly two years to remove, if we find much behind the seals. I am coming back in ten days and will try and see you.

Yours ever,
Carnarvon

Budge, like most archaeologists, was sceptical at first about the sensational reports from Luxor. In past decades an 'untouched royal tomb' had all too often proved in the end to be merely a grave-workers' store-room or a tomb skilfully reclosed by robbers. Although he was still not sure whether he would find Tutankhamun, Carter was outwardly self-confident. On 4th December, 1922, *he* invited the Cairo correspondent of *The Times* to his house for an interview. The assurance displayed by the excavator, hitherto so reserved, was remarkable, the more so as Lord Carnarvon was present at the interview.

Our impressions, [said Carter] gathered from our initial investigations, are that the chambers opened are really antechambers to the King's mausoleum, and from the seals on the doorway still unopened there is every indication that we shall find Pharaoh Tutankhamun. From the famous *papyri* at Turin giving a description of the tomb of Rameses IV, we know that the custom was that the King would not only be buried in his sarcophagus enclosed in three coffins, but that the sarcophagus itself was protected by a series of funereal canopies which, from the details of these *papyri*, seem to have been constructed of wood. Therefore, as this door is unharmed with the exception of a small hole made by the famous metal robbers in the reign of Rameses IX and reclosed by the inspectors of that monarch, we have every reason to hope that whatever may have happened to the metal objects of value the King himself will be found intact. . . [Full of self-confidence, Carter continued] What makes this find so fortunate and important is that this is the first instance in which a Royal tomb has been found with doorways intact as sealed by the hands of the inspectors of Rameses IX. Naturally we are most anxious to break further seals and enter, but this cannot be done with safety until the objects in the first chambers have been removed and preserved. We must therefore ask for the patience and indulgence of the archaeological world until we are able to carry out this. We hope that the next two months will suffice to place us in a position to investigate these further chambers.

It is astonishing how accurately Howard Carter predicted details of later discoveries. In one thing, it is true, he was mistaken: the seals with which the entrance to the tomb had been closed were not those of any Rameses; the break-in and subsequent re-sealing had taken place earlier. In fact, even the re-sealings bore Tutankhamun's name-sign.

The indescribable confusion in the antechamber, which first struck Carter and Carnarvon, was evidence that the grave-robbers had been there. Ornaments torn off, chests broken open, and smashed bits of gilded wood bore witness to excessive and irreverent human greed. The criminals, it seemed, had been disturbed in their sacrilegious activity and had to leave the tomb in a hurry. Who were these grave-robbers and why had they broken open the tomb?

The exact position of the royal tombs was known only to the priests and the construction-workers of Deir el Medina. While the priests handed down their knowledge officially, the grave-workers passed on the information unlawfully, and in this bribery would undoubtedly have played a significant part.

When the ancient cemetery officials who watched over the Valley of the Kings noticed the break-in at Tutankhamun's tomb, they closed the openings made by the grave-robbers with bricks and plaster and pressed their seal into the soft material.

In a report to *The Times*, Lord Carnarvon had stated that the outer doors had borne the seals of Rameses IX, hence that the break-in had taken place in his time (1127–1109). James Henry Breasted, however, who was later asked by Carter to examine the seals, established that the supposed seals of Rameses IX were in fact badly-preserved Tutankhamun seals. The tomb of the child-king had already been forgotten, after all, under Rameses VI (1142–1135). This is the only explanation of why the workmen who cut the tomb of Rameses VI out of the rock set up their huts over the entrance to the tomb of Tutankhamun. The tomb must in fact have been broken open shortly after its completion.

Thanks to the almost daily reports in *The Times*, the discovery quickly became a world-wide sensation. Admiration for Carter grew, but envy too was unmistakable. A mere layman – an experienced excavator, it is true, but without higher education – had stolen the scene from all the highly-qualified professors.

Not all of them gave such free rein to their feelings as the eminent British Egyptologist Alan Gardiner, who on 4th December, 1922, wrote with pique in *The Times*: 'All Egyptologists will look forward to a detailed publication of this kind, the more so in view of the fact that Mr. Carter is the finest living archaeological draughtsman.' The greatest discovery in the history of archaeology may have made Carter famous, but it did not by a long way make him an archaeologist – at any rate, not in the eyes of Professor Gardiner. He remained what he had been when he began thirty years previously, a draughtsman.

Whether it was done by mistake or by design will probably never be known, but Howard Carter sent Alan Gardiner a telegram. He asked him to come at once to Egypt, in order to undertake 'the philological work in connection with the papyrus find in the antechamber to the tomb'. If Gardiner had suspected what a fool this journey would make him look, he would have stayed at home in London.

In one of the first reports in *The Times*, Carter had mentioned a casket which obviously contained rolls of papyrus. These papyri were supposed to be deciphered by Gardiner. The

Professor, who had not been in Egypt for ten years, felt flattered; so the discovery would not after all proceed entirely without him. As he wrote in *The Times*:

> It is possible – it is even probable – that this papyri will turn out to be no more than 'Books of the Dead', as they are called, such as were buried with practically every king and person of note, and which consisted of incantations ensuring the dead king's welfare in the other world. On the other hand, these documents may throw some light on the change from the religion of the heretics back to the old traditional religion, and that would be exceedingly interesting.

No account ever appeared of Gardiner's examination of these papyri, for in the whole of Tutankhamun's tomb there was, in fact, not a single papyrus document. When the Professor arrived in the Valley of the Kings in the first days of January, and opened the casket with the supposed rolls of writing, he made a most painful discovery. The casket contained, rolled up, the Lord Tutankhamun's under-pants, a linen loin-cloth, and a change of underwear for the kingdom of the shades.

The Tutankhamun enterprise, as Carter quickly realised, was too big for him to handle on his own. But he had difficulty in convincing Lord Carnarvon of their need: that two or three assistants were not enough, that a whole archaeological team was required, if the tomb was to be studied with scientific care. Carter's call for help reached an expedition of the New York Metropolitan Museum, which, under the leadership of Arthur Mace, was about to end its excavations in Lisht, begun in 1906. Confirmation from New York came briefly by telegraph from Dr. A. M. Lythgoe, head of the Egyptian Department of the Metropolitan Museum: 'Do it!' The private-enterprise 'Tutankhamun' was now a public company.

The leader of the American team, Arthur Cruttenden Mace, was an Englishman who had studied in Oxford, at St. Edward's School and Keble College, where he graduated. He had actually wanted to become a university lecturer, but there was this cousin of his, Flinders Petrie, who was always urging him to go with him. In 1898, Petrie took Mace to Egypt with him for the first time, and he dug with him at Diospolis Parva and a year later in Abydos. In the autumn of 1901, Mace joined the Hearst Expedition of the University of California and worked with Dr. Reisner and A. M. Lythgoe in Giza and Nag ed-Deir.

In October 1906, when Lythgoe was appointed to set up an Egyptian department in the Metropolitan Museum, he asked Mace if he would dig for his museum. The Englishman agreed, applied for a concession for the pyramids of Lisht, and in the same year started to open the pyramid of Amenemhet I and the surrounding cemetery. There Mace found the famous tomb of Senebtisi. In the First World War, the 'American' Mace became a patriotic Englishman again; he served in the 2nd Battalion of the 29th London Territorial Regiment (Artists' Rifles), but was transferred on health grounds to the Army Service Corps, with which he ended up in Italy. At the end of the war, he went to New York; there he rose to be associate curator of the Egyptian Department of the Metropolitan Museum.

Carter got on well with Mace. For two years he was his mainstay in surmounting the numerous difficulties that were yet to befall them. And a second archaeologist proved to be a true friend: the American James Henry Breasted. He learned of the discovery on 7th December, 1922. He had landed at Aswan, having come by boat from Abu Simbel, and found a letter from Lord Carnarvon waiting for him. Carnarvon told of a tomb or cache that Carter had found in the Valley of the Kings, but without saying which. Breasted was convinced, nevertheless, that it could only be the tomb of Tutankhamun; he boarded his boat and sailed down the Nile to Luxor.

In Luxor rumours were circulating. The talk was of gold treasures and an unplundered royal tomb. No one knew any details. So far it had not been reported by any Egyptian paper. Carter had disappeared, said to have gone to Cairo; Breasted and his son Charles hired two donkeys and rode to the Valley of the Kings. As they passed the brown house in which Carter had lived during the years of fruitless digging, Charles Breasted couldn't help thinking of his first meeting with Carter. That was now nearly twenty years ago, a period in which Carter had gone through, more than once, all the heights and depths of an excavator's life. But he had always stuck to his conviction that Tutankhamun was buried in the Valley of the Kings. If anyone deserved this success it was Carter.

From a distance the Americans could already see the great pit that had been dug, just below the entrance to the tomb of Rameses VI. It was surrounded by soldiers with rifles at the ready. In the middle of the pit a pile of debris had been thrown up. On it was stuck a slab of limestone with the arms of the Carnarvons drawn roughly in black paint, Howard Carter's work. By it sat Carter's new assistant, A. R. Callender, a gun on his knees; he was guarding the pile of debris, which obviously covered the entrance to the tomb that had been found. Nothing more was to be seen.

Next morning, Carter arrived in Luxor on the night train from Cairo. When he heard Breasted was there, he took a cab and drove straight to the landing-stage on the Nile where the American's boat was tied up. Their greetings were rapturous.

Was this the crushed, reserved little excavator Howard Carter, the Carter that had been used to carrying out orders all his life? Breasted noticed the change at once: this Howard Carter was aware of his uniqueness, his success, his historic achievement. This Carter spoke like a man who was on the way to becoming one of the most famous archaeologists in the world.

'Think of it!' said Carter. 'Twice before I had come within two yards of that first stone step! The first time was years ago when I was digging for Davis, and he suggested that we shift our work to some "more promising spot". The second was only a few seasons ago when Lord Carnarvon and I decided to reserve clearance of this area for a time when we wouldn't interfere with visitors to the tomb of Rameses VI.'

Carter narrated all this with unusual self-confidence, but now and then he became so moved that his voice gave way. Then he broke off, paused for a moment and went on in a calmer tone, 'Forgive me, but I was moved like this when I peered in at the ineffable wonders of the first chamber, and thought of the long, barren years that had led up to this unbelievable consummation of all my hopes.'

As he was speaking, he rummaged in his coat pocket, pulled out an old letter and began to sketch on it the ground plan of the antechamber. He then touched various spots in the rectangle with his pencil and mentioned some of the treasures that had been found lying about.

In Cairo, Carter related, he had ordered a massive steel door for protection against grave-robbers. In addition, he had procured large quantities of wadding, collodion, paraffin wax, and materials for preparation and conservation. Now his concern was to get electric cables laid into the Chamber.

Breasted sounded almost timid as he asked when he might have a look at the tomb.

'We shall now re-excavate the entrance,' replied Carter, 'install the steel door – which was shipped on my train – and make many other preparations which will consume three days. On the third day from today, please cross the river as if on a routine visit to the Theban temples, climb the mountain as if for the view – and then drop down into the Valley. Plan to reach the tomb at three o'clock in the afternoon. Bring with you a complete change of underclothes – the temperature in the tomb is still such that after only a brief stay in it, one comes forth dripping with perspiration!'

Three days later, Breasted followed Carter's instructions. So as not to arouse any suspicion and unnecessarily attract a lot of bystanders, the American set out as though on a sight-seeing tour. Unobserved by the natives and the tourists, he at once climbed the path that he knew so well up to the cliffs and down again the other side: Carter was ready waiting.

The appearance of the pit had changed. Instead of the pile of debris, a deep shaft was to be seen, and a little shack had been erected. Next to Carter stood Callender, Burton, Mace and Herbert Winlock, who had brought with him his wife and one of his daughters. The men took off their jackets and made

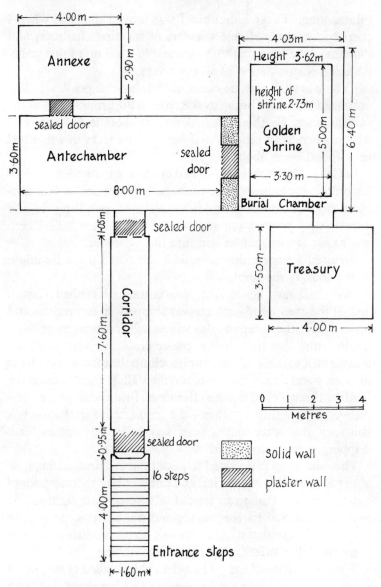

Ground plan of the tomb of Tutankhamun.

efforts to crack jokes, an understandable reaction in the tension of the moment.

'Are we ready?' asked Carter excitedly, but as correctly as a starter on a race track. 'Come, please!' Sixteen steps led into the depths, to a grill that was hung with a white cloth. Inside the tomb floodlights were shining, throwing shadows of the iron grill on to the cloth.

All my life, [wrote Charles Breasted] I shall remember the picture of that little group of men as they stood waiting with glowing eyes while Carter paused with his left hand at the upper corner of the white sheet, then suddenly drew it away.

Through the steel bars we saw an incredible vision, an impossible scene from a fairy tale, an enchanted property-room from the opera house of some great composer's dreams. Opposite us were three couches upon which a king had lain, all about were chests, caskets, alabaster vases, gold-embellished stools and chairs – the heaped-up riches of a Pharaoh who had died some three thousand two hundred and fifty years ago – before Crete had passed her zenith, before Greece had been born or Rome conceived, or more than half of the history of civilisation had taken place. In the brilliant light, against the white limestone wall, the colours of all these things were vibrant yet soft – a medley of brown, yellow, blue, amber, gold, russet and black.

The iron grill was closed with four locks and chains. As if in a spell the men stood behind Carter as he pushed the heavy grill aside. It almost startled them to hear him say, 'Will you not enter?'

The words were hardly necessary, but the excitement, the tension, was so great that each of them tried hard to seem as normal as possible, and naturally failed; it was painful. As none of the men seemed inclined to follow Carter's invitation, he turned round to face them: the men had tears in their eyes. Even Carter cried; no one uttered a word. Suddenly they began to shake each other by the hand and laugh sheepishly as they wiped the tears from their eyes. As James Henry Breasted wrote later, 'Emotion struggled with the habit of years to observe and to understand, a struggle in which my critical faculties were for the moment completely routed. . . Never was anything so dramatic in the whole range of archaeological discovery as this first view of what must surely be Tutankhamun's tomb.'

It took all Carter's powers of persuasion to convince Lord Carnarvon that the antechamber to the tomb could not be cleared overnight. In view of the uniqueness of the discovery, everything had to be photographed, recorded and catalogued before the first object could be removed. For his lordship this would all take too long; he went back to England. Carter was to let him know when work could be resumed.

In London, Lord Carnarvon met his friend Alan Gardiner.

'I can't get a night's rest,' he complained. 'As soon as I am in bed there are telephone calls. If I walk out of my house I am stopped by some press man.'

'I can understand your annoyance,' said Gardiner, 'but in view of the enormous public interest in the discovery such incidents are bound to occur. The newspapermen are only carrying out their duties.'

Geoffrey Dawson, editor of *The Times*, got wind of the fact that Carnarvon was staying with his friend Alan Gardiner. While Carnarvon and Gardiner were discussing the dubious fame of making a historic discovery, the telephone rang. Dawson wanted to speak to Carnarvon. Carnarvon said Dawson should come and see him there. Alan Gardiner recalls the following conversation: 'Dawson. . . explained. . . that he had come to ask him to give *The Times* exclusive rights in the story. Carnarvon said he'd never been in such a position before, but Dawson pointed out that by making *The Times* his sole agent for the distribution of news and pictures he would be saved an enormous amount of trouble. Carnarvon said he'd think about it.'

According to Gardiner, Carnarvon was uncertain whether he should sell *The Times* the exclusive rights. Only a conversation with the secretary of the Royal Geographical Society, which had marketed the Mount Everest Expedition in a similar way, removed his doubts.

Officially, Carter approved the press monopoly of *The Times*; personally, however, he was strongly against it, and even sabotaged it.

At the beginning of 1923, reports on the Tutankhamun affair suddenly appeared in American newspapers, giving more interesting information than that in *The Times*. In the *Chicago Daily News*, a certain George Waller Mecham reported regularly on the progress of the excavations. This Mr. Mecham, whom nobody in Luxor knew, was always very well informed. All the journalists were on the look-out for the mystery man, but not even the Reuter correspondent Valentine Williams, who was well-known for his crime stories, and who made the journey to Luxor specially, could lift the veil.

Three men followed the journalistic chase with great amusement: Carter, James Henry Breasted, and his son Charles.

Charles was then twenty-six. 'Night after night,' he later admitted, 'somewhere between midnight and four in the morning, I wrote Mr. Mecham's dispatches, took them in a carriage through the streets of sleeping Luxor to the government telegraph office in the railway station, where I filed them with a drowsy, tarbooshed effendi.' So as not to upset relations between Carter and Breasted senior, Charles admitted to Carter one evening that *he* was Mr. Mecham. Carter said that was his affair: that he would forget what Charles had told him. Young Breasted's advantage lay above all in the fact that he didn't have to be on the spot to write his reports. He only had to set down on paper what he heard each evening from his father, who worked with Carter during the day. And so it was that Mr. Mecham was never identified.

The fame of the discovery, which Carter had gratefully enjoyed at first, became a burden after only a few weeks. Newspapers all over the world reprinted the reports of *The Times*, and let loose a flood of good wishes and telegrams. The little post office at Luxor, in normal circumstances mainly a receiving office for picture post-cards and telegrams, couldn't cope with the onslaught. Postal traffic trebled and personnel was doubled.

> Beginning with letters of congratulation, [wrote Carter] it went on to offers of assistance, ranging all the way from tomb-planning to personal valeting; requests for souvenirs – even a few grains of sand from above the tomb would be received so thankfully; fantastic money offers, from moving-picture rights to copyright on fashions of dress; advice on the preservation of antiquities, and the best method of appeasing evil spirits and elementals; press clippings; tracts; would-be facetious communications; stern denunciations of sacrilege; claims of relationship – surely you must be the cousin who lived in Camberwell in 1893, and whom we have never heard of since; and so on and so on. Fatuous communications of this sort came tumbling in upon us at the rate of ten or fifteen a day right through the winter.

Carter was astonished how many friends he suddenly had. For nearly fifty years he had lived the life of an outsider, in isolation, withdrawn and self-sufficient; suddenly everyone wanted to know him, had always known him: 'Howard, old fellow!' First it was hundreds, then thousands, who came with letters of introduction from 'a friend', so that they might be allowed the honour of viewing the tomb. For, unlike all the other tombs in the Valley of the Kings, this one was not open to view. In the luxury hotels of Luxor, there was only one topic: 'Have you seen the tomb yet? No? You must produce a letter of introduction. Go to Mr. So-and-so, he's a personal friend of Howard Carter's.'

Every morning, as the sun threw its first low rays on the bordering hills of the Valley, crowds of people made the pilgrimage past Carter's house to the Wonder of the World, as it was now called. They came in horse-drawn cabs, in sand-carts, on donkeys and on foot, equipped like campers, and settled down along the wall that had been built round the entrance to the tomb. Under airy sunshades, the gentlemen conversed, the ladies knitted, and the hotel servants brought picnic baskets. The start of Carter's work each morning resembled the triumphal procession of a silent-film star – hand-shakes, applause, cheers, snapshots, presents, notes, letters. And the more unfriendly and morose Carter's reaction, the more his standing grew. The tourists, who streamed to Luxor from all over the world, tried by every conceivable trick to make his acquaintance and get into the tomb. American travel bureaux sold package tours that included a viewing of the tomb, without ever having made contact with Carter. Tourists lay in wait for him and offered large sums to be shown round; one tried to get into the tomb dressed as a telegraph boy; another came as a lemonade seller.

Under the headline 'Tourists besiege the tomb' *The Times* wrote on 18th January, 1923:

Today another crowd, reinforced by tourists off a Nile steamer, congregated outside the tomb, expecting that after yesterday's rest some interesting objects would be brought out, but they were doomed to disappointment.

Although Mr. Carter had everything in readiness, his plans were upset by the difficulty of putting in place the new steel gate for the tomb of Seti II, in which all objects removed are placed for treatment. This work, which was started yesterday afternoon, occupied the entire morning and afternoon of today and seriously interfered with the experts' activities as well.

From Cairo a delegation of the newly-resigned government paid a visit; they came privately and brought wives and children with them: ex-Premier Ebdel Khalek Sarwat Pasha, ex-Minister of Finance Ismail Sidky Pasha, and ex-Minister of Information Wassif Simeika Pasha. Carter had to shake hands, be friendly, arrange tours of inspection, answer questions and share in the marvelling – no light task for a man to whom, in this situation, ministers, tourists, people in general, were a burden; who wanted only one thing in the world: to evaluate scientifically the discovery of his life.

But the ex-excellencies were delighted and insisted on expressing their delight; it was all far more marvellous than they had imagined; the beauty of what they had seen was unique and indescribable. Sarwat Pasha told Carter that he intended travelling on up-river the next day to Wadi Halfa; it was his first holiday trip since 1914. Carter listened, but in thought he was miles away. And when the excellencies departed with their families, that was another day gone.

> The scene at the tomb [reported the *Daily Telegraph* on 25th January] awakened memories of Derby Day. The road leading to the rock-enclosed ravine. . . was packed with vehicles and animals of every conceivable variety. The guides, donkey-boys, sellers of antiquities, and hawkers of lemonade were doing a roaring trade. . . When the last articles had been removed from the corridor today the newspaper correspondents began a spirited dash across the desert to the banks of the Nile upon donkeys, horses, camels and chariot-like sand-carts in a race to be the first to reach the telegraph offices.

The press monopoly of *The Times* led to increasing tension in journalistic circles. Correspondents of other papers used increasingly outrageous tricks to break the predominance of *The Times*. Bribes were paid and offered – above all to the workmen. Under the headline 'Tutankhamun Ltd.' came a broadside from the London *Daily Express*, on 10th February, 1923:

> While we have admiration for the faith and persistence which have brought so magnificent a reward to the labours of Lord Carnarvon, it is difficult to approve the manner in which he has seen fit to exploit his discovery. . . the tomb is not his private property. He has not dug up the bones of his ancestors in the Welsh mountains. He has stumbled on

a Pharaoh in the land of the Egyptians. . . by making an exclusive secret of the contents of the inner tomb he has ranged against him the majority of the world's most influential newspapers.

Six days later, *The Times* hit back:

Discreditable and unfounded aspersions have been cast on Lord Carnarvon's work. He has been charged with creating a monopoly of news from Luxor, and even of commercialism. . . no charge could be more false. He supplied the news through *The Times* solely because he thought it would be the best way, in fact the only practical way, of supplying it fully and independently to all newspapers throughout the world who wanted to take it. The character of the work compelled him to distribute news of it through an agent.

The Times had informed its readers that Carter would be opening the sealed burial chamber of Tutankhamun's tomb on 17th February, 1923. In letters to the editor, readers wanted to know what might be expected behind this wall, whether it was not too risky an undertaking, or where entrance tickets for the opening were to be had.

On that 17th February Howard Carter could have earned more money than in the whole of his life. But that is unlikely to have been in his mind; above all, it was not in his power. Who was to be present at the opening, and who not, was decided solely by Lord Carnarvon.

It is quite astonishing how many people subsequently claimed to have been present at that historic moment, the first and probably only opening of an untouched pharaonic tomb in modern history. Newspaper articles and books are always cropping up by 'one who was there'; yet the antechamber to Tutankhamun's tomb was not, after all, a theatre auditorium with hundreds of seats; it measured less than thirty square metres.

Carter testifies to the presence of the following people:

Lord Carnarvon, Lady Evelyn Herbert, H. E. Abd el
Halim Pasha Suleman, Minister of Public Works, M.
Lacau, Director-General of the Service of Antiquities, Sir
William Garstin, Sir Charles Cust, Mr. Lythgoe, Curator
of the Egyptian Department of the Metropolitan Museum,
New York, Professor Breasted, Dr. Alan Gardiner, Mr.
Winlock, the Hon. Mervyn Herbert, the Hon. Richard
Bethell, Mr. Engelbach, Chief Inspector of the Depart-
ment of Antiquities, three Egyptian inspectors of the
Department of Antiquities, the representative of the Gov-
ernment Press Bureau, and the members of the staff –
about twenty persons in all.

Among the latter was, *ex officio*, Arthur Merton, correspondent
of *The Times*. Only *he* could report next day, as eye-witness,
what had taken place the day before *in camera*. The reporter of
the *Daily Telegraph* made a virtue of necessity and supplied a
detailed account of what was to be seen and heard outside,
before and during the breath-taking proceedings within the
tomb:

Mr. Callender opened the massive dungeon door leading
from the entrance to the steps and a number of chairs were
taken down.
 'We're going to have a concert! Carter's going to sing a
song!' said Lord Carnarvon very audibly, glancing up at
the pressmen whose presence seemed to disconcert him.
For the next three hours every sound and every incident
were noted and interpreted. Sometimes it was a piece of
masonry that was brought up, sometimes we heard Lady
Evelyn's exclamations, sometimes the sound of chisel blows
or the hammering of wood. The excitement of the watchers
on the parapet grew intense as they saw labourers carrying
out blocks of masonry and baskets of minor debris.

What did take place in those minutes down below?
Alan Gardiner was an eye-witness. He recalls:

As Carter removed the upper part of the wall we saw beyond it what seemed to be a wall of solid gold, but as the rest of the masonry was taken away we realized we were looking at one side of a vast outer shrine. We had seen such shrines depicted in ancient papyri, but this was the real thing. There it was, splendid in its blue and gold, and almost filling the entire space of the second chamber. It reached nearly to the ceiling and the space between it and the walls at the sides was not more than about two feet.

First Carter and Carnarvon went in, squeezing their way through the narrow space, and we waited for them to return. When they came back they both lifted their hands in amazement at what they had seen. Then the rest of us entered, two at a time. I remember Professor Lacau saying to me jokingly, 'You'd better not attempt it; you're much too stout.' Anyway, when it came to my turn, I went in with Professor Breasted. We pushed our way through and then turned left, so that we were opposite the front of the shrine, which had two great doors. Carter had drawn the bolt and opened these doors, so that we could see that inside the great outer shrine, which was seventeen feet long and eleven feet wide, was another, smaller shrine, also with double doors, with the seal still unbroken. In fact there were in all four of these gilded shrines, one inside the other like a Chinese nest of boxes, and within the fourth was the sarcophagus, which we were not to see until a year later.

Already within a few weeks of the discovery, the Tutankhamun affair had become politics. The British, who through the discovery had undoubtedly become the leading excavating nation, were afraid that the agreement made in 1904, which guaranteed French leadership of the Egyptian Department of Antiquities for thirty years, might now work out unfavourably. Wallis Budge, of the British Museum in London, was reported as saying on 1st December, 1922, 'The laws which governed excavations made by foreigners in Egypt used to allot to the excavator one-half of the "find". Under Maspero these laws were interpreted generously, and all must hope that such will be the case in respect of the present discovery.'

Carter had spent half a lifetime alone, with only one goal in which he believed constantly before him. Now, all at once, at the zenith of success, his work had become an affair of the British Empire, an affair of the whole nation. The treasures of the tomb of Tutankhamun were seen less as an art-historical sensation than as a collection of trophies of national prestige.

'One cannot help hoping,' declared Alan Gardiner, 'that Lord Carnarvon, who has worked for so many years in Egypt without any adequate compensation for all his efforts, will be able to bring home what is not absolutely essential for the purposes of the Cairo Museum. There is nothing so educative as ocular demonstration, the very purpose for which our museums were instituted, and it is very much to be hoped that M. Lacau will show as enlightened a generosity in this respect as his distinguished predecessor M. Maspero would undoubtedly have done.'

The excavation, finding, trading and exporting of antiquities were regulated by Law No. 14 of 12th June, 1912. This law replaced a corresponding decree of 1897, which had proved inadequate. Eleven years had been needed to frame the new law; for eleven years the politicians had haggled and wrangled with the Comité d'Égyptologie in Cairo about such questions as, for instance, what should in fact be regarded as an antiquity. The legislators finally arrived at the view that antiquities were 'objects of all periods – Pharaonic, Greek, Roman, Byzantine and Coptic; buildings, as well as objects of industry or art; inscriptions graven on rocks; walls and houses of sundried bricks as well as those of stone; in fact all the remains of man's occupation in earlier times'.

The law required every finder of an antiquity to hand it over to the Department of Antiquities. If he could show that his find had not come from an illegal excavation, he was entitled to half of the find or half of its equivalent value. If the find was so divided by the Department of Antiquities, then the finder was allowed to choose *his* share.

Archaeological excavations, which required special licences, were allowed to be made only by archaeologists authorised by governments, universities, academies and learned societies, and by private individuals who could produce the necessary qualifications. If their own experience was insufficient, a qualified archaeologist could be called in at the request of the administration. The transport and export of antiquities could be effected only with the permission of the Department of Antiquities. In granting export permits, the Department of Antiquities collected 1.5 per cent of the declared value. Carnarvon's concession, which had to be renewed every year by application, provided that first-class finds were to be handed over to the Department of Antiquities. The excavators could claim only second-class material and duplicates; here too, export licences were issued by the Department of Antiquities. These provisions had been stiffened because, in the past, irreplaceable cultural assets had been taken out of the country, partly with the consent of the authorities, partly through reprehensible juggling by excavators.

'Mummies of the Kings, of Princes, and of High Priests,' to quote Article 8 of Carnarvon's concession, 'together with their coffins and sarcophagi, shall remain the property of the Antiquities Service.' And if Carter were to find an untouched tomb, he would have to hand over its contents, without appropriating a single piece, to the Museum.

In the case of Tutankhamun, Article 10 was the decisive, debatable point:

In the case of tombs which have already been searched, the Antiquities Service shall, over and above the mummies and sarcophagi intended in Article 8, reserve for themselves all objects of capital importance from point of view of history and archaeology, and shall share the remainder with the Permittee.

As it is probable that the majority of such tombs as may be discovered will fall within the category of the present article, it is agreed that the Permittee's share will sufficiently recompense him for the pains and labour of the undertaking.

This Article, which was certainly not drafted by a lawyer, was ambiguous; at any rate, it left every possibility open to the Department of Antiquities. Since Tutankhamun's tomb had undoubtedly been broken open, Article 10 came into force, and assured the concession-holder of at least a part of the contents. The head of the Department of Antiquities, however, declared the whole contents of the tomb to be of 'capital importance'. As a result, Lord Carnarvon was not entitled to a single piece from all of Tutankhamun's grave-treasure. This was the opinion also of Howard Carter. And that helped to aggravate the already strained relations between his lordship and the excavator.

Nut, mistress of the sky, the feminine counterpart of Amun-Re.

7 Preserving the evidence: the mysterious life below ground

> *He had a lot to contend with –*
> *official interference, irritating*
> *delays, misunderstanding and a*
> *surfeit of unwelcome publicity, and*
> *perhaps he was not the*
> *best-tempered of men.*

Alan Gardiner

Only now did the real work begin, the saving of all the treasures. Carter had learned from Petrie and Naville that not only the found object itself was important, but also the circumstances and the position in which it was found. If the excavator records the exact position of an object, this enables him on other occasions to find objects in a similar position. Luck, often an archaeologist's most important adjunct, is thereby largely excluded. Howard Carter had established that the grave-gifts in every tomb were arranged according to a quite definite plan. Once one object had been found, it was not difficult in an unplundered tomb to detect the others.

It was for this reason that he attached such great importance to preserving the evidence below ground with scientific exactness. Before it was touched by a human hand, every object, from the smallest to the largest, had to be photographed, measured *in situ* and, immediately after its rescue, described exactly. All the data and information was entered by Carter on cards 12 cms. by 20 cms., which were ruled in squares on the front side and in lines on the back. They are preserved today at the Griffith Institute in Oxford. Let us take a card at random from Carter's file.

48D. Stick with crook composed of Asiatic and African prisoners. Dimensions of stick proper, 2.2 centimetres. But for handle and head and arms and legs of prisoners, stick entirely covered in gold leaf on gesso.

(a) Handle of ivory.

(b) Plain bands with five incised lines.

(c) Chevron pattern all the way down.

(d) As (b).

(e) Feather pattern on three sides; on top is relief running entire length.

(f) An Asiatic and an African prisoner bound back to back. Binding shown as raised bar.

Cleaned with damp brush, sprayed with celluloid in amyl acetate and treated with melted paraffin wax.

Usually there was time only at night for this work of card-filling, and not infrequently the nights in the laboratory in the tomb of Sethos II proved all too short; besides card-filling, there was the preserving, repairing or assembling of broken finds waiting to be done. In addition, wage-books had to be kept, bills paid, disputes settled and the excavation workers, with their wives and children, treated medically. The one free day in the week, Friday (following Islamic custom), was just sufficient to clear up everything left undone during the week.

A fashion phenomenon of the 18th Dynasty, and especially of the Amarna period, which Tutankhamun still followed, gave Carter particular trouble. The latest thing at that time was necklaces, collars, pendants and girdles of faience spangles threaded together. These tested the excavator's patience more than all the other grave-goods; Carter hated them. Although

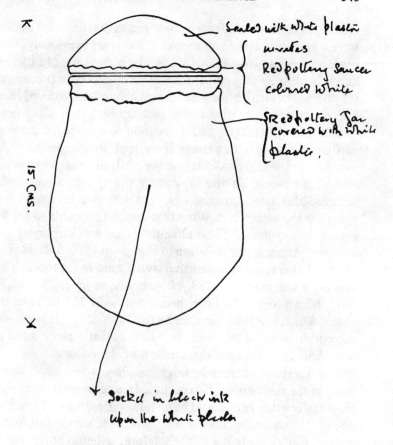

Sealed with white plaster invates

Red pottery saucer coloured white

{Red pottery Jar covered with white plaster.

15. CMS.

Jocked in black ink upon the white plaster

Contents: Sticks of a plant broken up into short lengths.

Umbelliferae. {Probably a species of {Chaerophyllum

A page from Carter's diary.

chains, collars and pendants were found in the tomb just as they were when placed there more than 3,000 years previously, they couldn't be handled. They couldn't be picked up and carried away, because, although the faience beads had been preserved, the threads on which they had been strung had decayed, and Carter had no alternative but to pick up each individual bead with a pair of tweezers, and press it on to a prepared piece of cardboard spread with a sticky layer of plasticine. In the end a necklace in the right order lay on the card. But that was not the end of the work. In the laboratory the spangles had to be rethreaded. Carter sometimes worked with twelve needles and thread at the same time. What that meant I was able to see for myself in a collar of Tutankhamun's that was displayed at a Nefertiti/Akhenaten exhibition in Europe in 1974–5. It was one of a total of seventeen collars that were found in the tomb. This fine piece was made up of 93 yellow beads, 40 green, 50 red, 71 blue, 60 white and 57 blue, hence a total of 371 links in the chain, which was held together by two lotus-shaped clasps – an incredible work of patience, in which no little piece must be lost. And that was only the smallest of the collars.

The question whether he might not have overlooked something in the rescue operation occupied Carter almost every day. How easily a tiny bead could be lost, how great was the risk that one of the workmen concerned might cause something to disappear! Carter made it a rule, therefore, to let no object out of his sight, from its registration in the tomb and its removal to the laboratory to its registration in his card index. Whenever the workmen carried something away, Carter always walked alongside.

This absolute thoroughness proved to be particularly helpful in the scientific research. Thus one number, for instance, puzzled Carter greatly: there were exactly 413 figures of servants, so-called *ushabti*, in Tutankhamun's grave-treasure. Why precisely 413? The assumption that some of the servant-figures might have been lost or stolen was obvious. But Carter, who was quite sure that neither robbery nor any other kind of loss was involved, thought it over and came upon a plausible explanation: for each of the 365 days of the year Tutankhamun had one servant; for each week, which at the time of the 18th Dynasty still had ten days, there was an overseer, and for each month a superintendent. This amounted to 365 + 36 + 12 = 413.

The figures of servants in Tutankhamun's tomb were made of various materials – pottery, alabaster, sandstone, granite and wood. It was the wooden figures that caused particular difficulty. Some were coated with a layer of gesso and overlaid with gold leaf. And precisely these, the most beautiful figures, began to perish of their own accord under the influence of the change of atmosphere: the wood shrank, the layer of gesso came away, the gold peeled off.

A painted casket, which Carter admired in particular, set the team special problems. The casket was of wood coated with a layer of gesso, and painted. They knew that after a certain time the valuable painting would come away. Any special preparation, however, was not to be thought of until the little chest had been emptied. And that would take all of three weeks. Why such a great labour?

The problem can only be understood by reading Howard Carter's description of the contents of the casket:

The first thing we saw was on the right a pair of rush and papyrus sandals, in perfect condition; below them, just showing, a gilt head-rest, and, lower again, a confused mass of cloth, leather, and gold, of which we can make nothing as yet. On the left, crumpled into a bundle, there is a magnificent royal robe, and in the upper corner there are roughly shaped beads of dark resin. The robe it was that presented us with our first problem, a problem that was constantly to recur – how best to handle cloth that crumbled at the touch, and yet was covered with elaborate and heavy decoration. In this particular case the whole surface of the robe is covered with a network of faience beads, with a gold sequin filling in every alternate square in the net. These – beads and sequins – had originally been sewn to the cloth, but are now loose. A great many of them are upside down, the releasing of the tension when the thread snapped having evidently caused them to spring. . .

In removing the individual objects from the casket, Carter had to be constantly on guard lest in removing one object he destroyed another, and perhaps more valuable one, lying beneath it. It would have been perfectly possible to fix the garment with melted paraffin and lift it out in lumps. But what would have been the value of such an unsightly object? For Carter there were two possibilities: either he could try to rescue the material in the largest possible pieces – and thereby destroy the bead embroidery. Or he could rescue the embroidery – in which case, in picking it out, the material would be lost. Carter decided on the second solution. 'Later, in the museum,' he wrote, 'it will be possible to make a new garment of the exact size, to which the original ornamentation – bead-work, gold sequins, or whatever it might be – can be applied.'

The casket was not yet completely empty when the first cracks appeared in the top layer of paint. Carter, on the chemist's advice, had carefully cleaned, and thus freshened, the colours with benzine; then the whole had been sprayed with a solution of celluloid and amyl alcohol. The treatment proved to be insufficient; the solution had to be washed off again. Carter turned to the last resource, hot paraffin wax. Would the colours, would the layer of gesso stand the hot liquid? Carefully he applied the paraffin. The colours at once seemed to glow. The brittle material, however, completely absorbed the paraffin. And that indeed was the answer. Not only the layer of paint, not only the gesso, but even the underlying wood had to be impregnated, so that no further movement could take place. The process was hair-raising; the surface of the casket had to be pre-heated in the sun, and the paraffin brought nearly to boiling point. Blisters thrown up in the gesso through the action of the hot paraffin could be pressed flat, once cooling had begun. On the one hand, the paraffin had to be made hot enough to penetrate the material at once, but on the other it had to be kept short of a temperature at which the layers of paint and wood might begin to burn.

The most admired piece to come out of the tomb was the young king's golden throne. It was made of wood and completely overlaid with sheet gold. Its small size and artistic decoration show that the chair had been prepared for the king while he was still a child. It had obviously been made a little higher later on, when Tutankhamun had grown: ingenious craftsmen had mounted washers several centimetres thick under the lion's feet. The level of the seat had been raised in this way by at least six centimetres. This gorgeous piece of royal furniture is worked in the typical Amarna style. The inside of the back-rest is decorated with a domestic, almost intimate scene between Tutankhamun and his lovely consort Ankhesenamun. Similar representations of Akhenaten and Nefertiti are known to us. The scene on the throne shows the queen, dressed in a transparent white gown and a high crown of feathers, anointing Tutankhamun as he sits in an arm chair. The young Pharaoh rests his right elbow negligently on the back of the chair and turns his left shoulder towards his wife. His face is young, almost childlike, yet he has a distinct stomach bulge with three cross-folds, the unmistakable sign of Amarna art. Equally typical of the Amarna style are the King's wig-ribbons fluttering in the breeze. Shining dominantly over the two figures is the sun-disc of Aten, its rays, which end in hands, bestowing *ankh*, or life, on the royal couple.

Semi-precious stones, coloured glass, faience and stained ivory – a great variety of materials worked on gold was in keeping with the traditions of the artist craftsmen of Amarna. All this, and the use of his earlier name, Tutankhaten, in one of the royal cartouches, raises the question of how such an undoubted relic from the heretical period could have survived the restoration of the old religion. And how did it come to be in the tomb?

More than two and a half months had passed since the opening of the tomb before the chemist, Alfred Lucas, made the first bacteriological examination, initially in the burial chamber. Lucas, a criminologist, had been head of the Forensic Medicine Institute in Cairo for several years; he was regarded as a great authority on poisons and ballistics, and had been relieved of his duties for the investigations in Tutankhamun's tomb. Nevertheless, he committed the unforgivable mistake of not taking bacteriological swabs until the morning after the opening of the burial chamber, on February 18th, instead of before the first person had entered it. This led – as we shall see – to speculations that can no longer be refuted.

One thing is certain: Lucas was chiefly interested in the chemical analysis of materials, and attached no great importance to the problem of bacteria. He took five swabs in all: from the rear wall of the chamber, from the bottom ledge of the outer shrine, and from some foot-mats. To take them, he used sterile pads supplied by the bacteriological laboratory of the Royal Naval cordite factory at Wareham, whose main concern was the manufacture of solid rocket fuel. He sent the five specimens by post to Wareham, work in the tomb continuing in the meantime. The results of the test gave four negative and one positive. Lucas calmed the fears of those taking part in the excavation by saying that the organisms on the fifth swab had been 'brought into the tomb from outside'. With that the problem was dismissed. The fungi that covered all the walls of the antechamber, the main chamber and the stone sarcophagus were not considered to be of special significance.

Dr Alexander Scott, another chemist, who conducted tests in the tomb at the same time as Lucas, disagreed with his colleague's view that the tomb had been free of germs. He wrote in *his* report that the numerous brown patches that could be seen everywhere on the walls were mould or bacteria that had fed on the size used as whitewash, or on egg-white. But he too did not go any further into the question of a possible bacterial contamination of the tomb. Instead, he and Alfred Lucas collected dead insects, which lay about the floor in large numbers. He sent them to the entomologist of the Ministry of Agriculture, who passed them on to the entomologist of the Royal Agricultural

Society in Cairo, where they were identified as a kind of beetle that fed mainly on dead organic matter. The species is still found in Egypt today and has scarcely altered.

Even at that time, while the discovery of the century was receiving ever more publicity, voices were raised suggesting that Tutankhamun's tomb had been discovered a generation too soon. Carter's master, Flinders Petrie, now seventy, posed the question: 'Is the world fit to assume responsibility for all these treasures of the past . . . to guarantee them for some more thousands of years of existence? Or is all this exposure the last stage?' And Arthur Weigall, ex-Inspector-General of the Egyptian Department of Antiquities, made a similar point: 'Have these wonderful objects survived the siege of nearly thirty-three centuries only to be shown to us of this one generation and then to fall to pieces because conditions are not ready for their preservation?'

Weigall knew what he was talking about; he could still see all too clearly in his mind's eye that sobering episode fifteen years previously, which had shocked archaeologists all over the world. It had occurred during the discovery of tomb No. 55, where the excavators had found the supposed body of Akhenaten. Leaning against a wall of the tomb were the side pieces of a burial shrine intended for Tiye. Weigall, who was then supervising Theodore Davis's excavations, recalls, 'We were able to photograph them and to copy the inscriptions; but a few hours after the introduction of the outside air the plaster-work had cracked and crumbled and fallen off the wood beneath.'

How long would the priceless treasures from Tutankhamun's tomb last? Would they fall into dust one day, disintegrate into nothing? Chemical methods of preservation were still in their infancy at that time. The first century of archaeology had gone by, the century of chemistry had only just begun.

Work in the tomb was interrupted almost every day, because the Ministry of Public Works announced the visit of some dignitary or other. It was then Carter's thankless task to examine the letters of introduction, which were quite often forged, and, with as friendly a face as possible, explain to the guests who were stealing his time the mysterious life below ground.

There were two possible ways of getting to view the tomb, either by personal permission of Carnarvon and Carter or though a letter of introduction from the Ministry in Cairo. At Lord Carnarvon's instigation, Carter gave permission only very rarely; even fellow archaeologists were not allowed to visit the tomb. The reason for this provocative edict was the exclusive agreement with *The Times*, which forbade even Egyptologists to enter the tomb if they were connected with any newspaper. Since nearly every archaeologist at some time or other published something in some newspaper, the Tutankhamun tomb was taboo to most experts. This didn't exactly sweeten the atmosphere.

The clause in the agreement could be circumvented, however, by getting permission from the Ministry of Public Works. Viewing permits could certainly be obtained there, but in such cases Carter was not allowed to give any information. Only *The Times* might have that. 'What right,' asked the Cairo newspaper *Al Ahram*, 'has an excavator to Egypt's sacred past?'

The situation became explosive when Cairo journalists came to Luxor, at the invitation of the government, in order to write about the discovery in the Valley of the Kings. Unfortunately, the newspapermen arrived before the necessary letters of introduction from the Ministry. Carter gave no information; he was not allowed to. The reporters were permitted just a glimpse into the underworld, across a barrier set up at the entrance to the antechamber. The treasures already rescued, in the tomb of Sethos II, he didn't show at all. The tone of the newspaper articles can be imagined. The Minister of Public Works declared, 'It is an unheard-of thing that we Egyptians should have to go to a London newspaper for all information regarding a tomb of one of our own kings.'

The restraint imposed on the excavators enveloped the activity below ground in an air of mystery. Luxor at the beginning of 1923 was full of rumours. Two aeroplanes, it was said, had landed in the Libyan desert behind the Valley of the Kings and had taken the most valuable treasures abroad. Famous people had been observed leaving the Tutankhamun tomb with gold and jewellery under their clothes.

All this strained Carter's nerves beyond measure. And day after day fresh visitors poured in – politicians, heads of state and other potentates. The British High Commissioner for Egypt and the Sudan, Lord Allenby, came along with a whole company of soldiers, who had to stand in line for the passage of their commander-in-chief. Lord Allenby departed but the soldiers remained, to repeat the performance for the Queen of Belgium. The arrival of the Dowager-Sultana, with all her retinue, was like a scene from musical comedy. Arthur Weigall, Inspector-General of the Department of Antiquities, who witnessed the event, recalls:

> There were soldiers springing to the salute; officers with clanking swords shouting orders; kinema operators running up the hillsides, while native boys climbed behind them carrying their apparatus; crowds of European and American visitors in every kind of costume from equestrian to regatta; Egyptian notables looking very hot in western clothes and red tarboushes; tall black eunuchs in long frock-coats; dragomans in bright silken robes; and so forth.

It was more curiosity than interest that brought the Sultana to the Valley of the Kings. She took a gracious look through the opening in the wall of the burial chamber – and vanished; but another working day had been lost. This Tutankhamun, Carter's Tutankhamun, had become an object of display for the whole world.

Arthur Weigall said he felt sorry, not for Carter, but for Tutankhamun. The opening of the tomb seemed to him like the disturbing of a sleeping man, and the massive invasion like a blasphemy. It was as though someone had been woken up in an alien age, and was being stared at by thousands of eyes, filled not with reverence but with curiosity.

Dusk sent the gapers away. As shadows fell over the Valley of the Kings reverence returned. It was quiet. Only the occasional murmur of one of the guards broke the uncanny peace. Flickering points of light wandered from one tomb to another – the guards with their lanterns. Only at the back, at the end of the Valley, was a bright gleam of light to be seen: Carter was working in his laboratory, a man possessed, renovating history.

Shortly before midnight, the approach to Tutankhamun's tomb, flanked by two armed policemen, was lost in darkness; Carter made his way home. It was the hour when voices sighed through the Valley, voices such as that of the Theban priest Neferhotep who whispered there:

How calm is this justified Great One. His beautiful destiny is fulfilled. Men have passed over since the time of the gods, the rising generation takes their place.

Ra shows himself in the morning, and Atum goes down in the fabulous land of Marun in the west. The men beget, the women conceive, and every nose breathes air – day breaks, and their children go like them into the tomb.

Celebrate the day happily, O priest! Put salve and fine oil on thy nose and garlands and lotus flowers on the body of thy sister, whom thou lovest and who sits by thee. Let singing and music be heard. Throw all evil behind thee and remember thy friends, till that day comes when thou shalt arrive in the land that loves peace. . .

The quiet Englishman had come to the end of his tether. Ten days after the opening of the third door, he had the entrance to the tomb filled in, locked and barred the laboratory, and cleared off. He disappeared for a full week. Nobody has ever discovered where he went; all at once he was there again.

Lord Carnarvon took Carter to task, but he remained impenitent. He couldn't go on working in that way. Each laid the blame on the other. 'This painful situation,' wrote James Henry Breasted, 'resulted in such strained relations between Carter and Carnarvon that a complete break seemed inevitable. Alan

Gardiner and I succeeded in pouring oil on the waters, but in so doing we both fell from Carter's good graces. The man is by no means wholly to blame – what he has gone through has broken him down.'

The hour of their greatest success had turned the two men into enemies. Fifteen years of dependence and humiliation; fifteen years of having to say 'yes', even when it went against his own convictions; fifteen years of hope, worry and despair had left their mark on Howard Carter. Was it any wonder that it all now erupted? Carnarvon sensed this; he tried to be conciliatory and sought out Carter at his house at the entrance to the Valley of the Kings. The man he found there was a bundle of nerves, stuttering, confused in speech, rummaging in mail-baskets, grumbling and swearing.

'Pull yourself together, Carter,' snapped Carnarvon at his excavator. One word led to another.

'Leave my house,' roared Carter, 'and never set foot in it again!'

Carnarvon went, and he was indeed never to cross that threshold again, for he had only a few more weeks to live.

8   Carnarvon's death: curse or legend?

> *The large number of visitors to Egypt and persons interested in Egyptian antiquities who believe in the malevolence of the spirits of the pharaohs and their dead subjects, is always a matter of astonishment to me, in view of the fact that of all ancient people the Egyptians were the most kindly and, to me, the most lovable. . . I have heard the most absurd nonsense talked in Egypt by those who believe in the malevolence of the ancient dead; but at the same time, I try to keep an open mind on the subject.*
>
> Arthur Weigall
>
> *There are more things in heaven and earth, Horatio, Than are dreamt of in your philosophy.*
>
> William Shakespeare

Lord Carnarvon was shocked. Such a thing had never happened to him in his whole life. The very man who was most indebted to him, this Carter who had been living at his expense for fifteen years, had thrown him, George Edward Stanhope

Molyneux Herbert, fifth Earl of Carnarvon, out of his house!
Catastrophe seemed inevitable.

Next day Carnarvon did not appear at the tomb. He had a
rendezvous at the Winter Palace Hotel with John Maxwell and
an Australian millionaire called McIntosh. The two Englishmen were complaining about the difficulty of finding backers
for the excavations of the Egypt Exploration Society. On the
spur of the moment, Mr. McIntosh said he would like to
support the Society for seven years at the rate of £500 per year.
(This corresponded at the time to the value of a motor-car.) In
addition, the rich Australian promised to set up an offshoot of
the British Egypt Exploration Society in New South Wales.
Carnarvon was enthusiastic.

Agreements made over whisky only acquire significance
when they are fixed in writing. On the following day, therefore,
Lord Carnarvon wrote a letter to 'Mr. McIntosh, New Winter
Palace Hotel, Luxor.' In it he expressed his thanks for the kind
donation of £500 for seven years to the Society, and for Mr.
McIntosh's readiness to set up a branch of the Society in
Australia. It was the last letter that Carnarvon wrote. Even
while writing it he was shaken by violent attacks of fever. 'I feel
awful,' he had said at breakfast that morning, when his temperature was already up to 104°F. For twelve days attacks of
fever alternated with slight improvements. His lordship
thought his poor condition was due to a mosquito bite on the
chin, which he had cut while shaving.

But he was not a man to be worried by a feverish infection.
The doctor in Luxor put him on a diet and strict bed-rest, but
that didn't stop his lordship. He drank a bottle of wine every
evening as usual: not the sour red wine of Egypt – Lord Carnarvon had first-class French wines, of which there were ample
stocks in the cellar of Highclere Castle, sent to him regularly, in
Luxor.

As his condition visibly deteriorated, Carnarvon asked his
family doctor in England to come out to him. It took barely a
week for the doctor to get there, and when he arrived he at once
arranged for the transfer of his patient to a clinic in Cairo. He

was examined, and the suspected malaria was not confirmed; so Carnarvon insisted on leaving the clinic. He moved into the Continental Savoy Hotel, where he always stayed. The attacks of fever became worse, and his lordship began to be delirious.

Lady Almina came out to Cairo; Carnarvon's son, who was on military service in India at the time, was summoned to Egypt, and Carter received a telegram from which it emerged that Lord Carnarvon was dangerously ill. But Carter made no move. He continued his work in the tomb.

'Mister, Mister!' One of his workmen came running up in excitement. Carter had sent him to his house during working-hours to fetch something. The man had found the house empty; the two servants had ridden to market in Luxor. Breathlessly the messenger reported what had happened. As he was going into the house he heard a feeble cry like that of a human being. When he turned round he saw a cobra in the canary's cage, which was just eating Carter's pet bird.

'It was the King's cobra!' said the messenger excitedly. 'It has taken its revenge on the bird, because it betrayed the site of the tomb – and now something terrible will happen!'

This event made a strong impression on Howard Carter, who was anything but superstitious. He travelled to Cairo next day and visited the mortally ill Lord Carnarvon in his hotel. But he no longer recognised him. The two men were never reconciled.

Carnarvon's feverish delirium became ever worse. 'A bird is scratching my face,' he repeated again and again. 'A bird is scratching my face.'

This sentence, spoken in a coma, was later to preoccupy the archaeologists. As Dr. Ali Hassan, Director-General of the Egyptian Museum in Cairo, pointed out, 'This sentence is of particular interest because something similar appears in a curse-text from the First Intermediate Period, which says that the Nekhebet bird shall scratch the face of anyone who does anything to a tomb.'

The ancient Egyptians viewed tomb-sacrilege as a monstrous crime, because tomb and mummy were the earthly dwelling of the Ka, the preserving life-force which lived on after a person's death. The food and drink in the tomb were also intended for the Ka, not for the corpse. The destruction and plundering of the tomb or the mummy rendered the Ka homeless and nameless. That was the worst retribution that could fall on an Egyptian. Curse-formulae go back to the beginnings of Egyptian history. In the tomb of Harkhuf in Aswan, which dates from the 6th Dynasty (2423–2263 B.C.), the threat can be read on the wall: 'Whoever enters this tomb. . . on him will I pounce as on a bird; he shall be judged for it by the great god.' And Ursu, a wealthy manager of mines, a thousand years later, had these words chiselled on a funerary statue made for him: 'Whoever lays hands on my property, whoever desecrates my tomb or carries away my mummy, the sun-god shall punish him. He shall not bequeath his goods to his children. He shall have no joy in life. He shall thirst in his grave, and his soul shall be destroyed for ever!'

Did Lord Carnarvon know these funerary texts? Were his feverish dreams a coincidence? Or was there something more behind them?

The vulture goddess Nekhebet was the goddess of Upper Egypt. Buto, the serpent goddess, ruled over Lower Egypt. Vulture and cobra, as symbols of the two lands, glittered on the forehead of the pharaoh. Carnarvon undoubtedly knew of this symbolism, but we may be equally sure that his lordship did not know the curse-texts. He always had a horror of tomb-texts – especially if the tomb had not been excavated under his patronage. But this was only the start of a chain of mysterious events.

The only living witness of these events is Lord Carnarvon's son, the present Earl of Carnarvon, now over eighty. His lordship is in many respects a replica of his father, although he had no great affection for him, as he freely admits. This came about because his father believed that small boys should be seen but not heard. As a result, he and his sister led pitiable, shadowy existences as children. The present Earl, the sixth, was not allowed to use the main entrance or to set foot in the drawing-room; he had to sneak up to the nursery by the back stairs. Only on very rare occasions, at Christmas or Easter, or at a large party for the races or a pheasant shoot, was the young lord spruced up, brought into the dining-room after lunch and shown off like a prize-winning poodle. Then he sometimes received in addition a present of a pound – as consolation for the painful programme, for he was also kept short of cash.

It can be imagined that all this did not exactly promote love for his father. So much the greater is his enjoyment of his inheritance today. 'Happy Highclere' as he likes to say – the neo-Gothic castle built by the architect of the London Houses of Parliament – is 'small, but mine own.' His lordship is flippant about his stately home, but the vast castle with its hundred rooms is in fact occupied only by him, his secretary Mary Povey, his butler and a handful of domestic servants. His lordship has been twice divorced.

How does he see his father today, and the mysterious circumstances of his death? Does he believe in the pharaoh's curse? Carnarvon's answer is worthy of Solomon: 'Whenever I am asked, I say I believe in the curse, and I don't believe in the curse; but there are the facts.'

These facts are still ever-present in his lordship's memory. He got to Cairo on 4th April, 1923, and hurried at once to the hotel where his father was lying, already unconscious. Carter and Lady Almina, his mother, were with him. The doctors had already given him up. The following night, at 1.50, there was a knock at the young lord's door. A nurse brought him the news that Lord Carnarvon had died. The sixth Earl of Carnarvon, as he now was, got up and went to his father's room. As he opened the door, all the lights in the hotel went out. The hotel bedroom with the dead peer was enveloped in a ghostly darkness. They looked for candles, but couldn't find any. Finally, after five minutes, the lights in the hotel went on again.

Next day, when the young lord went to Field Marshal Lord Allenby, to discuss arrangements for conveying the body back to England, he heard that at 1.50 the previous night the whole of Cairo had been without electricity. An enquiry had produced no explanation for this failure. Even more puzzling, however, was the fact that the lights of the city, with its population of a million, went on again without any intervention by technicians. But that was not all. At Highclere Castle, at the same moment, allowing for the difference in time, Susan, Lord Carnarvon's fox terrier bitch, began to howl. His lordship's favourite dog, which had even accompanied him on journeys to Egypt, until it lost its left front leg in an accident in 1919, fell over as though struck by lightning, and died. The facts are attested by Mrs. McLean, the Scottish housekeeper.

George Edward Stanhope Molyneux Herbert, fifth Earl of Carnarvon, was buried on 30th April, 1923, within sight of Highclere Castle, on Beacon Hill, where he had played as a child, and as an adùlt had searched for archaeological treasures. One man was missing: Howard Carter. He carried his anger with his lordship beyond the grave. Only the closest relations and friends and the domestic staff were present. Among them was J. G. Maxwell, who wrote in an obituary, 'His loss to Egyptian Archaeology and Egyptology is irreparable and to all it is a great sorrow that Lord Carnarvon should have died thus, in the zenith of his fame, when his name was a household word on the lips of nations – for alas he never saw his work completed. So it remains for us all and for posterity to carry it on in a manner worthy of his name.'

After the interment, an unknown woman appeared at Highclere Castle. She said her name was Wilma, that she had mediumistic powers, and that the spirit of the dead man lived on in her. When the sixth Earl of Carnarvon received her, she merely said, 'Don't go near your father's grave! It will bring you bad luck!' Then she vanished. Lord Carnarvon took the strange advice to heart and to the present day has never once visited his father's grave.

At the same time, James Henry Breasted was also shaken by a strange fever that returned every day. His son Charles described it as a 'feverish malaise', which now all at once became worse. It always began in the afternoon with an aching throat, fits of shivering, and a feeling as though his blood were burning in his veins. Breasted suspected malaria. He had contracted the disease once before, in Iraq. But the English doctor who examined him shook his head; it was not malaria. The laboratory report was negative, and even quinine, which he prescribed, had no effect. Instead, like clockwork, the attacks of fever set in punctually every afternoon. For six weeks Breasted kept to his bed, but then could stand it no longer and resumed his researches at the Tutankhamun tomb. Twice a week he had himself and a horse-cab ferried across the Nile, so that he could drive to the Valley of the Kings, for he was far too weak to ride on a mule. The effect was uncanny when James Henry Breasted appeared in the royal tomb with a white mask over his mouth.

The Breasteds occupied two rooms on the ground floor of the fashionable Winter Palace Hotel. One day a new guest moved into the room next door. He introduced himself as Professor La Fleur. He struck Breasted as 'a cultivated and pleasant-spoken' person. The tall, slim man with a jaunty goatee beard lectured in English literature at a Canadian university. His great desire was to view Tutankhamun's tomb. Armed with a couple of letters addressed to Carter, he set out for the Valley of the Kings. When he returned to the hotel in the evening, he was overjoyed, for his wish had been fulfilled; but he was also ill, in fact desperately ill, according to the Breasteds' English doctor, who was hurriedly summoned. That night Breasted's son Charles sat at his typewriter writing his usual report for the *Chicago Daily News*. He recalls, 'At about three o'clock. . . my room door stood open. Suddenly I realised that the coughing had grown much fainter and less frequent. I stepped down the hall to La Fleur's door and listened. The coughing had stopped, everything was still.' Charles felt that something terrible must have happened. Then the door was opened from the inside and the grave face of the doctor appeared in the doorway. Young Breasted didn't dare ask any questions; the doctor merely nodded: Professor La Fleur was dead.

The death certificate which the doctor filled out gave as cause of death 'inflammation of the lungs'. La Fleur had had a cough and fever; what else could the doctor have diagnosed? The management of the luxury hotel was alarmed: a guest had died.

There was great concern to get the body out of the hotel without attracting attention; the illustrious guests from all over the world must not be allowed to notice anything. Two hotel servants dragged in a long wicker basket. The dead guest was laid in it and covered with a blanket. Before the day was even dawning and the first guests seeking out the luxurious breakfast-room on the first floor, the body had disappeared. Charles Breasted and the doctor packed the Professor's last belongings into his suitcase and deposited it in the baggage-room. Hotel servants put clean sheets on the bed. Next evening the Americans had a new neighbour. The Professor was said to have left.

Breasted himself was dogged by mysterious illnesses all his life – one day during a lecture at Bryn Mawr College his left arm became purple and swelled up like a balloon – but he reached a good age. He was seventy when he died in New York on 2nd December, 1935, a few days after returning from an Egyptian trip. The doctors of the Rockefeller Institute for Medical Research found a virulent haematolytic streptococcal infection.

But back to 1923. Lord Carnarvon's death was only the beginning of an uncanny series of deaths. The same year saw the deaths of Lord Carnarvon's brother, Colonel Aubrey Herbert, the Cairo archaeologist Achmed Kamal, and the American Egyptologist William Henry Goodyear. In 1924, the British radiologist Archibald Douglas Reed and his fellow-countryman Hugh Gerard Evelyn-White died. Reed died on the way to Luxor, where he was to have X-rayed Tutankhamun's as yet unopened mummiform coffin, using a portable apparatus. Evelyn-White, a classical archaeologist formerly of Oxford, had joined the Metropolitan Museum's expedition in 1909 and had dug in the Theban necropolis.

In the same year, Carter's assistant Arthur C. Mace gave up his job. Shaken by attacks of fever, he was often too weak to make his way to Tutankhamun's tomb. He spent the following four years in sanatoria in England, on the Riviera, in Switzerland, and in New York; he kept trying to get his scientific work into order and prepare it for publication, but in vain. He died, aged fifty-four, on 6th April, 1928.

Two years previously, Carter's teacher Edouard Naville, Carnarvon's friend George Jay-Gould, the British industrialist Joel Woolf, the papyrologist Bernard Greenfell, the American Egyptologist Aaron Ember, and the British nurse who had looked after Lord Carnarvon in Cairo until he died, had all lost their lives. Naville was over eighty, but Ember, who came from Russia, had studied in Germany and held a chair at the University of Baltimore, died at the age of forty-eight in mysterious circumstances. On 1st June, 1926, he tried to rescue a manuscript from his burning house in Baltimore; he had been working on it for years – the Egyptian Book of the Dead. The British industrialist Joel Woolf travelled out from England to view the tomb. On the boat home he fell into a coma and died. A similar fate overtook the American multi-millionaire George Jay-Gould, who complained of severe fever a day after viewing the tomb. A few hours later he was dead. Bernard Pyne Greenfell had visited Tutankhamun's tomb for the last time two years before his death. The papyrologist from Oxford was regarded as the leading excavator of Roman documents in Egypt; he died at fifty-seven. Carnarvon's nurse was only twenty-eight. She had married a rubber planter from Tanganyika and died in childbirth. In 1929, the newspapers announced the deaths of Lord Carnarvon's wife, Lady Almina, Carnarvon's friend and executor John G. Maxwell, and Carter's secretary Richard Bethell. Bethell was only thirty-five; he was found dead in bed one morning, from circulatory failure.

The mysterious circumstances now became grotesque. Bethell's father, the seventy-eight-year-old Lord Westbury, when he heard of his son's death, threw himself from the seventh floor of his London house. The hearse that took his lordship's mortal remains to the cemetery ran over a small boy at a busy crossing.

When the archaeologist Harry R. Hall died the following year – he had been a draughtsman on the Tutankhamun team and in 1924 had succeeded Wallis Budge as Keeper at the

British Museum – scientists began to look into the annals of Egyptology. The result was staggering.

Since the beginnings of Egyptology in the last century, dozens of archaeologists and researchers have met an unexpected, untimely and inexplicable death. At the same time, it should not be concealed that a series of prominent Egyptologists – including Richard Lepsius, Adolf Erman, Alan Gardiner, Gaston Maspero, and Edouard Naville – reached an advanced age. But that does not account for the unexpected deaths of a far greater number of scholars.

William Berend, a New York banker who made a journey to the Valley of the Kings with Gaston Maspero, a friend of his student days, died at the age of twenty-nine. Thomas Bromhead, an English scholar, stopped on the Nile on his way to Persia in the last century; he died at thirty. Also thirty when he died was the Scottish lawyer, collector and excavator Alexander Henry Rhind. The librarian at Cairo Museum, Joseph Galtier, a French orientalist, was thirty-four when he died quite unexpectedly on 2nd April, 1908. The French draughtsman Prosper Marilhat died at thirty-six on the way to Egypt. He had travelled the land of the Nile sixteen years previously with the German expedition of Carl Alexander Freiherr von Hügel, and had returned to France on the boat that carried from Luxor the 3,200-year-old obelisk which stands today in the Place de la Concorde in Paris.

The American amateur archaeologist Robb de Peyster Tytus, who assisted Naville at the excavation of the palace of Amenophis III at Thebes, only reached the age of thirty-seven. The English traveller Vere Monro, who travelled in Egypt and Nubia and died in Malta on the way back, was granted no more than thirty-nine years. George Bethune English, an American artillery officer born in Cambridge, Massachusetts, who took part in Ismail Pasha's expedition to Dongola and Senaar, died prematurely at forty-one after his return to Washington.

The French Egyptologists Jean François Champollion and Jean Lesquier each lived only one year longer. Champollion, who found the key to the decipherment of the hieroglyphs without previously setting foot on Egyptian soil, died in 1832 after his first journey to Egypt. Lesquier, whose researches in Egypt were confined to the Graeco-Roman epoch, was, like Champollion, only forty-two when he died, on 28th June, 1921, at Neuilly-sur-Seine. Champollion's pupil, the Italian Ippolito Rosellini, who accompanied his master on his Egyptian expedition, lived only one year longer than him. He died a few years after accepting a chair in oriental languages in Pisa.

Did the god-kings of the empire of the Nile avenge themselves on the Americans Henry Gorringe and Eckley B. Coxe Jr., and on the German Egyptologist Georg Möller, who all died at forty-four? Was it because Gorringe had taken that great obelisk from Alexandra to the New World, where it can be seen today in New York? And because Coxe, a rich businessman, financed the excavations of Pennsylvania University in Nubia and Egypt? And because Georg Möller in his research had specialised in the burial customs of the ancient Egyptians? The curse – let us for once so call these unusual deaths – reached them everywhere – America, Europe, Asia. Georg Möller died on 2nd October, 1921, in Sweden, of a shivering fever. The son of a German businessman, he was born in Caracas, Venezuela, went to school in Germany and at twenty-eight became scientific attaché to the German consulate-general in Cairo. At Abusir he uncovered prehistoric graves, and at Deir el Medina he found the tombs of noble Egyptians. Tombs were his hobby. A few months after his appointment as an honorary professor, he died, far from Egypt and the Valley of the Kings.

Edward Ayrton, who with Theodore Davis had discovered the tombs of Queen Tey and the pharaohs Horemheb and Siptah, and the cache of material from the construction of Tutankhamun's tomb, died at the age of thirty-one in an obscure manner in Ceylon. He had left Egypt in 1910 after successful activity as a discoverer in order to devote himself to the study of Indian languages at Oxford. A year later, in October, he went on behalf of the Archaeological Survey of India to Ceylon, as Director of the Archaeological Institute. After only a short while, his friends in Luxor received troubled letters;

Ayrton was homesick for Egypt. At the next opportunity, he wrote, he would come back. But he never saw Egypt, the green Nile and the red-brown cliffs of the Valley of the Kings again. In the spring of 1914 his body was found in the sand of a lagoon. Beside him lay his companion, also dead, and nearby two guns. They had been on a hunting expedition. No signs of injury or any effects of violence could be detected on either Ayrton or his companion; their clothes were dry and the bodies did not give the impression of having been in water for even a short time. But since the death of each and every person requires a plausible official explanation, the coroner wrote on the death certificate: drowned.

The uncanny list could be continued at will. Such well-known names would crop up as that of the British Consul-General and excavator Henry Salt; the engineer, actor and archaeologist from Padua, Giovanni Belzoni; or the British diplomat Sir Eldon Gorst. They all died at an age that is usually called the prime of life. Was it really all only chance?

How did the sixth Earl of Carnarvon put it? 'I believe in the curse, and I don't believe in the curse; but there are the facts.'

Among them is the following. A few years ago, when I was researching for my book *The Curse of the Pharaohs*, I had an appointment at the Omar Khayyam Hotel with Gamal Mehrez, at that time Director-General of the Egyptian Museum in Cairo. I wanted to know what he thought about the curse.

'Certainly,' said Dr. Mehrez, 'if you add up all these mysterious deaths it could undoubtedly give cause for thought. Especially as one or two curse-formulae occur in ancient Egyptian history.' He smiled self-consciously and went on, 'But I simply don't believe in it. Look at me. All my life I have had to do with pharaonic tombs and mummies. I am surely the best proof that it is all coincidence.'

Indeed, no man in the world had ever had so many mummies under his roof as Dr. Gamal Mehrez. The mummy gallery of the Cairo National Museum is a thrilling accumulation of mummified Egyptian history. Amenophis III lies there, grinning broadly with caved-in eyes; so do Sethos I, slim and delicate, and his son Rameses II, aquiline of nose and with a fuzz of flaxen hair. At the time Mehrez's answer made me think. I became even more thoughtful, however, when the newspapers announced four weeks after this conversation that Dr. Gamal Mehrez, Director-General of the Egyptian Museum in Cairo, had died suddenly and unexpectedly of circulatory failure. He was fifty-two years old. His last interview has been with me. He 'happened' to fall down dead as transport-workers carried the carefully packed gold mask of Tutankhamun out of the Museum to take it to the airport. Waiting there were two jet planes of the Royal Air Force, which brought the valuable piece to London for the Tutankhamun exhibition.

Ever since the April days of 1923, when the main Egyptian dailies, *Al Ahram* and *El Mokkatam*, announced Carnarvon's death on their black-bordered front pages, and referred to the pharaoh's curse, the world has been haunted by stories and films which may be agreeably hair-raising but in no way do justice to the problem. And the special interest of occultists in the subject, far from shedding light on it, has enveloped the curse-phenomenon in even greater darkness. But every now and then we sceptical realists of the last quarter of the twentieth century are startled by scientific experiments which show that there are, after all, manifestly more things in heaven and earth than are dreamt of in our philosophy.

Pyramids have always had a special interest for natural scientists. In 1959 the Czech radio engineer Karel Drbal took out a patent, No. 91304, for a small hollow pyramid that caused strange things to happen. Fishes under the pyramid, aligned in a north-south direction, became dehydrated within thirteen days; they lost two thirds of their weight and were suddenly mummified. Blunt razor blades under this geometric construction regained their former sharpness within six days. The patent was granted, though Karel Drbal could offer no explanation.

The pyramids, it seems, do not owe their shape to chance; the ancient Egyptians were already conducting empirical experiments. Following in their footsteps came the American nuclear physicist Luis Alvarez, Professor at the University of California, Berkeley, and winner of the Nobel Prize in 1968. He visited the pyramids of Giza for the first time in 1962 and was interested to hear that archaeologists were still not sure whether there might not be hidden chambers in them. The Professor, well acquainted with all the physical possibilities, at once came up with a theory on how to tackle the problem. The pyramids must be X-rayed. But no X-ray apparatus in the world is big enough or powerful enough to penetrate even the smallest of the Egyptian pyramids, and so Alvarez pursued a quite different idea. He concerned himself with the middle one of the three great pyramids of Giza, the one in which Giovanni Belzoni had discovered an empty burial chamber in 1818. The room was so plain that archaeologists simply couldn't believe that a king had been buried there. Since then, generations of researchers and adventurers have sounded the Chephren pyramid for a perhaps undiscovered chamber, but in vain.

In the chamber discovered by Belzoni, 130 metres below the tip of the pyramid, Alvarez set up electronic apparatus weighing in all some thirty tons. It was a considerable feat just to get the sensitive instruments inside the pyramid. The internal passages were not more than 120 centimetres wide, and so the technicians had first to dismantle their valuable equipment and then reassemble it in the vault within. The most important instruments were so-called radiation detectors, with which the incidence of cosmic rays can be measured. It took three months to get the laboratory under the Chephren pyramid into working order; the Six Days' War finally interrupted the enterprise, but in the spring of 1968 the scientists were at last able to go to work.

The principle was as follows: cosmic radiation is so powerful that it can penetrate even the stone of a pyramid, over four million tons of it, though the braking effect of the stone on muon particles is greater than that of air. As applied in practice to the pyramid experiment, this meant that, if the muon incidence remained constant under continual variation of the angle of measurement, there was no further chamber; if the muon incidence increased in an otherwise constant field of measurement, there was a hollow space. That was the theory; in practice things turned out differently.

In the first place, all the measuring instruments went mad; the muon incidence was greater than expected and the physicists in the pyramid at a loss. As Professor Luis Alvarez said at the time, 'Call it sorcery or the curse of the pharaohs, call it what you like, but there is something here that we can't explain!'

The fact that a scientist of repute was at a loss in the face of certain phenomena must give even a sceptic food for thought.

A dispassionate analysis of the premature deaths reveals three different causes of frequent occurrence: severe attacks of fever with delusions and presentiments of death; strokes, with failure of circulation; and cancers of sudden onset which in a short time lead to death.

Because what cannot be must not be, archaeologists usually dismiss the curse-formulae with a wave of the hand. Yet these same archaeologists accept, literally and in detail, all the other texts handed down. In the meantime, science has taken up the subject. Serious researchers have proposed interesting theories, though they are unable to prove them. There is talk of deadly bacteria and poisons, of radioactivity and nerve gas, and of mysterous radiation from the universe. Hardly a year goes by without a claim by some scientist or other that he has found a possible new solution.

The physician and biologist Dr. Ezzedin Taha of the University of Cairo reported the results of some interesting research on 3rd November, 1962, before press representatives in Cairo. Taha maintained that he was on the track of the legendary curse of the pharaohs. Studies of archaeologists and museum employees over a long period of time had shown that these men had suffered from a fungoid infestation that caused feverish inflammation, especially of the respiratory ducts. After microbiological investigations, Dr. Taha established that the fungi could survive in burial chambers and mummies for thousands of years. The researcher declared, in his own words, 'This discovery has destroyed once and for all the superstition that scholars working in ancient tombs have died through a kind of curse. The scientists were victims of pathogenic agents with which they came into contact in the course of their work. There are people, even today, who still believe that supernatural powers are to be attributed to the pharaohs' curse, but that belongs in the realm of fairy tales.'

Those were the unambiguous words of a level-headed scientist. They seemed rather less persuasive, however, when shortly after that press conference Dr. Ezzedin Taha, together with two of his colleagues, drove from Cairo to Suez. On the dead straight, little-frequented desert road, seventy miles from the capital, Taha's car suddenly crossed to the other side of the road and went straight into a car coming in the opposite direction. Taha and his colleagues were killed outright; those in the other vehicle were rescued, with injuries. These witnesses confirmed that they had seen the scientist's car coming from a long way off, and that it had suddenly driven straight at them. Because of their report, an autopsy on Taha's body was ordered. The result: a circulatory failure had brought the biologist's life to an abrupt end; at the moment of the accident a dead man had been sitting at the wheel. Dr. Taha, it seems, was on the wrong track.

Bacteria and poisons would in themselves be an obvious and de-mystifying explanation of the so-called curse of the pharaohs, especially of the fact that some archaeologists lost their lives in their early years, while others reached an advanced age. For it is indeed in the nature of infections to attack one person and pass another by without trace. But all attempts at explanation so far, however interesting they may be, are mere hypotheses. Which is why there are so many of them.

Dr. John Wiles, a South African geologist, climbed into the cave system of a Rhodesian range of mountains in the 1950s in order to investigate bat droppings as a possible source of fertiliser. In his tour of the caves, 150 feet below ground level, the geologist encountered tens of thousands of bats. Back in the daylight, he complained of heartburn, muscular pains and a high fever. A doctor thought that Wiles had contracted an inflammation of the lungs in the hostile cave-world. As the fever grew worse, he sent his patient to the Geoffrey Hospital in Port Elizabeth. There the chief physician, Dr. Dean, found on examining the geologist symptoms similar to those described by American doctors in a professional journal. The Americans had discovered the same clinical picture in men who had devoted themselves to exploring Inca caves. Dr. Dean took a blood sample from the mortally sick Wiles and sent it to the U.S.A. for examination. The result was not surprising. The American specialists confirmed that the South African geologist had been struck by the same cave-disease as the American Inca explorers. It was called histo-plasmosis, and its germ was transmitted through the droppings of bats. It was possible to save John Wiles with antibiotics.

A similar puzzling disease was discovered by physicians in the 1870s in Europe. During the building of the St. Gotthard tunnel, so many workmen went down with a strange 'tunnel disease' that the project was seriously endangered. There were not enough beds in the Swiss clinics to provide medical care for all the patients; workmen from St. Gotthard were taken as far as Frieburg. A Swiss doctor finally discovered the cause of the attack: a tiny threadworm in the faeces of the tunnel-workers. Two poison-glands in the head of this hookworm produce the pathogenic substance which enters the blood stream via the intestinal blood vessels and destroys the red corpuscles. The sickness was known as 'miner's anaemia' (*Bergarbeiteranämie, anémie des mineurs*) in the German pits and in the Belgian mining district. Perhaps archaeologists too were struck by this pit disease. Attacks of weakness and anaemia are frequent symptoms.

The two last-named possibilities are thus a perfectly natural explanation; in these two cases there can be no question of a curse. It is another matter, however, with poison. If the pharaohs had protected their tombs with highly effective poisons, the deaths would definitely not have been coincidence. And the ancient Egyptians were masterly poisoners. They obtained prussic acid from peach-stones and aconitine from monkshood – five milligrams of either are fatal.

Poisons in general played a significant part throughout antiquity. The ancient Greeks carried out executions in a 'refined' manner – with prussic acid; Socrates had to drink a cup of hemlock, Medea eliminated her rival with the poison of meadow saffron, and Mithridates IV, King of Pontus, had only one passion besides waging war – poison. From fear of one day falling victim to an attempt at poisoning, he gradually accustomed himself to all poisons by taking regular small doses, so that eventually he was immune.

Cleopatra, the last Egyptian queen, was one of the most considerable poisoners of history. She had no scruples about trying out her own recipes on slaves, and even her lovers went in fear of her arts. Antony never dined alone with the beautiful queen; he always had a food-taster beside him. The subtlety with which Cleopatra went to work is recounted by Pliny. Antony sat with his beloved at wine, and his taster had first to sample even that. He did so, and as he survived the sip Antony took the cup. Cleopatra put her hand seductively to her hair, plucked a flower from her garland and threw it into her guest's wine. He took it as a gesture of coquetry and put the cup to his lips. But the beautiful Cleopatra snatched it from him. She sent for a convicted felon and told him to drink the wine. The man did so and fell down dead. The Queen then informed a perplexed-looking Antony that it was not the wine that was poisoned but the flower. She had merely wanted to demonstrate by her gruesome act that it would have been an easy matter for her to poison Antony – if she had wanted to. He could have saved himself the taster.

The quality of Egyptian poisons was proverbial, the achievements of Egyptian toxicologists legendary. Roman emperors had their poisoners trained on the Nile. Caligula, Claudius, Nero and Caracalla maintained extensive collections of poisons. Caracalla is supposed to have invested seven and a half million denarii in his strange hobby.

In Africa today we are still finding a large number of highly effective poisons which act by paralysing the heart. Best known are *acocanthera schimperi* and the amorphous glyco-side, quad-bain. The strophanthus poison can produce equilibrium disturbances, hallucinations and states of confusion, merely through contact. Toxicologists have established that this poison causes a heart fibrillation that can lead to death. Infection can follow even from perspiration. Powerful poisons on the wall-surfaces of tombs or on grave-goods could thus have a fatal effect. And the stability of such poisons for thousands of years in the hermetically sealed atmosphere of the burial chamber, screened from the incidence of any light, has also been affirmed by scientists.

The ancient Egyptians built pyramids and temples that have been a technical mystery to posterity for thousands of years: would such a people have abandoned their god-kings to robbers and adventurers without protection?

Even those who take a negative or sceptical view of the curse, such as Arthur Weigall, Inspector-General of the Department of Antiquities, quoted at the start of this chapter, are sometimes confronted with mysteries that shake their view of life. In the case of Weigall it was a simple photograph. In the course of excavations in western Thebes, in the tomb of a vizier of the 18th Dynasty, Weigall had come upon the mummy of a priest who had obviously appropriated the tomb and sarcophagus in order to save his heirs money. What had happened to the mummy of the rightful owner of the tomb one can only guess. The mummy with its sarcophagus was taken to Luxor, where Weigall locked it up in the store-room of the Department of Antiquities. Every time the Inspector entered the room he felt an unaccountable sense of apprehension in the presence of this mummy, which lay in its open coffin. This was all the more remarkable as Weigall was accustomed to the sight of mummies. He had spent many a night alone with a mummy in a tomb, and had often used an occupied sarcophagus as a picnic table. But this mummy seemed to attract the archaeologist as though by magic.

This strange feeling roused his curiosity. One morning he

went into the store-room and, all on his own, set about undoing the bandages in which the impious priest had been wrapped, more than 3,000 years before. With his usual precision, Weigall took notes on the progress of the work, made sketches, and photographed the various stages of the job. The linen cloths that had covered the face were of such fine quality that Weigall took them home with him, together with the stripped mummy, to show them to friends. The mummy was put in the portico outside the house and the linen cloths Weigall placed in a drawer in his guest-room.

During this time, the archaeologist had visitors, a lady and her little daughter. Weigall thought no more about the mummy-cloths and put the guest-room at the visitors' disposal. Two days later the girl became gravely ill. The doctor arrived but could form no diagnosis. The little girl's condition grew visibly worse.

Next morning the mother came running to Weigall with the mummy cloths in her hand. 'Here,' she cried in great distress, 'take this horrible stuff and burn it; and for goodness' sake send that mummy away, or the child will die!' Weigall, as mentioned, was rather a sceptic, but he humoured the hysterical woman. That very evening the cloths and the mummy, packed in a box, were sent to Cairo. Two days later, the child was on her feet again, and Weigall forgot the incident.

It was not until a few weeks later that he was given a sharp reminder. He had developed the film he had taken during the unwrapping of the mummy. He couldn't believe his eyes: staring at him from one of the photographs, transparent and shadowy, was a face, as though an uninvited guest had interposed himself between camera and mummy. 'It can't have been faked,' said Arthur Weigall. He showed the uncanny picture to numerous experts, but never received an explanation.

Arthur Edward Pearse Brome Weigall was short and stocky, but he was no coward. At that time, in the winter of 1908, he had as guests in his villa on the Nile the well-known American painter Joseph Lindon Smith and his wife. Smith, a Bostonian

who had studied in Paris, had taken the hearts of all archaeologists by storm on his first visit to Egypt in 1898, because he was
able to copy ancient reliefs as no one else could. He had painted
for Davis in Thebes, for Quibell in Saqqara, and for Reisner in
Giza, and wanted to continue his work that winter in the tombs
of the nobility in Thebes. Weigall, then twenty-eight, and his
guest, nearly twenty years older, had a large tent put up on the
other side of the Nile, below the tomb-world of Sheik Abd
el-Kurna. They spent their days in the shadows of the tombs
and their nights in their tent.

During a long walk which the two made after dusk, and
which took them as far as the necropolis of Biban el Harim, the
Valley of the Queens, an idea occurred to them: the moon,
shedding its soft beams into the semi-circle of the Valley like
stage-lighting, prompted them to put on a show in that impressive open-air theatre. The piece was conceived that very night.
The subject was the drama of Akhenaten, who, robbed of his
tomb and his mummy, wandered the necropolis as a ghost. It
was a piece with three characters. Weigall's wife was to play
Akhenaten – the part of the youthful dreamer had to be played
by a woman; Mrs. Smith was to take the part of Akhenaten's
mother Tiye, and Lindon Smith was to represent a messenger
from the underworld. Stage manager and director: Arthur
Weigall.

The project was entirely serious. The high society of Luxor
was invited to the first night, but the first night never took
place. During the dress rehearsal Mrs. Smith had just finished
her first monologue when she was prostrated by a piercing pain
in the eyes, and within two hours she had fallen into a sort of
delirium, in which she poured forth all manner of phantasies.
'The story of how at midnight she was taken across the deserted
fields and over the river to our house at Luxor, would read like
the narration of a nightmare,' wrote Weigall. Mrs. Smith was
suffering from highly disturbed vision and was taken next day
to the clinic in Cairo. A day later, Mrs. Weigall had also to be
conveyed to Cairo; she had collapsed in unaccountable circumstances. Weigall recalls, 'For the next two or three weeks, Mrs

Smith's eyes and my wife's life hung in the balance and were often despaired of. Mercifully, however, they were both restored in due time to perfect health; but none of us entertained any desire to undertake the rehearsals a second time.'

Howard Carter had never believed in the curse of the pharaohs – at least, that is what he maintained. He was a fatalist; he took life as it came. But he would certainly not have let himself be deflected from the Tutankhamun enterprise even if it had been sure to bring him an early death. The pharaoh had him in his spell.

9   The burial chamber: treasures for eternity

*With the profound silence that
reigned the emotion deepened, the
past and present seemed to meet –
time to stand and wait, and one
asked oneself, was it not yesterday
that, with pomp and ceremony,
they had laid the young king in
that casket?*

Howard Carter

The previous year Howard Carter had still put up at one of the
cheap hotels of the city. When he arrived in Cairo from London
on 8th October, 1923, he stayed at the exclusive Continental
Savoy. Two days later, he travelled on to Luxor.

Lord Carnarvon's widow, Lady Almina, had taken over the
digging concession, at Carter's insistence. It was agreed with
the Department of Antiquities that the work in the Valley of the
Kings was to be finished within a year. Who could have
imagined that it would take another nine, of agonising toil?

In the train to Luxor, Carter reviewed the past year. Only a
year before, he had travelled to Luxor with beating heart; he
had staked all on one card, and had won. But the success, the
triumph, was not what he had imagined it would be. And he
still could not grasp that Carnarvon was dead. For fifteen years
he had always stood behind him – even when he was not in

Egypt. Now all at once, when he, Carter, was the uncrowned king in the Valley of the Kings, he missed his lordship, his gruff instructions, his condescending orders. Would he in fact have the strength to complete this Tutankhamun enterprise alone? Did he possess sufficient authority to hold together all those taking part in the project?

The workmen, he knew, were on his side. He could rely on his foremen, the *reises*. There were five of them altogether: Achmed Gurgar, Hussein Achmed Said, Gad Hassan, Hassan Abu Owad and Abdelad Achmed.

Achmed Gurgar was the man who had spotted the first step to Tutankhamun's tomb. Between him and Carter there was a very special relationship; he spoke an amusing English and always addressed Carter correctly as 'Sir'. Carter had a letter in his pocket which Achmed had written to him in England during the summer break; he drew it out and read it yet again:

Kurna, Luxor
5th August 1923

Mr. Howard Carter Esq.

Honourable Sir,

Beg to write this letter hoping that you are enjoying good health, and ask the Almighty to keep you & bring you back to us in Safety.

Beg to inform your Excellency that Store No. 15 is alright, Treasure is alright, the Northern Store is alright. Wadain and House are all alright, & in all your work order is carried on according to your honourable instructions.

Rais Hussein, Gad Hassan, Hassan Owad, Abdelad Ahmed and all the gaffirs of the house beg to send their best regards.

My best regards to your respectable Self, and all members of the Lord's family, & to all your friends in England.

Longing to your early coming.

Your most obedient Servant
Rais Ahmed Gurgar

Excavation workers were occasionally a source of much trouble to archaeologists. Although it was not difficult in Egypt, then as now, to engage hordes of unemployed as labourers, most researchers remained faithful to their workers and in spite of higher costs took them with them from one site to another. This naturally had its reason. If it was difficult enough in the first place to explain to these simple people the purpose of this grubbing about in the sand, it was still more difficult – assuming this was successful – to persuade them not to let the finds disappear into the fold of their long garments, and thence on to the black market.

The British archaeologist Leonard Woolley was the first to employ a premium system, under which for every find they made the workmen were paid roughly what it was worth on the black market. This increased Woolley's budget, but also his quota of finds; small finds, especially, suddenly cropped up in astonishing numbers.

Out of the mass of workmen – Carter at times had 100, Petrie and Woolley even 300 to 400 – the archaeologists would appoint one or more foremen, so-called *reises*. These *reises* had marked themselves out by a special flair and by their intelligence. In face of the men of science, however, they sometimes displayed the minds of children. Woolley, for instance, spoke with a grin about his foreman Isgullah, with whom he had carried out excavations in Nubia. This Isgullah came along one day with a swollen cheek, caused by a bad tooth, and asked his master to pull it out. Woolley was a 'doctor', a D.Phil. in fact, but how can one explain to a Nubian foreman that a Doctor of Philosophy cannot pull a tooth? Woolley got out of it by saying that he didn't have the necessary instruments on hand, and without pincers it was impossible to deal with a tooth. Isgullah turned and went out; when he came back he had two enormous pairs of pincers in his hand and asked Woolley to get to work. After a look into his suffering foreman's mouth, Dr. Woolley said the tooth could be saved; it only needed a strong medicine. Under Isgullah's critical eye, 'Doctor' Woolley mixed a draught of potassium iodide, which he carried with him in his first-aid box, and handed it to the patient.

'How can that help?' he grumbled. 'That only goes to my stomach, which is all right; the pain is in my tooth!' Still grumbling, Isgullah let himself be persuaded, poured down the medicine with disgust and disappeared.

Woolley was surprised and relieved when he met his grinning foreman next morning at work; yes, everything was all right again.

'But Isgullah,' said Woolley, 'that can't be so; you said yourself that the medicine couldn't help.'

Isgullah looked grave. 'It was a very good medicine; it really worked miracles. In the night, while I was asleep, I swallowed the bad tooth; it went down into the medicine, and when I woke up, there it was again in my mouth, and it was cured.'

That is only one of the many foremen's stories that archaeologists like to tell. Howard Carter was far too serious a person to relate anecdotes about his foremen. But perhaps that was why they liked him so much.

Achmed was standing by the train when Carter arrived. For years the Englishman had tried to puzzle out how it was that whenever he arrived in Luxor one of his foremen was always at the station, to load his luggage on to a donkey, even when he had given no indication of his coming. It was not until much later that he discovered the secret of this infallible presence: when Carter was on the way – and the workmen knew, of course, that the excavations began every year at roughly the same time – the *reises* took it in turns. Each day a different one met every train arriving fom Cairo. And since there were only two trains a day from Cairo, it was not such a great imposition. They were on station duty every five days.

Carter's house, the laboratory, everything, was in order. The last, exciting stage, as everyone thought, could begin.

The golden shrine which Carter believed to contain the mummy of Tutankhamun set the researchers some problems. How had that magnificent structure, 5.18 metres long, 3.35 wide and 2.74 high, got there? Even when taken to pieces the shrine wouldn't go through the doorway to the burial chamber; above all, it would have been impossible to assemble its awkward components in the confined space.

There was only one explanation: the wall between the burial chamber and the ante-chamber could not have been put up until after the shrine had been assembled over the sarcophagus. The door-opening, which would have been left free, had a purely symbolic character. So in order to get to the mummy, Carter had to the follow the opposite course to that of the tomb builders; he had first to pull down the dividing wall and then dismantle the shrine into its component parts – as it had been when fitted together over three thousand years before.

The two folding doors at the east end were closed with simple bolts; they bore no seals, but also no sign of any violent opening. Uncertainty was in the air: had the grave-robbers who had rummaged through the antechamber, but then left it largely unplundered, laid hands on the mummy of the king?

Howard Carter drew back the bolts. They offered no resistance. The gilded panels swung open as easily as the door of a room. An electric lamp on a stand threw its fierce light on to the inside as it emerged from the darkness. Carter saw a second shrine, and the bolt that closed this second door bore a seal. Doubts were over: the seal was intact; no human hand could have touched King Tutankhamun's mummy since it had been laid to rest. 'I think,' wrote Carter, 'at the moment we did not even want to break the seal, for a feeling of intrusion had descended heavily upon us with the opening of the doors. . .'

The overwhelming moment, the certainty that they were standing right by the body of the legendary king, made Carter re-close the doors of the outer shrine. He turned first to a low opening in the wall at the eastern end of the burial chamber. As he shone in a light, he caught his breath: all the art treasures stored in the antechamber were as tinsel and pinchbeck compared to what was piled up here, each on top of the other. This was the king's treasury.

On a golden chest in front of the entrance, sitting ready to spring, was a jackal, the sacred animal of the god of the dead,

Anubis, who watches over all the secrets of the tomb. The chest still stood on its carrying-frame, just as it had been when the priests set it down. Behind this chest Carter noticed a tall Canopic shrine. Four young girls in transparent garments held their outstretched arms protectively against the gilded side walls. It was hard to recognise in these charming creatures the goddesses Isis, Nephthys, Neith and Selkit. This shrine, like the coffin shrine, was of gesso-gilt wood and it covered a vast block of alabaster, which was inscribed all over with hieroglyphs and had four cavities in its upper surface. In these four cavities stood four miniature coffins containing Tutankhamun's viscera; each cavity had a lid in the form of a head in the likeness of the king. These four heads, after Carter had removed the roof-like lid of the precious receptacle, stood out from the block of alabaster.

The four figures of the tutelary goddesses that watched over the outer shrine were repeated in high relief on the alabaster container. 'My arms,' says Isis in an inscription, 'shelter what is in me. I protect Imsety, who is in me, Imsety of the Osiris-king Nebkheprure, the justified.' And Selkit says, 'I place my arms on that which is in me. I protect Qebehsnewef, who is in me, Qebehsnewef of the Osiris-king Nebkheprure, the justified.'

The goddesses' words require a brief explanation. Imsety and Qebehsnewef, who are protected by the goddesses Isis and Selkit, are demi-gods, so-called sons of Horus. There were four altogether: Imsety, Hapi, Duamutef and Qebehsnewef, who were associated with the viscera, i.e. the liver, lungs, stomach and intestines. These lesser divinities were protected by the full goddesses Isis, Nephthys, Neith and Selkit. Selkit, for instance, watched over the dead king's intestines.

Only after the Canopic chest had been taken to the laboratory did Carter notice something odd. The inscriptions on the inside of the Canopic coffins had been retouched here and there. What had been altered? What was posterity not supposed to know? The traces of later re-working were confined to the cartouches of Tutankhamun's name. These had been engraved over another name. Carter had come across such usurpations, such seizures of works of art, in his excavations with Edouard Naville at the Hatshepsut temple of Deir el Bahari. In the present case, viscera containers had been appropriated for Tutankhamun which had originally been made for Akhenaten's co-regent, Smenkhare.

In the far right-hand corner of the treasury stood twenty-two black chests, high, narrow little cupboards, which were furnished on their front sides with two small doors. The doors were sealed with the usual cords. Carter opened one chest after the other; each contained a standing figure of a divinity. These were the gods that Tutankhamun had restored to their thrones after the heretical Amarna period.

Lying on top and alongside each other were fourteen model boats. These were to serve the king in his progress in the hereafter: lighters with deck-cabins for passengers and crew, like those that were used on the annual pilgrimages to Busiris and Abydos; gondolas and barges for outings; fast, fully-rigged ships, which carried the dead to the fields of the blessed.

Amid all the confusion Howard Carter made a gruesome discovery. When he opened two doll-sized mummiform coffins, in which he expected to find symbolic figures, he discovered the mummies of two premature babies. On later examination they were identified as girls in the fifth and seventh month, and must undoubtedly have been Tutankhamun's daughters. To the present day, however, the two children are surrounded by mystery: after Carter had taken them to Cairo, they disappeared without trace.

The boxes, caskets and chests in the treasury were crammed with ornaments and valuable jewellery, whose salvage demanded much time. The work was complicated by the fact that the contents of the chests and caskets were no longer in the position in which they had originally been placed more than 3,000 years before. The grave-robbers, who in pharaonic times snatched up the most valuable articles and left behind only the 'inferior' ones, must have rummaged through all the boxes and scattered their contents on the floor. When the cemetery officials noticed the break-in, they cleared up hastily, before reclosing the tomb, and replaced the scattered ornaments in their receptacles. But the tomb guards naturally didn't know what belonged where. They filled one box after another at random, and so it was that Carter found bits of the same piece in different receptacles, a puzzle that required high concentration and great experience to solve.

There has been much speculation as to why the cemetery officials of the 19th Dynasty took so little care in restoring order in the tomb after the break-in. It's unlikely that they were anxious to close the tomb as fast as possible, from one day to the next, for before the cemetery officials resealed the tomb, their chief, a man called Maya, had a small funerary chest made, and an inscribed wooden mummy with Tutankamun's features, and added these to the gifts of the robbed king. The preparation of this later, carefully-made grave-gift could not have been managed in a few days.

Carter was unable to remove all these treasures until the vast burial shrine had been dismantled. To do this it was necessary to clear the narrow passageway that had been left between the wall and the shrine. Lying on the ground in the northern passage were eleven steering paddles. These were to help the pharaoh pass over to the Other Side. Next to a bouquet of persea and olive twigs lay four wine jars which bore the dates of the regnal years 5 and 9, and the source, 'Domain of the Aten on the western river bank'. The seals with which the jars had been closed had been broken by the grave-robbers.

In the south-east corner of the passage round the shrine stood an alabaster lamp which has no counterpart in the three-thousand-year history of ancient Egypt. It consisted of a chalice-like cup on a pedestal, framed by two figures of Hah, the god of eternity. The chalice was smooth on the outside and undecorated. What appeared at first sight to be simple work turned out on closer inspection to be a lamp of exceptional refinement. If one poured oil into the alabaster chalice and lighted the floating wick, the bowl glowed from within and the ghostly image of a well-loved scene appeared on the inner wall: Tutankhamun and his consort Ankhesenamun, festooned with garlands. The trick behind this apparition was a second, painted cup within the first; the images on this, when the lamp was burning, were projected on to the smooth surface of the outer bowl.

Among the numerous small objects that Howard Carter found in the narrow passage were a silver trumpet and two six-foot Anubis emblems; these are worth mentioning. The trumpet is still playable today – it could be heard recently in a radio broadcast. The function of the Anubis emblems, lotiform poles of about human height, each with an animal skin tied to it and a base in the form of an alabaster flower-pot, is so far largely uncertain. Further vessels were filled with natron and a kind of resin.

The long-awaited moment had come. Carter opened the doors of the burial shrine. On the floor between the first and second shrines stood two unguent jars of alabaster. The larger was vase-shaped and flanked by two pot-bellied male figures with pendulous breasts, symbolic of Hapi, the god of the Nile. The smaller was cylindrical in form. It stood on ball feet, which had been worked into human heads and represented Egypt's enemies, bearded Asiatics and Negroes with ear-rings. Leaning against the side was a whole collection of sticks and staves.

A wooden framework in front of the second, inner shrine was hung with a linen cloth. This pall hung down from the roof of the second shrine. Sewn on to it were gilt marguerites of bronze, which in places had torn the cloth with their weight, and Carter fixed it with a compound of rubber and chlorine in an organic, zylene solvent. This made it possible to wind the cloth on to a roller and take it to the laboratory. There it disintegrated when Carter had later to stop work.

But the immediate problem was the dismantling of the outer shrine. This vast structure was made of oak planking 5.5 centimetres thick, overlaid with gesso and gold; its weight amounted to several tons. The component parts – roof, side walls and doors, each weighing between 250 and 750 kilograms – were held together by wooden tongues. Carter carefully widened each joint so that he could insert a thin saw-blade; he then sawed through the wooden peg and so was able to dismantle the shrine into its various sections.

The second shrine was smaller, each section weighing less. Taking it apart, Carter thought, would hardly present any problems. But he was mistaken. Even the outside of this second catafalque differed from the first. The outer shrine was furnished with five bands of hieroglyphs, in which the signs for *djed* (stability) and *thet* (blood of Isis) provided ornaments. The second shrine was decorated with representations of gods and genii in hollow relief. Simple cords with clay seals closed the folding doors. Carter undid the seals and opened the doors. As expected, a third golden shrine came into view. By the doors, also sealed, lay bows and arrows.

The dismantling of the second shrine offered unexpected difficulties, because the tongues that held it together were of bronze. There was no question of sawing through them. Carter had to loosen each tongue carefully and pull it out with pincers. In the process, some damage to the gilt work here and there was unavoidable.

Within the third shrine was yet another. Carter was sure this must be the last. The tension grew. How would the King appear to them?

For over three thousand years no human being had ever seen the mummy of a pharaoh in its original state. The temptation to work faster, and so less carefully, was great. Carter had to contain himself for eighty-four days.

Two gold fans, each made up of thirty white and brown ostrich feathers, lay alongside the innermost shrine. One bore the name of Akhenaten. Such fans, which originally wafted fresh air over the pharaohs, developed in the course of the centuries into symbols of power. Until quite recently similar fans were carried behind popes.

Of particular interest were the fan-shaped stocks which carried the feathers, feathers which, as an inscription proclaimed, 'His Majesty captured on a hunt in the desert east of On' (Heliopolis). A raised relief on one of the stocks shows the

Triumphal procession of a pharaoh through Thebes.

youthful king with stretched bow on his chariot, a pose which
was later to be a favourite one of Rameses the Great, in
particular. The Pharaoh's arrows have already hit two ostriches.
Tutankhamun reins back the rearing horses with his behind; he
had passed the reins round his backside so as to have his hands
free – a dare-devil pose which one would not have expected
from this childlike pharaoh. The continuation of the story
appears, like a comic strip, on the reverse side of the stock: two
attendants have laid the dead ostriches across their shoulders
and are walking home in front of the king, standing in triumphant pose on his chariot. Tutankhamun now wears a sumptuous robe. The king, says an inscription in the background, has
shot like the cat-headed goddess Bastet, and his horses were as
strong as bulls.

The fourth catafalque differed again completely from the
three outer ones. The tabernacle-like shrine had a cornice and

roof made in one piece. Its weight alone was a problem to the excavators.

More than eighty sections were finally propped around the antechamber, when Carter had dismantled all four shrines. Now standing free was the royal sarcophagus itself, of yellow-brown quartzite, protected at its four corners by the winged goddesses Isis, Nephthys, Neith and Selkit. In order to get at this massive block of stone, Carter erected scaffolding over the sarcophagus, which took up all the room. As he relates, 'We bumped our heads, nipped our fingers, we had to squeeze in and out like weasels, and work in all kinds of embarrassing positions. I think I remember that one of the eminent chemists assisting us in the preservation work, when taking records of various phenomena in the tomb, found that he had also recorded a certain percentage of profanity!'

The sections of the four burial shrines were numbered and furnished with orientation marks, north, south, east and west. Carter discovered, however, that the undertakers in 1338 B.C. had worked in a very slovenly manner, mixing up the sections and reversing the directions.

This may have been a pardonable fault [wrote Carter], the chamber being too small for correct orientation, although there were other signs of slovenliness. Sections had obviously been banged together, regardless of the risk of damage to their gilt ornamentation. Deep dents from blows from a heavy hammer-like implement are visible to the present day on the gold-work, parts of the surfaces in some cases had been actually knocked off, and the workmen's refuse, such as chips of wood, had never been cleared away.

Only now was it possible to see the paintings on the golden walls of the burial chamber. The long wall behind the sarcophagus showed a life-sized Osiris, the god of the dead, being embraced by Tutankhamun. Behind the king is his Ka, his protective spirit, the same size and with the same physiognomy.

Next to this, with her back to the Ka, is the goddess Nut. According to Heliopolitan mythology, Nut is the daughter of Shu, the god of the air, and personifies the sky. Because she swallows the sun-god Ra every evening, and gives birth to him again the next morning, in Egyptian eschatology she also symbolises resurrection. In the wall-painting the goddess Nut holds out her hands invitingly to Tutankhamun, standing facing her. The young king, in a white loin-cloth and with a convenient short wig, is obviously equipped for a long journey; he holds a walking-stick in his right hand and in his left a sceptre and the key of life.

In a third scene, next to this on the right, we meet Tutankhamun as a mummy. Only his face and hands are left free of bandages. A very young-looking Ay, dressed in the leopard-skin of a priest and the royal head-dress, steps towards the mummy to perform the ritual opening of the mouth. The hook-shaped instrument which this requires can be seen in Ay's hands; further instruments lie ready on a little table. With the opening of the mouth, which must always be performed by the pharaoh's successor, the dead person, by means of magic formulae, is supposed to be given back the use of his organs.

All these scenes are framed by priests and relations, who draw the mummy of the king on a sledge, and by the sacred ape of the sun-god Ra.

In the whole tomb only six colours could be seen: white, black, blue, red, yellow and green. Lucas analysed the white as diluvial chalk and the black as powdered charcoal; blue proved to be limestone copper silicate, and red was made from red ochre. The chemist took a sample of yellow from one of the brilliant yellow chests; the colour was yellow sulpharsenide (arsenic sulphide). Green was based, not as in other tombs, on malachite, but on a powered mixture whose composition resembled that of the blue.

The real difficulty of ancient Egyptian painting was the mixing of the paints so as to make the colouring-matter stick. The use of turpentine and oil was not known. The tomb painters are presumed to have mixed their colours with egg-white, gum or size, but their use cannot be proved after such a long time. The finished wall paintings were varnished with a glass-clear resin that liquefied with heat. This resin sealed in the colours hermetically; hidden behind it is the secret of why in some places the colours look as fresh as though they had been applied only yesterday.

Hordes of tourists blocked Carter's way every morning when he rode up to the tomb on his donkey. In order to escape these tiresome gadflies, he began after a while to steal into the Valley of the Kings before sunrise, and to disappear unseen. The heavily guarded tomb was his best hiding-place – until the trick was rumbled. After that the bystanders and sensation-mongers used to chant several times a day, 'Carter, Carter, Carter', until he appeared, received the applause of the crowd and, like a sacred apparition, vanished again into the dark hole in the rock.

The hope that the first finds, sent to Cairo and exhibited in the Museum, would satisfy the curiosity of the masses proved to be false. Quite the contrary – the exhibition of the first finds became the best advertisement for a visit to the Valley of the Kings.

The tension grew, once it leaked out that the opening of the sarcophagus was imminent.

This information did not come from Carter, but so many people and institutions had in the meantime got a say in the enterprise that it was hard to know who was in control. The Ministry of Public Works had its under-secretary of state on the scene of action. He represented the government, and invited archaeologists and diplomats at his discretion.

Pierre Lacau, Director-General of the Egyptian Department of Antiquities since 1914, kept Carter on a tight rein with orders and instructions; he prescribed press communiqués, announced visitors and times of visits, and even supervised the scientific staff. After barely two weeks of the work, Carter would have gladly given it all up.

When James Henry Breasted arrived in the Valley of the Kings on 12th February, the day on which the sarcophagus was supposed to be opened, he met a wretched-looking man. Carter said he felt ill, and handed Breasted a letter from the Ministry of Public Works, which laid down the scientific programme for the next two days. 'This,' said Carter, 'is what has made me ill.'

Breasted himself had been afflicted for some days with mysterious attacks of fever and 'periods when his blood burned in his veins'. The suspicion of malaria, however, could not be confirmed by the doctor. Wearily, Breasted sat down in the shadow of the steps that led into the tomb. From down below he could hear Carter giving directions; he was installing block and tackle. The lid was to be raised after the midday break.

At about one o'clock Carter and his assistant Callender came up the steps, dusty and tired. 'Come along,' said Carter, turning to Breasted. Together they went to Tomb 41 which, since the discovery, had served as dining-room and recreation room. A kitchen had been set up in the nameless tomb, with two native cooks and a servant to see to the refreshments. In the entrance to the tomb, where daylight still fell, was a long table covered in a white cloth, with round-backed tea-shop chairs to left and right. The room was little more than six feet wide. Carter went ahead and sat down at the far end of the table, in the seat which had once been Lord Carnarvon's regular place, but which had always been left empty since his death. The men looked surprised. Down the left-hand side sat Alfred Lucas, Harry Burton and James Henry Breasted, and opposite them, A. R. Callender, Arthur Mace and Alan Gardiner.

On the table in front of Carter lay bundles of letters and newspapers. Indifferently he pushed them aside. The lunch proceeded in silence. It seemed as though each of them was thinking of the coming event. What sight would await them when the lid of the sarcophagus was raised?

Shortly before three o'clock Carter rose from table and he and his colleagues went across to Tutankhamun's tomb. Waiting at the entrance were the Under Secretary of State, Mohammed Zaglul Pasha, a few government officials and some archaeologists. Without a word they disappeared one after the other into the mouth of the tomb.

The treasures of the antechamber had been removed. Standing there now were the side walls and roof of the outermost shrine. The burial chamber lay about a metre below the floor level of the antechamber. From the massive scaffolding over the reddish gleam of the sarcophagus hung two blocks and tackle. Carter had worked for days, preparing to raise the lid of the sarcophagus, for it was not without problems. Running through the middle of the slab, weighing nearly one and a half tons, was a crack. So it was treated with the greatest care. This crack was not due to any injury, however; it was a natural one and had already been patched up and painted over by Tutankhamun's craftsmen.

The ancient stone-masons would undoubtedly have prepared a new lid for the sarcophagus if they hadn't been pressed for time. In contrast to the quartzite sarcophagus, the lid-slab was made of granite. This suggested that some accident must have occurred. 'It may be,' wrote Carter, 'that the intended lid was not ready in time for the burial of the king, and that this crudely made granite slab was substituted in its place.'

Howard Carter had placed angle-irons along the sides of the lid. The pulleys could go into action. Those present felt that 'in the young king's case,' as Carter wrote, 'a dignity had been added even to death. With the profound silence that reigned the emotion deepened, the past and present seemed to meet – time to stand still and wait. . .'

None of the men spoke a word. Harry Burton cranked away at a film camera. Two powerful electric lamps lit up the small room. The heat became increasingly unbearable. At one pulley stood Callender, at the other Carter. But it was not he who gave the order; it was the man behind the film camera. With a sinister cracking and creaking the lid-slab now began to quiver and eventually to rise, a millimetre at a time, but quite perceptibly, until it started to swing uncertainly and hovered a few centimetres above the sarcophagus – too little as yet for one to be able to see anything inside.

How would they find the king?

For fifteen months this question had agitated not only Howard Carter. Archaeologists, tourists and people all over the world had been talking their heads off. Now the moment was here which would answer that question; now the seconds were becoming minutes, the minutes stretching out like hours.

Among the onlookers in the antechamber was James Henry Breasted. He gazed alternately at the mechanical scene with the pulleys and at the wall-paintings lying behind it, gleaming in yellow and gold, in which Tutankhamun's successor, the old Ay, was performing the ceremony of opening the mouth on the mummy of the king who had died so young. Breasted recalls:

> The painted pharaoh on the wall seemed to me at that moment to take on a strange reality. I felt a puzzling sense of unworthiness as I looked up at him. Why did he seem so calmly superior? On my left and looking down upon the sarcophagus of his ancient ancestor, stood a representative of the government of modern Egypt. He beamed upon the preparations below with an expression of smug assurance and sluggish curiosity and the general air of good-natured inefficiency so characteristic of the modern Egyptian. Over on the wall stood Ay, still calmly extending his censer, still burning the last incense to the soul of his departed predecessor.

As far as anything could be seen through the slowly widening crack, a fine, dusty linen cloth lay arched over an indeterminate shape. On it were some little fragments of granite. Those present were puzzled, almost disappointed. Finally the granite slab hung about half a metre above the sarcophagus.

Carter took a torch. Cautiously, as though he might destroy something with the rays of light, he shone it inside. Then he announced, and it sounded solemn, 'In the sarcophagus is a coffin. The coffin rests on a golden bier in the form of a lion.'

The photographer Harry Burton was busy now with a still camera; he set up his tripod at the foot of the sarcophagus, clicked his shutter and turned to the head. The sounds he made brought relief in the oppressive silence. 'In the midst of this,' Breasted recalls, 'and reminding one for all the world of the routine efficiency of modern undertakers' assistants, Carter and Mace stepped quietly forward to the head of the sleeping figure and loosening the shroud on either side, slowly and carefully rolled it back off the head toward the feet.'

The cloth was carbonised and fragile, and in places disintegrated into nothing at the slightest touch. A second linen cloth came into view, so thin that under it the golden figure of a king glimmered through, the face and the arms, with crook and flail crossed over the breast. 'Gorgeous was the sight that met our eyes,' wrote Carter, 'a golden effigy of the young boy king, of most magnificent workmanship, filled the whole of the interior of the sarcophagus.'

Thus had deeply religious people laid Tutankhamun to rest 3,263 years before, so that Osiris might take him one day into his realm of shades, to be born a second time, before he might stroll for ever along the banks of the heavenly rivers that flow round the galaxies, and enter a time in which memory no longer has meaning. The golden shell that enveloped the dead pharaoh was the image of a youth of timeless beauty; idealised, more beautiful than the natural model, it was the perfect template for the rebirth.

Were the archaeologists not in the very act of serving as midwives? Were they not witnessing at that very moment the rebirth of a pharaoh, a forgotten pharaoh? It was the golden shell, radiating power, pomp and glory, that became a model for the imagination of future generations, not the wretched, torn skeleton of the murdered youth that was to fall into their hands much later.

The eyes of the golden king, inlaid with aragonite and obsidian, were alive. But they looked at no one. Directed majestically upward, sure of immortality, they seemed to disdain a glance at the intruders. Over them arched eyebrows of lapis lazuli glass. 'Many and disturbing were our emotions awakened by that Osiride form,' wrote Howard Carter. Cobra and vulture, the emblems of Upper and Lower Egypt, and the symbols of kingship, gleamed on the forehead. The vulture, the divinity of Upper Egypt, pointed to the south; the cobra, the divinity of

Lower Egypt, to the north, corresponding to the geographical positions of the two countries. The body, wrought in the form of a mummy, showed the pharaoh as Osiris, as personified resurrection. Blue glass and red stones on a gold ground outlined a feather pattern. This gilt coffin was 2.25 metres long and 70 centimetres high. Its dimensions alone convinced the excavators that there were several more coffins nesting one inside the other.

The tension had eased. None of the men in the antechamber felt any desire to open the golden mummiform coffin. Not an hour had gone by since they had entered the tomb, but the experience had been so overwhelming that it seemed natural for them to turn, one after the other, towards the exit and to climb the sixteen steps to the radiant blue sky.

The emotions that stirred them were expressed thus by Breasted: 'We came away with a sense of having glimpsed the era and the last rites of Tutankhamun.' And Howard Carter wrote, 'Our inner thoughts still lingered over the splendour of that vanished Pharaoh, with his last appeal upon his coffin written upon our minds: "Oh Mother Nut! Spread thy wings over me as the imperishable stars".'

Next morning, Carter crossed the Nile to Luxor at crack of dawn and sought out Breasted in his hotel. Carter was fuming. From a bundle of records and letters he pulled out a telegram. It was signed by Marcos Bey Hanna, the newly appointed Minister of Public Works. The Minister had learned through one of his officials, who made his presence felt at the excavations, that on 13th February, i.e. that day, Carter had invited the wives of the British and American scientists taking part in the enterprise to view the tomb. In the Minister's opinion this viewing required authorisation by the ministry. Since this had not been obtained, Marcos Bey Hanna banned all the wives and members of the archaeologists's families from entering Tutankhamun's tomb. At the same time, in the early hours of the morning, police had been assembled at the tomb with the obvious intention of checking everyone who tried to go in.

Carter and Breasted agreed to suspend their work under

these conditions. Angry and on edge, with hands behind his back, Carter paced up and down the hotel room, dictating a public announcement to Charles Breasted. He worded it sharply, abusively and laboriously, in his customary manner. Breasted shook his head each time and said, 'You can't say that!' Carter began again. At least twenty different versions were jotted down by Charles Breasted; they became increasingly conciliatory and the last ran as follows:

13th February, 1924

Notice

Owing to the impossible restrictions and discourtesies on the part of the Public Works Department and its Antiquities Service, all my collaborators in protest have refused to work any further on the scientific investigation of the discovery of the Tomb of Tutankhamun. I am therefore obliged to make known to the public that immediately after the press view of the tomb this morning between 10.0 a.m. and noon the tomb will be closed and no further work carried out.

(Signed)   Howard Carter

This announcement was fixed in great haste to all the noticeboards in Luxor. The town again had a scandal, the smart people on the hotel terraces something to talk about.

The press conference in Tutankhamun's tomb became a triumph for Carter. The excavator had the whole of public opinion on his side. In the circumstances, he thought, the Cairo Ministry would climb down, and in a few days the controversy would be settled. So Carter left the heavy covering-slab hanging by its ropes over the sarcophagus, locked the tomb and retired indignantly to the Winter Palace Hotel, where he held a council of war with Breasted.

A day later came a telegram from Cairo: Carter was to resume work within forty-eight hours, and without any conditions. Should this not occur, he would be forbidden ever to set foot in the tomb again, and the Countess of Carnarvon would have her concession withdrawn.

Carter refused. He applied to the Mixed Tribunals in Cairo, a ministerial mediation committee, but its mills ground very slowly. With every day that passed Carter became more uneasy. Still hanging by two thin ropes over the golden mummiform coffin of the king was that one-and-a-half-ton slab of granite. Was it in fact still hanging? Perhaps it had already crushed the precious coffin. Perhaps Tutankhamun had thus eluded the sight-seers of posterity, greedy for sensation.

The tomb was surrounded day and night by militia. There was no chance for Carter to get in. At Breasted's insistence, he sent a telegram to the Minister of Public Works, asking to be allowed to enter the tomb just once more, in order to lower the granite slab; the consequences would otherwise be incalculable. The answer was, 'No'. Marcos Bey Hanna now accused the excavator of negligence, and held him responsible for all the consequences. Lady Carnarvon had her concession withdrawn, with immediate effect. The government, said the Minister, would take over the tomb officially on 22nd February, 1924. Carter shivered at the thought: by then, the mummy of the king might have been crushed by the slab.

During these days of waiting and anxiety, Carter ran around Luxor aimlessly, like a hunted stag. The Breasteds, with whom he stayed between times, tried to console him and give him advice, 'which for the most part,' the son Charles recalls, 'he was nervously too exhausted and emotionally too upset to follow'. They were the most troubled days of Howard Carter's life.

On the morning of 22nd February, Charles Breasted rode by donkey to the Valley of the Kings. He wanted to give Carter, who had stayed behind with his father in the hotel, an account of what happened. Had the ropes held? Charles Breasted sat down on the surrounding wall, guarded by soldiers at the entrance to the tomb, and waited upon the events that were pending. Access was barred by an iron grill, the key of which was held by Carter, who was sitting in the Winter Palace Hotel.

While Charles Breasted was waiting, the tragedy of the situation came home to him. In 1905, when he was eight years old, he had met Carter for the first time, not far from there. That was now nearly twenty years ago. During that time, Carter had done nothing but look for this tomb. He had discovered it, contrary to the predictions of distinguished scholars. He had gained Egypt world-wide prestige, and brought more tourists into the country than the greatest optimists, with vast publicity efforts, could have imagined. He had sacrificed his nerves, and turned down large sums of money, for the sole purpose of losing no time in clearing the tomb and preparing the finds. He had quarrelled with Carnarvon because he thought all the treasures should remain in Egypt. And now soldiers were gathered to prevent him from entering 'his' tomb, whose precious treasure, the gilded royal mummy, might at any moment be crushed under a ton or so of stone.

At about two o'clock Pierre Lacau arrived; behind him, a government delegation, and behind them a few workmen with a great load of tools. The scene was theatrical: at the entrance to the tomb, Lacau struck a pose which he thought suitable to his position as head of the Department of Antiquities, drew a letter from Howard Carter from his pocket and began to read it aloud. The content: Carter declined to give up the key to the tomb. Two lawyers standing behind Lacau took notes zealously. Then the workmen stepped forward and began to saw at the heavy padlocks. But were they not already too late?

The sawing at the two iron gates lasted until late afternoon. When the second door could be opened, Lacau stormed into the tomb. After only a few moments he came back, and from the expression on his face it was clear that the worst had not happened. As it turned out, the ropes had stretched so much that the lid-slab was almost back on the sarcophagus. Lacau and his gang went to Carter's laboratory in the tomb of Sethos II. There too they broke open the door. The Tutankhamun enterprise was now a purely Egyptian affair.

In the meantime, Carter had gone back to his house, from where he had a good view of the return of the official procession. 'He looked disconsolate and worn,' Breasted reported, 'but was quite calm and evinced no rancour as I described the latest in the long series of strange episodes which had attended and had finally deprived him of the greatest archaeological discovery in the history of the orient.'

The cause of these continual incidents must be sought in Egypt's political situation. The ending of the British protectorate and the subsequent recognition of the Egyptian King Fuad had released national emotions that threatened to smother all foreign activity in the country. These 'arrogant, self-conscious, sweepingly victorious Nationalists' – as James Henry Breasted once called them – often overshot the mark. Certainly, Egyptology had hitherto been mainly an affair of the British, French, Italians and Germans, but for that very reason there were no Egyptian Egyptologists of distinction. Who was to continue Carter's work?

Carter went to Cairo for the hearing of the court of arbitration. His lawyer, Sir John Maxwell, enjoyed a high reputation in Egypt. He had once been commander-in-chief of the British army in Egypt and a good friend of Lord Carnarvon's. The two had got to know each other out there. Sir John had gone to the Nile in 1882 with the British occupation troops and had risen with unprecedented speed and that not merely because he enjoyed the protection of his uncle, Sir Francis Grenfell, the commander-in-chief of the Egyptian army.

Uncle Francis had also awakened his nephew's interest in archaeology; at least, John had always looked on with interest whenever the old Field Marshal had exchanged his sabre for a spade, and his highly decorated uniform for a plain working-suit, and, in between supply and attack, gone on a dig. Lord Grenfell had been President of the Egypt Exploration Society, and when he died John Maxwell had taken over.

The administrators of the Carnarvon estate also sent to court a lawyer called Maxwell. F. H. Maxwell, however, was tainted by the fact that, a few years before, he had accused the present Minister of Public Works, Marcos Bey Hanna, of treason, and demanded the death penalty for him. And Marcos Bey Hanna was now representing the opposing party – a circumstance that was not calculated to moderate the situation.

Because he was bound to fear the worst, Howard Carter sent a telegram to his friend James Henry Breasted in Luxor asking him to appear as extra-judical mediator. Breasted went to Cairo, despite his poor health, worked out an acceptable compromise and secured an adjournment of the court hearing.

The compromise was perfectly feasible; even the two lawyers advised Carter to accept it, but he was no longer in control of his faculties. 'He lost all control of himself,' related James Henry Breasted, 'and became very high-handed and arrogant. He appears so overcome by his misfortunes as to be incapable of major decisions.' Breasted toyed with the idea of giving up his role as mediator, but then shrank from such a step when he realised that more was at stake than the arbitration of a dispute: it was a matter of the future of archaeology in Egypt.

The Breasted compromise was finally the basis of the court hearing. Quite unexpectedly the government declared its agreement to the resumption of the work by Howard Carter. The only condition was that Carter must renounce all claims in writing. This was almost grotesque, for Carter had in any case always advocated that the whole of the tomb-treasure should remain in Egypt. It was for this reason, after all, that he had fallen out with Lord Carnarvon. But Carter wanted a victory

Girls in transparent dress with stringed instruments and double-flute.

right down the line. Stubbornly he stuck out for a moral condemnation of the government.

In the meantime, Breasted tried to bring at least Carnarvon's executor and the government closer to each other. He argued that the Egyptian government should show its generosity and, in view of their enormous significance for Egypt, reward the unpaid services of the British and American archaeologists. This could best be done by presenting, in Lady Carnarvon's name, some of the many duplicates from the tomb-treasures to the British Museum in London and the Metropolitan Museum in New York.

The unexpected happened. The warring parties came to terms without Carter's consent. March 11th was fixed for the signing of a suitable agreement. But in the middle of this ceremony a government lawyer burst in. He said no such agreement could ever be signed, for, only the previous evening, the lawyer for the Carnarvon estate had accused the government of forcing its way into Tutankhamun's tomb 'like a bandit'. At that, the government representative left the conference chamber.

A last attempt at mediation ended with the offer by the Minister of Public Works that Breasted should take over the digging-concession. Breasted declined categorically. He couldn't do that to his friend Howard Carter.

Embittered, frustrated and full of anger, Carter went back to England. The newspapers hailed him as a martyr; a hero had lost his battle-field.

10 Carter's triumph: face to face with Tutankhamun

A word may fittingly be said here in defence of the unwrapping and examination of Tutankhamun. Many persons regard such an investigation as in the nature of sacrilege, and consider that the king should have been left undisturbed. From what I have said as to the persistent robberies of the tombs from the most ancient times up to the present, it will be understood that when once such a discovery as that of the tomb of Tutankhamun has been made, and news of the wealth of objects contained in it has become known, to leave anything whatever of value in the tomb is to court trouble.

Douglas E. Derry

Multicoloured rockets shot up over the Valley of the Kings; the rock walls in which three dynasties of Egyptian pharaohs had found their last rest echoed with the din of exploding detonators. Nowhere, the Egyptians believed, could they demonstrate their regained independence more fittingly and

ostentatiously than here in the resting-place of their great an-
cestors. The British excavators had been sent to the devil; the
Tutankhamun tomb was once more firmly in Egyptian hands.

The sarcophagus with the pharaoh's mummy had been temporarily closed. The tomb was now made accessible to visitors,
and the rush was indescribable. In the English-language *Egyptian Gazette* an eye-witness reported, 'a pathetic note was provided by two of Mr. Carter's trusted Egyptian foremen faith-
fully guarding a heap of their master's property, not far from
the mouth of the tomb for the discovery of which they had
served him with such unflagging fidelity and perseverance.
Their saddened faces left no doubt as to their thoughts. . . at
seeing the careless throng passing into the tomb which to them
and their master represented the almost sacred crowning of the
labour of a lifetime.'

Howard Carter in the meantime was on a lecture tour of the
United States of America. The Americans hailed him as the
greatest excavator of the century. Yale University in New
Haven conferred an honorary doctorate on him. Carter often
spoke before an audience of more than 3,000. His fees in dollars
enabled him to forget all material cares for the next few years. If
he had seen Tutankhamun's mummy, which still lay concealed
in its golden coffin, for only a brief moment, he would have
been happy. As it was, the triumphal journey through America
filled him also with melancholy. It was highly uncertain
whether he would ever see his Tutankhamun at all.

On his way back to England in December 1924, Carter broke
his journey in Spain. The Academy of Sciences in Madrid did
themselves the honour of conferring on the by now world-
famous archaeologist a further honorary doctorate. Carter was
proud of this and quite liked to hear himself addressed there-
after as 'Doctor Carter'.

While he was there, the British ambassador in Madrid passed
on to Dr. Carter a telegram from London. This requested him
to go as fast as possible to Cairo and resume work on the tomb
of Tutankhamun. What on earth had happened, Carter
wondered.

In Cairo, on 20th November, 1924, an Egyptian nationalist had shot the commander-in-chief of the British army, Sir Lee Stack, in broad daylight. The situation was explosive. The British could use this political murder as the pretext for a reinstatement of the protectorate. British armed forces were in the country now as ever. In Cairo all held their breath. In this highly explosive situation the Egyptians decided on a step which, more than any other, was calculated to smooth feelings between Egypt and Britain: the government formally invited Howard Carter to resume work on Tutankhamun's tomb. The gesture was completely unexpected, especially by Carter. He could now do nothing else; he had to accept. The invitation was not a request from a public authority to a scholar; it was a diplomatic order. He saw his return to Egypt as a personal victory: he had been called back. To the public he was a martyr who had suffered for his convictions. His popularity was greater than ever. As a guest of the government he stayed at the Continental Savoy Hotel, where the first contacts between the new Minister of Public Works and the recalled excavator took place. So as not to lose face, the Minister asked Carter if he would kindly state his agreement in a formal exchange of letters. The whole thing was a farce; the letter and the reply, in French, were written on the same day. But Carter knew, of course, how matters stood in the country, and agreed. The text of the two letters follows.

Cairo, 13th January, 1925

His Excellency
the Minister of Public Works,
Cairo.

Your Excellency,

I have the honour to inform you that on 29th December, 1924, I addressed a letter to His Excellency the President of the Council of Ministers in which I suggested that work be resumed in the tomb of Tutankhamun on the basis of the general conditions laid down in the draft authorisation conveyed to Almina, Countess Carnarvon, last June, while requesting that the question of ownership of the objects referred to in Article 12 of the said authorisation to set aside until such time as the work shall be finished and all the objects contained in the tomb deposited in the Cairo Museum. Last Wednesday a meeting took place between M. Lacau and Badawi Pasha on the side and Merzbach Bey and myself on the other, in the course of which I had the opportunity to indicate my thoughts on the subjects of this authorisation.

Taking advantage of the desire which both His Excellency the President of the Council and also Your Excellency have been pleased to express to see the work in question resumed, I venture to submit to you that Almina, Countess Carnarvon, would be grateful to Your Excellency if you would be willing to grant the authorisation to resume work on the conditions which have already been conveyed to her, together with the points which the solicitor of the Ministry of Public Works and the Antiquities Service have agreed to incorporate in the said authorisation.

Upon receipt of Your Excellency's assurances that he has no objection to granting the authorisation on these conditions, Almina, Countess Carnarvon, will make a point of renouncing, and causing the executors of the will to renounce, all actions, claims and pretensions whatsoever, not only in respect of the Tomb of Tutankhamun and the objects originating from it, but also with regard to the cancellation of the authorisation and the measures taken by the Government following that cancellation.

Confident that in a spirit of goodwill Your Excellency will be pleased to grant the said authorisation, I beg him to accept the assurance of my high esteem.

(Signed) Howard Carter

The Minister replied on the same day.

Ministry of Public Works,
Minister's Office,
No. 133–2/4.
Cairo, 13th January, 1925

M. Howard Carter,
Continental Savoy,
Cairo.

Dear Sir,

I have the honour to acknowledge receipt of your letter of today's date, in which you inform me that Almina, Countess Carnarvon, seeks to obtain authorisation for the resumption of work in the tomb of Tutankhamun on the conditions communicated to her last June, together with the points which my solicitor and the Antiquities Service have agreed to incorporate in the said authorisation.

Filled with a sincere desire to see the work resumed, I have no objection to granting the authorisation on the conditions mentioned, provided that Almina, Countess Carnarvon, renounces, and causes the executors of the will to renounce, all actions, claims and pretensions whatsoever, not only in respect of the tomb of Tutankhamun and the objects originating from it, but also in regard to the cancellation of the authorisation and the measures taken by the Government following its cancellation.

Anxious to show its gratitude for the wonderful discovery, the Government, while considering itself under no obligation in respect to the objects found in the tomb, intends, in accordance with the suggestion made by M. Lacau shortly after the discovery, to give Almina, Countess Cararvon, at its discretion a selection of duplicates as representative as possible of the discovery, provided that these duplicates may be subtracted from the whole without damage to science.

In addition, to save the excavator from any disagreeable comments, if the mummy of the King is transported to

Cairo, the Antiquities Service alone will undertake the transfer and assume responsibility for it.

Please accept, Sir, the assurance of my marked esteem.
The Minister of Public Works,
(Signed) M. Sidky.

A day later, at the end of this farce, Howard Carter boarded a train to Luxor, where he was received like a hero. Natives and tourists accompanied the famous excavator from the station to the Nile ferry and from there to his house at the entrance to the Valley of the Kings. The *reises* were surprised to find that Carter had put on weight; his emaciated face had filled out; his gait had grown heavier.

By the time he had gathered his old team round him and got his house and the laboratory in order, ten days had gone by. On the morning of 25th January he appeared at the entrance to the tomb in a grey flannel suit and hat, and with a stick in his hand. The stick, 1.30 metres long and surmounted with a figure of Tutankhamun in gold, was one of the Pharaoh's ceremonial sticks which Carter had found between the first and second shrines. Like a herald, he knocked three times on the ground. That was the sign for the tomb to be opened.

Carter entered the pharaoh's tomb like a schoolboy setting foot in a lady's boudoir for the first time. Although he had descended the narrow passage a hundred times, his heart beat faster. Would he succeed at last in uncovering the mummy of Tutankhamun? The political conditions that had brought him so unexpectedly back to this place could be reversed again just as quickly: there were enough points of friction between Egypt and Great Britain. There was the Suez Canal Zone, which the British still kept in their hands, or the Anglo-Egyptian condominium in the Sudan. In addition, the internal political situation in Britain was not exactly stable. The first Labour government had just been replaced, after only eleven months, by the Conservatives again, and on the Continent all eyes were on Germany, where a man called Hitler had just been released from custody, and the first President, Friedrich Ebert, had died.

It would be a mistake to think that Carter hastened the work because of the uncertain political situation. On the contrary, his world was the tomb and the laboratory; what was happening on the surface of the globe interested him little or not at all. A small world, and yet so big. And as he was proceeding on the assumption that he couldn't in any case recover the mummy before the start of the hot season, he shifted his activities first to the laboratory.

There, in the tomb of Sethos II, Tutankhamun's treasures were piled up into a vast warehouse. Sethos's funerary equipment had in its time undoubtedly been on a far smaller scale than that of Tutankhamun, for Sethos II, who reigned barely a century and half after the child-king and for only six years, was an unimportant pharaoh. Practically nothing has been handed down from his reign (1200–1194) except for a legal report of an attempt at manslaughter that became notorious during the building of his tomb. Now, however, his tomb was furnished with riches beyond anything he could have conceived.

Carter set about packing up the individual finds. In Cairo he had procured a mile of wadding and as much again of surgical bandages; in addition, sacks of bran, the best packing material for breakable objects, stood ready.

The excavator's card-index in the meantime recorded 3,000 finds, from tiny little ornaments to bulky articles like chariot parts and the life-sized guardian statues. Carter was faced with the complicated task of conveying these 3,000 pieces, undamaged, to Cairo, 500 kilometres away. Neither the excavators nor the authorities had considered leaving the treasures on the spot, or in Luxor. For that, the security risk was too great.

In weeks of work Carter and his assistants packed up everything, including the bulky articles, into eighty-nine wooden boxes. These were finally stowed for transport in thirty-four heavy packing-cases. The cases, some very weighty, had then to be got out of the Valley of the Kings over a rough desert road down to the bank of the Nile. Waiting there, was a steamer chartered by the Department of Antiquities. The idea of using a motor-car for the purpose proved impracticable. Lord Carnarvon had in fact brought an open tourer to Luxor shortly before he died, but the vehicle had to be dug out of the desert sand by the workmen too often to be useful.

After unbelievable difficulties, Carter managed to get hold of a field railway. This means of transport seemed to him ideal for conveying the tomb-treasures, because it involved the least risk of bumps and crashes. Only three cars and five pairs of rails were available, however; so the cars had to be loaded up, the rails dismantled behind and relaid in front.

This procedure, from the tomb of Tutankhamun in the Valley of the Kings across five and a half miles to the bank of the Nile, was made even more difficult by the temperature; it was already the middle of May and over 37°C (100°F) in the shade. But the treasures in the cases, some of which had been prepared with paraffin wax, were not supposed to be exposed, if possible, to the direct rays of the sun. Carter resorted to wet cloths, which he spread over the cases during their journey.

Fifty labourers were allocated according to an exact plan, some pushing the cars, others dismantling, carrying and laying the rails, escorted by a squad of guards in uniform and fez, carbines over their shoulders: certainly a strange sight. Towards midday the rails became so hot that they could no longer be handled. Carter urged the work on. By ten o'clock on 15th May the trek had reached the Nile and he could breathe again.

In that heat an opening of the coffins was not to be thought of. Carter filled in the entrance to the tomb, locked up the laboratory, and took the next boat to England. He had actually thought of taking a holiday, but nothing came of it. Tutankhamun's discoverer was passed round from one reception to another, from lecture to lecture. He spoke to the Royal Institute as well as to small clubs. The slides he showed were a sensation. 'The Wonders of Egypt' wrote a popular magazine, the *Illustrated London News*, and celebrated the event on several pages. There was no doubt about it, Howard Carter was a star.

On 23rd September, 1925, he set off again on the journey back to Egypt. The work in the tomb of Tutankhamun was now entering its fourth year.

In the Museum in Cairo, where the tomb-treasures were now on exhibition, he was overcome by a feeling of pride when he stood before the fruits of his labour. The pharaoh's throne meanwhile had darkened. Carter suggested treating it, like the other objects, with paraffin wax. At the Museum he met the deputy director of the Department of Antiquities, Edgar. He asked him to have the electric light available from 11th October, so that work in the tomb could be resumed at once. 'Past experience had taught us,' wrote Carter, 'that it would be well to resume our work on the tomb of Tutankhamun as soon as the decline of the great heat rendered it practicable, our aim being to carry it out with due scientific procedure, with the least possible interruption and to be able to open the tomb to the public as early as possible during the tourist season.'

For the examination of the mummy, Carter secured the collaboration of the anatomists Dr. Douglas E. Derry and Dr. Saleh Bey Hamdi, and also that of the chemist, Alfred Lucas. The head of the Department of Antiquities, Pierre Lacau, was on leave in Europe, and sent Carter a telegram asking him to defer the unwrapping of the mummy until 10th November, as he wished to be present.

The Valley of the Kings welcomed its uncrowned king with temperatures of 35–45°C (95–113°F). For the time of year this was extremely unusual. It seemed as though the forgotten pharaoh were defending himself against the intruders with all the means at his command. But in the course of his thirty-five years and more as an excavator, Carter had grown used to such temperatures. He engaged twenty-five men and seventy-five boys as labourers. Larger numbers would not be required for the work that lay ahead.

'Familiarity can never entirely dissipate the feeling of mystery,' wrote Carter, 'the sense of vanished but haunting forces that cling to the tomb. The conviction of the unity of past and present is constantly impressed upon the archaeological adventurer, even when absorbed in the mechanical details of his work.' On 13th October he began operations. The heavy covering slab of the sarcophagus had already been removed; the researchers had decided to leave the coffins in the sarcophagus at first, and to raise one lid after the other. But that was a great deal easier said than done.

The first and second mummiform coffins were secured by silver pins with heads of pure gold. The pins of the third coffin were of 18–21 carat gold. The chemist Alfred Lucas, who examined the golden coffins on the spot, was struck in particular by differences in the colour of the gold used. Chemical analysis eventually revealed that the dull gold contained additions of silver and copper, and the gold with a grey sheen was alloyed with particularly large amounts of silver. In the gold with a reddish sheen Lucas analysed iron, silver, and copper which had oxidised.

The undertakers had enveloped the second coffin in a delicate, transparent linen cloth, which disintegrated, however, at the slightest touch. Carter noticed with concern that the gold of the second mummiform coffin was covered with a grey film. Moisture had obviously penetrated, or else the king's funeral had had to be fixed at such short notice that the mummy had not been completely dry.

Since work on the nest of coffins was proving to be increasingly complicated, Carter decided to try to raise the coffins out of the stone sarcophagus with the help of the two blocks and tackle. The coffins fitted so tightly into each other, however, that it was impossible to pass a rope under them. The only solution, albeit not a very elegant one, was to screw strong eyelets into the edge of the first gilded wooden coffin. These rings provided an attachment for the ropes of the hoisting-gear. The operation was successful. As the great coffin hovered over the stone sarcophagus, Carter laid planks across the sarcophagus and then lowered the coffin on to them.

Hardly had that been done when a new problem arose: how could he lift the second coffin out of the first?

20th October, 1925. Entry in Carter's diary:
The raising of a lid of a coffin or lifting the coffin itself
seems a comparatively simple job; but when one realises
that it is deep down in the interior of a sarcophagus where
it fits quite closely, that it is in a fragile condition, that it is
immensely heavy, that the overhead room in the chamber
is very limited, and that one does not even know whether
its wood is sufficiently well preserved to bear its own
weight, the reader will perhaps begin to realise what an
anxious work it really is.

None of the men in the tomb had realised that the burial
chamber was far too low to enable one of the inner coffins to be
lifted out of the outer one; below the scaffolding with the
hoisting gear there was a space of only eighteen inches. Eventually Carter evolved the following plan: the second coffin had to
be fitted with rings like the outer one. Through these the ropes
of the hoisting gear were to be drawn and the inner coffin raised
slightly. Then ropes were to be passed under the outer coffin,
the planks were to be removed, and the outer coffin was to be
lowered carefully into the sarcophagus. After the planks had
been replaced across the sarcophagus, the second coffin could
be lowered on to them.

This complicated technical manoeuvre succeeded, just as
Carter had planned. Now the lid of the second, inner coffin
could be removed.

What the men saw a moment later left them speechless. A
third mummiform coffin of solid gold appeared under a plain
linen cloth. So that was why the coffins had been so enormously
heavy. The innermost one alone weighed 224 kilograms. Eight
men could lift it with difficulty. Like the gilded wooden shells
in which it was enveloped, it was Osiride in form, with
Tutankhamun's features, and a stylised feather pattern on the
body. Red, blue and turquoise enamel had been melted into the
cells of the feather pattern.

This overwhelming sight was marred by a resinous mass, a
libation that had been poured over the coffin at the funeral. The

priests had not spared the unguents, so that the narrow space between the inner and middle coffins was filled with the black matter, sticking them together. Lucas at once investigated the fateful sticky substance, and established that it was composed for the most part of stearic acid – a solid crystalline fatty acid – and palmitic acid, which occurs with particular abundance in palm oil. Since both acids had only formed, however, through chemical decomposition, the identification of their original substances would be a problem. Carter thought they smelt of coconut oil, but Lucas took the view that the smell arose only from the decomposition: it was not the true smell of the substance. According to the chemist's analysis, the black mass that had been poured over the precious coffins was composed of 46 per cent fats, 19 per cent brown resin, and 35 per cent of unidentifiable brittle organic substances. Tar or mineral pitch was not present.

To work on it further, Howard Carter took the inner coffin, which was still stuck in the lower part of the middle coffin, into the antechamber. The researchers now had to look for a recipe for tackling the sticky black mass. From the way it had run down the sides, Lucas thought it must once have been liquid, and what had once been liquid could be liquified again, or dissolved or melted.

But first Carter wanted to open the last lid. The coffins nesting one inside the other had been, after all, a severe strain on the excavator's nerves. After the removal of ten gold pins with which the lid and the lower part were held together, the upper half could be raised without any difficulty. Spellbound, the men stared at the mummy of the forgotten pharaoh. 'At such moments,' wrote Carter later, 'the emotions evade verbal expression, complex and stirring as they are. . . But it is useless to dwell on such sentiments, based as they are on feelings of awe and human pity. The emotional side is no part of archaeological research.'

A cloth over the head concealed a gold death-mask. Carter drew it back: in fixed, majestic gaze Tutankhamun looked past the excavators. The body was firmly bandaged and covered with unguents; only the mask and the feet had been spared the libations. It was not easy to turn away from the youthful beauty of this majestic head, on whose brow gleamed the Nekhebet vulture and the Buto cobra, the symbols of Upper and Lower Egypt. A disintegrating necklace of blue faience beads and gold discs adorned the throat; on the breast hung a large scarab. The arms were crossed over the chest, the fingers encased in gold sheaths, and grasping the crook and flail. As Carter touched them the insignia crumbled into dust.

Wide gold bands, with which the bandages were held together, bore ritual inscriptions, such as an address of welcome from Nut, the goddess of the sky: 'I reckon thy beauties, O Osiris, King Nebkheprure; thy soul livest: thy veins are firm. Thou smellest the air and goest out as a god, going out as Atum, O Osiris, Tutankhamun. Thou goest out and thou enterest with Ra. . .' And Geb, the god of the earth, the prince of the gods, says on the same band, 'My beloved son, inheritor of the throne of Osiris, the King Nebkheprure; thy nobility is perfect: thy royal palace is powerful; thy name is in the mouth of the people, thy stability is in the mouth of the living, O Osiris, King Tutankhamun, thy heart is in thy body eternally. He is before the spirits of the living, like Re he rests in heaven.'

Unguents and libations had badly affected the mummy wrapping. The outer bandages were almost completely destroyed or carbonised by acids, but there was still the hope that they would be better further in.

'I then attempted,' wrote Carter in his diary on October 31st, 'to remove the mummy and mask from the coffin, but found that unfortunately both were stuck fast to the bottom of the coffin, and could not be under the present conditions raised out without using great force, endangering both the royal remains and that finely wrought mask.'

The excavators now placed all their hopes on Aten, the melting power of the sun. The next day twenty-five excavation workers carried the open coffin with the mummy to the laboratory in the Sethos tomb. There Carter exposed it to the rays of the sun. In the evening he found to his disappointment that the heat of the day had not been able to achieve anything, although the thermometer had risen to 65°C in the sun. The procedure was repeated the following day, but again without success.

So the mummy would have to be examined in the coffin. On 9th November, Howard Carter invited Under-Secretary of State Saleh Enan Pasha, the Director-General of the Department of Antiquities Pierre Lacau, the governor of the province Sayed Fuad Bey el Kholi, and Doctors Douglas Derry and Saleh Bey Hamdi, as well as Inspector of Antiquities Tewfik Effendi Boulos and Assistant Curator Mohammed Shaaban Effendi, to the autopsy on 11th November. Harry Burton, the photographer, and Alfred Lucas, the chemist, were already on the spot.

11th November, 1925. Entry in Carter's diary:
Today has been a great day in the history of archaeology, I might also say in the history of archaeological discovery, and a day of days for one who after years of work, excavating, conserving and recording, has longed to see in fact what previously has only been conjectural.

At about 10.35 Carter and Lucas began to paint the outer layers of the bandaging with liquid paraffin wax. They were fragile, and disintegrated at once at the slightest touch. When the wax had cooled, Dr. Derry applied his scalpel. All eyes were fixed on the glittering little blade in the doctor's hand. With a careful sawing movement he made a cut only a few millimetres deep from the chest to the feet. The upper layers could now be removed like orange peel. In the process, various pieces of jewellery and amulets came to light. They had been bound on to the body of the dead king as protection against evil powers. From the thirteen layers between throat and stomach alone, Howard Carter removed thirty-five amulets. Each piece had to be photographed, numbered and sketched; only then could it be withdrawn from the bandages.

The assumption that the state of the bandaging would

improve the deeper they got proved to be false. Quite the contrary: the closer Dr. Derry came to the body of the dead king, the more fragile and carbonised were the bandages. The original intention of sketching the method of binding the mummy had to be abandoned. The anatomist did record, however, the different qualities of linen in the bandages; the finest cambric was outside and inside, and a coarser stuff in between. As far as could be seen, the layers crossed on the chest, each running to the back over alternate shoulders.

Carter and Dr. Derry thought the best approach was to bare the king's body completely and then draw it from the gold mask, which was stuck fast to the coffin. This was to take place the following morning, 12th November.

Harry Burton was first on the scene. In developing the plates in the laboratory, he had spoilt some and had to take a few of the photographs again. After that, the excavators turned the mummiform coffin, which still stood in the entrance to the tomb of Sethos II, through 180°. Now the head was in a better light. In the course of the day the body was successfully bared to the skin from the stomach down.

The skin was leathery and greyish-white. The feet were shod in golden sandals and the toes, like the fingers, were encased in golden sheaths. On his right ankle the king wore a thin bangle. His forearms, too, were adorned with gold bracelets.

The abdominal incision made by the mummifiers was 86 mm, long and ran from the umbilicus to the anterior superior iliac spine. The usual gold plate over the wound was absent. As Dr. Derry reported:

The incision is situated somewhat differently from that described by Professor Elliot Smith in the royal mummies he examined; in these it was usually placed more vertically and in the left flank, extending from near the lower ribs to the anterior superior iliac spine. At a later period the incision was more often made in the lower part of the abdominal wall, parallel with the line of the groin, but always on the left side.

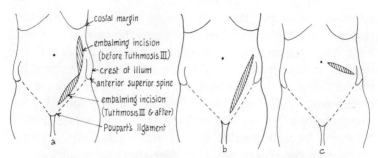

Our knowledge of the length and position of the abdominal incision made by the royal embalmers during the process of mummification is gained chiefly from the work of Elliot Smith. In his *Royal Mummies* he emphasises the fact that the position of the incision varied with different practitioners. The two positions shown in Fig. *a* were frequently used, while a third, Fig. *b*, was occasionally employed. The atypical site of the incision made in the case of Tutankhamun is seen in Fig. *c*. The line here chosen by the royal embalmers is one not noted by Elliot Smith. Derry records that the length of the abdominal incision appeared to be 86mm., but comments that the overlying resin may have obscured the original extent. This is feasible, since many incisions were as much as half as long again.

His majesty's penis, five centimetres long, had been bandaged in the erect position; pubic hair was completely absent. The left knee-cap was loose. When Dr. Derry raised it he could clearly see the lower end of the thigh-bone and the ephiphysis.

To anatomists the epiphyses are an unmistakable index for establishing the age of a dead person. In early years these end-parts of bones, which ossify separately, are not yet firmly knit to the main bone. Only after growth has finished does the connecting cartilage turn into bone, at about the age of eighteen to twenty. Since these ossifications were to some extent already present, while other bones, such as the upper end of the shin bone, as yet showed no change, Dr. Derry estimated Tutankhamun's age at death to be from eighteen to twenty years. The build was slight and fine-limbed. Carter thought they were dealing with the mortal remains of an adolescent.

The next day the two anatomists set about baring the arms. Although the head and upper part of the dead king's body were still swathed in bandages or under the gold mask, the team had already brought to light fifty-two amulets and pieces of jewellery.

On 14th November, the scientists turned to the trunk and the shoulders. Now it was already possible to raise the king's body carefully. On his back between the shoulder-blades were several parts of an ornament, which were stuck to the bottom of the coffin and could not be prised free. Now Dr. Derry and Dr. Saleh Bey Hamdi concentrated all their skill on Tutankhamun's head, which was still hidden behind the gold mask. Libations and unguents had stuck head and mask together so strongly that in all seriousness Howard Carter suggested using hammer and chisel. But then someone else in the team had a better idea: why not try using hot knives? And indeed, knives heated over the fire dissolved the resinous mass, so that after only half a day of this careful melting-work the mask could be raised. Just a few bandages were left, clinging to the inside.

This was the moment for which Howard Carter had been waiting for three years: he was face to face with the forgotten pharaoh. Although the eye sockets were empty, it seemed to Carter as though the king were looking at him. The nose had been plugged: this was supposed to prevent it from being compressed under the weight of the gold mask, but the precaution proved to be useless, for the nose had suffered badly. The raised upper lip bared the teeth in a hideous grin. The ears were comparatively small, with lobes pierced by holes almost a centimetre across. Tutankhamun was bald. The hair on the wide skull, which had a very pronounced rear part – circumference of head, 54.7 centimetres – had apparently fallen victim to the barber – why, is so far not clear. In its place the king wore a skull-cap embroidered with little beads – perhaps it was just the fashion.

The royal mummy measured 1.64 metres from head to foot. Dr. Derry estimated the king's height during life at 1.68 metres. Measurements of the life-sized guardian statues of Tutankhamun, which stood at the entrance to the burial chamber, gave close confirmation of this height.

At that time Carter still held the view that the mummy found

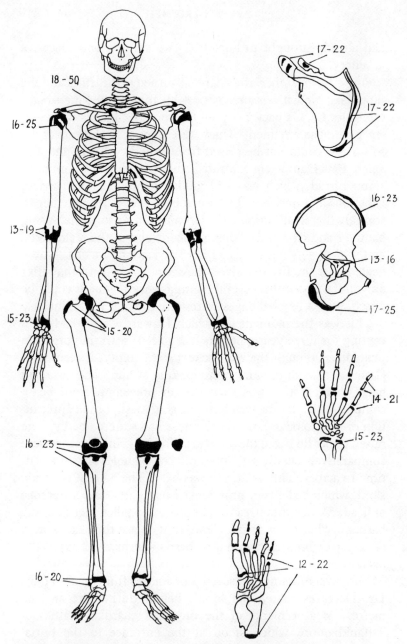

As an indication of the approximate ages between which the epiphyseal ends become fully calcified and unite, the diagram illustrates the range most generally accepted. These figures refer, however, to Europeans, and it is recognised that among Eastern peoples maturation tends to take place earlier.

in the tomb of Tiye was that of Akhenaten. Only later could it be shown that the remains were really those of Smenkhare. Comparative measurements of the skulls of the mummies show the family relationship between the two.

	Tutankhamun mm.	Smenkhare mm.
Length of skull	187	190
Breadth of skull	155.5	154
Height of skull	132.5	134
Forehead breadth	99	98
Height of face: upper	73.5	69.5
Height of face: total	122	121
Breadth of jaw	99	99.5
Circumference of head	547	542
Height	1168 (5'6")	1166 (5'5¼")

On 18th November the uncovering and examination of the mummy were brought to a close. The Director of Antiquities, Pierre Lacau, departed, with the report of the professors of anatomy. The doctors followed a day later.

Neither Dr. Derry's report nor Howard Carter's records made any reference to a regrettable but undeniable fact: during the work in the tomb of Sethos II, Tutankhamun's mummy had been well and truly torn apart. Only later did it appear from examinations of the mummy, which remained in its tomb, that the excavators had not been exactly careful in their handling of the forgotten pharaoh. The head had been detached, as had the hands, arms and legs. For a photographic record, which showed the king naked, the individual parts had been placed in their correct positions. This undoubtedly verified the fears of those who held at the time that the tomb had been discovered a generation too soon.

Carter now still had before him the task of separating the inner gold coffin from the second shell. It was a very difficult problem, the excavator recalled; at least two bucketfuls of the hardened resinous substance had been tipped over the coffins.

Heat, as Carter had discovered in freeing the head from the gold mask, was the only way to tackle this stuff, but heat would also destroy the coffins. The outer mummiform coffin carved of wood and overlaid with gold leaf, was especially vulnerable. The inner coffin, on the other hand, of solid gold with an average thickness of 3.5 mm., could stand far higher temperatures.

It took Howard Carter seventeen days to solve this problem. The inner gold coffin, with Tutankhamun's death-mask still attached to it, was lined with plates of zinc. Carter then laid the adhering coffins upside down over two trestles, covered the upper, outer coffin with wet cloths, and placed two primus stoves underneath. Three hours went by; then the resinous mass became viscous, like thick syrup; it seemed as though the inner gold coffin was slipping very slowly downwards, a millimetre at a time. It took another hour before the operation was successful and the wooden coffin could be lifted off the gold one. Carter could now also free the gold mask from the inner coffin.

On 31st December, 1925, he wrote with telegraphic terseness in his diary, 'Left for Cairo with Lucas with 3 cases containing the coffin 255 and mask 256a and handed them over to the Museum.'

Howard Carter returned to Luxor on New year's Day, 1926. For him the Tutankhamun enterprise was still far from over.

11   The mummifiers: reconstruction of a transformation

*For every Egyptian, however,
death was a desirable
transformation, the passage to the
true and eternal life.*

Christiane Desroches-Noblecourt

'Mr. Carter, what did Tutankhamun die of?'

'Mr. Carter, why were so many treasures put in Tutankhamun's tomb?'

'Mr. Carter, how was Tutankhamun's mummy prepared?'

'Mr. Carter! Mr. Carter!'

Tourists and culture-seekers from all over the world assailed its most famous excavator. Carter had become an Egyptian monument, like Abu Simbel or Karnak. By his house, by the laboratory, by the entrance to the tomb, there were clusters of people everywhere, trying to catch a glimpse of the great man or to touch his sleeve. Who had actually made whom famous? Carter Tutankhamun, or Tutankhamun Carter?

Between 1st January and 15th March, 1926, Carter channelled 12,000 visitors through the tomb, and 278 applications were received for a viewing of the laboratory. Regular scientific activity – the annexe and the treasury still held their secrets – was for the moment not to be thought of. 'The burial chamber and sarcophagus were now empty,' wrote Carter, 'and we were able, for the first time, to consider more closely the funerary customs followed in the burial of a Pharaoh, as revealed to us by Tutankhamun's tomb.'

Was this tomb really the poorest pharaonic grave in the Valley of the Kings? Up to now archaeologists and historians have answered this question in the affirmative, mainly on two grounds: Tutankhamun's tomb is the smallest and decoratively the most modestly appointed royal tomb, and it is the tomb of a pharaoh who, in his nine-year reign, did not achieve any great deeds, either politically or culturally, and who cannot be compared with Tuthmosis III, Amenophis III, or Akhenaten. What treasures might there have been in, say, the vast, luxuriously appointed tomb of Sethos I, before it fell into the hands of the grave-robbers?

Most recently, however, a growing number of scientists have asserted the opposite. They believe that Tutankhamun's tomb-treasure was the richest ever to be buried with a pharaoh.

A prominent advocate of this theory – and until a second untouched pharaonic tomb is found it remains theory – is the Cairo Egyptologist Labib Habachi. Dr. Habachi refers to traditions according to which there was a shortage of gold in Egypt towards the end of the 18th Dynasty. Most of the then-known mines were exhausted. The abundant gold treasures in Tutankhamun's tomb, however, contradict this – the inner mummiform coffin in Cairo Museum alone weighs several hundredweight, and is of pure gold. Where did it come from?

Habachi maintains that Tutankhamun's tomb-treasure was made from all the gold that had been used by Akhenaten at Tell el Amarna. When Tutankhamun died, Amarna was already an empty ghost town. That Akhenaten's capital was 'overflowing with gold' is well documented. The eccentric pharaoh had met his need for gold by stripping the sanctuaries of Amun at Thebes. Among these monuments were, for instance, the two 30-metre high obelisks of Queen Hatshepsut, which were covered with electron, an alloy of gold and silver. At any rate,

Akhenaten had so much gold that he could throw it about, as can be seen in a relief in Ay's tomb.

For the descendants of the heretic king, Habachi believes, it was a kind of overcoming of the past when they melted down all the gold objects from Amarna, and used them to make Tutankhamun's tomb-treasure. Valuables from earlier times, which Akhenaten had taken over but left in their original state, were spared also by Tutankhamun's undertakers. They gave the dead pharaoh some forty extra grave-gifts that came from his predecessors, going back to Tuthmosis III, even including a fan with the cartouche of Akhenaten. 'I believe,' said Labib Habachi, 'that the gratitude of the Egyptians for the religious restoration was so great that all classes of the people showed their veneration for the pharaoh by overloading his tomb with the riches of the past.'

According to pharaonic custom, the planning of the king's tomb was begun on the day he ascended the throne. Ever since the pharaohs of the New Empire had chosen the Valley of the Kings for their last resting-place, these plans had become ever more complicated, and demanded ever more care. For there was a great danger that, in the course of their work, the stone-cutters would strike one of the already existing tomb-passages, which were often more than 100 metres long. So there must have been secret maps in which the position and ground-plan of *all* the royal tombs were recorded. It seems that these maps really did have a note of all the tombs – except one, that of Tutankhamun. The effacement of his name carried on by Horemheb had obviously been so thorough that only 200 years after his death nothing was known any more about his tomb. This is the only explanation for what seems to be an architectural mistake in the planning of the tomb of Rameses VI, for out of the sixty-two tombs in the Valley of the Kings, only two get in each other's way, that of Tutankhamun and that of Rameses VI.

Responsibility for work on the tomb, which sometimes went on for decades, lay not with the pharaoh himself but with his vizier, who in the case of Tutankhamun was Ay. But while it was usually the custom for plans and tomb-texts to be submitted to the pharaoh for his consideration, this might have been omitted with Tutankhamun, for he was only nine years old when these decisions arose. In his case it was probably Ay alone who decided. But was it also Ay who decided that the tomb to be built for his protégé, who was the official ruler of Egypt, was to be the smallest and most insignificant in the whole of the Valley?

If a pharaoh died before the completion of his tomb, work was stopped at once. Even debris would be left lying about. It would be cleared away only in so far as was necessary for the pall-bearers to get through with the coffin; then the tomb-builders turned at once to the tomb of the new king. There was definitely nothing provisional, however, about Tutankhamun's resting-place. It is an architecturally complete building, albeit inferior in decoration and of small size, and this was all doubt-less by intention and probably in keeping with the slight signifi-cance accorded the pharaoh during his lifetime.

Technically, Tutankhamun's tomb posed no problems. The construction-workers of Deir el Medina, who worked in groups of forty to sixty men, didn't have to contend either with porous stone that was hard to work, as in Queen Hatshepsut's second tomb 150 years earlier, or with a poor air supply, as in the construction, some fifty years later, of the tomb of Sethos, which led deep into the mountain. Sufficient air came through the approach to the antechamber, only 8 metres long. Light was thrown into the interior with the aid of mirrors set up outside the entrance: the guides of El Qurna are still masters of this technique today. In constructing the burial chamber and the treasury the 'Attendants at the Places of Truth' were allowed to fall back on the usual sources of light – extra-large wicks, which were made of twists of linen cloth, soaked in sesame oil and sprinkled with salt, which reduced the formation of soot. The wicks, about 35 centimetres long, were held like torches in the hand or placed in earthenware bowls, for which wall-niches were cut. Since the workmen kept an exact account of work done and materials used, we even know how many wicks were used per day: on an average, fifty.

The time of year in which Tutankhamun was laid to rest has been determined to within exactly six weeks by the archaeologist Percy E. Newberry, who was a trained botanist. He managed to do this with the help of the flowers, wreaths and fruits which were given to the dead king in his tomb, and which Newberry could identify with complete accuracy. On the third coffin lay a floral collarette made up of leaves, flowers, berries and fruits. Newberry recognised date-palm leaves, the flowers of cornflowers and of *Picris coronopifolia*, the berries of woody nightshade, and eleven fruits of the mandrake. A garland of flowers on the chest of the second mummiform coffin had been put together from olive leaves, cornflowers, the leaves of the wild celery, and petals of the blue water-lily. The uraeus on the facial mask of the second coffin was adorned with the so-called 'Wreath of Justification', which was placed on the coffin to the accompaniment of magic formulae, as prescribed by the Book of the Dead. This wreath too was composed of cornflowers, olive leaves and petals of the blue water-lily.

The flowers of the blue water-lily didn't fit into Percy Newberry's scheme. Today the water-lily comes into flower in standing water in Lower Egypt, from July to November. Cornflowers and *Picris*, on the other hand, are in full bloom in March and April, at harvest time, which is also the time when the fruits

Relief in the temple at Karnak: plants and animals which Tuthmosis III brought back from his Asiatic campaigns.

of the nightshade ripen. Newberry concluded from this that Tutankhamun had been laid to rest between the middle of March and the end of April, and he thought the water-lily had been cultivated in garden tanks at Thebes, where it would flower much earlier.

It is remarkable that the Egyptians, the most communicative people in world history, have described every sphere of human life, even death, extensively. Representations and texts contain detailed accounts of burial rites, but the ritual and technique of embalming, which was so typical and innate in them, they took with them to the grave. Archaeologists, historians and doctors today are thrown back on a few references, which give, however, only a rough idea of what happened in those days to the body of a dead pharaoh.

The Greek historian Herodotus, who described the customs and manners of the ancient Egyptians in the fifth century B.C., must – as always – be taken with discretion when he asserts:

There are a set of men in Egypt who practise the art of embalming, and make it their proper business. These persons, when a body is brought to them, show the bearers various models of corpses, made of wood, and painted so as to resemble nature. The most perfect is said to be after the manner of him who I do not think it religious to name in connection with such a matter [Osiris]; the second sort is inferior to the first, and less costly; the third is the cheapest of all. All this the embalmers explain, and then ask in which way it is wished that the corpse should be prepared. The bearers tell them, and having concluded their bargain, take their departure, while the embalmers, left to themselves, proceed to their task.

First, with a hooked tool they draw the brain out through the nostrils; to be precise, they draw out only a part of the brain, the remaining part being removed through the introduction of decomposing substances. Then, with a sharp Ethiopian stone they cut the body down the abdomen and take out the viscera. When they have cleaned it and washed it out with palm wine, they wash it again with crushed aromatics. Then they fill the abdomen with pure crushed myrrh, cassia and the usual spices, with the exception of incense, and after carrying out this filling they sew it up again. Then the body is placed in natron for seventy days, and covered entirely over. After the expiration of that space of time, which must not be exceeded, the body is washed, and wrapped round, from head to foot, with bandages of fine linen cloth, smeared over the gum, which is used generally by the Egyptians in place of glue. . .

All the same, Herodotus is one of the few ancient sources in which the process of mummification is described. In 1908, a German professor of anatomy re-enacted the work of the mummifiers experimentally. The venture was highly secret. Anatomy assistant Gustav Hagedorn had already prepared everything when Professor Karl Sudhoff appeared early one morning in the anatomy department of Leipzig University. The head of the Medical History Institute, who came from Frankfurt, had chosen a week-end during the summer holidays for his experiment, because there was hardly anyone about in the clinic.

Together, Sudhoff and Hagedorn ascended the bare staircase to the dissecting rooms on the second floor. In Room 1 the body of an unknown suicide lay on the dissecting table. But on the instrument table, which was usually arrayed with numerous scalpels and knives, nothing was to be seen except for a slightly curved hook about thirty centimetres long. This original mummy hook had been discovered during excavations in Egypt financed by James Simon, a private collector of Berlin, who had made it available to the professor of anatomy.

Hagedorn closed the door and handed the rubber gloves to the professor, who took the hook, pierced the nasal septum of the corpse with the front, sharp end, and thrust the instrument about 20 centimetres into the interior of the skull.

At first Professor Sudhoff said nothing about the

experiment. Not until three years later did he reveal his secret and publish his findings.

> Penetration of the lamina cribrosa [Sudhoff reported], was managed at once; equally easy was the rupturing of the lamina perpendicularis, indeed the complete destruction of the superior and inferior ethmoidal conche. . . The cranium was then entered and the tentorium ruptured, and all resisting parts of fixed membranes inside the cranium, by hooking with the point of the hook or by thrusting with its curved, blunt side; the brain, easily reduced to a pulp, was stirred round and the body then laid on its stomach, when, with a little help from the hook or its handle-end, the brain ran out virtually completely in 15 to 20 minutes. . .'

Herodotus reported what priests had told him, or rather, what he had understood of it. Like much in Herodotus, his retelling becomes perfunctory, and in places incorrect, as when he says, for instance, that the bodies were embalmed with natron. Natron (ancient Egyptian *neter*, soda) is today a scientifically imprecise term for sodium. Now sodium does not have a preserving but a dehydrating function; it is supposed to extract all moisture from the body, thus protecting it from decay. The principle is still applied today: flowers laid in sodium for a few days become stiff and dry like immortelles; they no longer wilt, but keep their fresh appearance.

That was exactly what the ancient Egyptians wanted to achieve with their complicated mummifying technique. What was the purpose behind it?

Deep-rooted in Egyptian religion was the notion of resurrection. The Ba and the Ka, which temporarily left the body at its death, were supposed to return to it. The Ba was the bearer of the immortal forces, the Ka a kind of protective spirit; it was born with the person but survived his death. On their return, the Ba and the Ka were supposed to be able to find their corporeal shell again, and so it must not be exposed to decay. In addition, every mummified corpse represented an imitation of Osiris, the god of the dead. His was the power, according to popular belief, to bestow eternal life on the dead person.

The ancient Egyptians will undoubtedly have discovered by experiment that the technique of embalming was defective so long as the dead body contained soft tissues and internal organs. The removal of the brain proved to be the most difficult procedure, for the exterior had, if possible, to be left undamaged. We don't know when the mummy-hook for the macabre procedure of drawing out the brain through the nose was first used, but Professor Sudhoff's experiment showed that it was feasible. Copper mummy-hooks are preserved in the British Museum in London, in the Louvre in Paris, in the National Museum in Leiden, and in the Egyptian Museum in East Berlin.

As Sudhoff showed, the removal of the brain required a single curved hook. The medical historian even suggested that the washing out of the skull with some kind of clyster, as described by Herodotus, would have been unnecessary, because the corpse would in any case be laid in a solution of sodium or common salt.

The removal of the internal organs was much simpler. Herodotus's description is filled out by Diodorus. According to him, the corpse was placed on the ground and a scribe marked the line of the cut on the left side of the body. 'Then the cutter takes an Ethiopian stone and cuts the flesh as the law prescribes.' The Ethiopian stone, mentioned also by Herodotus, could have been obsidian, which occurs on the upper reaches of the Nile. Obsidian is a characteristic material of the Middle Eastern neolithic period, a rock-glass used especially for cutting-tools, arrow-heads and scrapers. It received its name from the Roman, Obsius, who is supposed to have discovered the stone in Ethiopia.

Nothing further has come down to us on the dissection. Only Diodorus observes that the heart and kidneys remained in the body. He didn't know why, and it remains equally puzzling to us today.

Karl Sudhoff reconstructed the work of the Egyptian

mummy-surgeons in great detail. According to this, the diaphragm would have been opened from below, and the bronchi or trachea cut through to release the lungs; likewise the aorta under the aortic arch. The dissector would have put his right arm through the opening in the left of the abdominal cavity, and after that had been emptied, the thoracic cavity would have followed. The diaphragm would have been perforated and the lungs and large vessels removed through its opening.

How are we to picture this? Did the mummifiers tear the viscera out of the dead person's body?

We know that, down to the 21st Dynasty (1070–945 B.C.), the liver, lungs, stomach and intestines were preserved in Canopic jars. The four sons of Horus had to guard them: Imsety the liver, Hapi the lungs, Duamutef the stomach, and Qebehsnewef the intestines. Modern anatomy takes the view that for the removal of the individual organs there were only two alternatives.

By the first, the dead person would be left for a few days, until the process of decomposition had set in; then the organs could be taken from the inside of the body with the bare hand.

But [Professor Sudhoff argued] a putrefaction of the body so far-reaching that the diaphragm could be broken through easily with the hand; that the trachea and the aorta, or the ligamenta lata and even the vagina, could have severed by probing and tearing with the tips of the fingers; and that cutting instruments would not have been needed for this; such a far-reaching putrid collapse of the tissues would have made any keeping apart of the individual contents of the abdomen and chest, even if only to a certain desired degree, a complete illusion; after that, whatever remained would undoubtedly have been reduced to an indefinable pulp by the manipulations of the embalmers.

There remains only the second alternative: the dissectors must have used a knife with a hook-like blade on the inner side. Such bronze knives, the length of an average hand, have been brought to light in various excavations. The sharpened point of the blade is curved to one side; the rest of the knife is blunt. So the instrument could be introduced as it lay in the surgeon's hand. Since the lower end of the knife is broadened like a chisel, it was also used for scraping. A better instrument for the dissection, Professor Sudhoff believed, could hardly have been invented.

The operation followed a hallowed ritual, which was why the surgeons belonged to none of the usual occupational classes; they were priests, so-called Ut priests. It was the Ut priests also who continued treatment of the surgically prepared corpse. Contrary to Sudhoff's view, that the bodies were placed in a *solution* of sodium, modern science takes the view that the bodies were treated dry. They were covered with dry natron, a natural mixture of sodium carbonate, bicarbonate, chloride and sulphate. This procedure, lasting thirty-five days, extracted all moisture from the body. The use of the dry method is probable if only because dissecting tables, on which the dehydrating process could take place, alone have come down to us and not steeping-troughs.

Since the dead, after this chemical treatment, had usually assumed a rather unattractive appearance, the mummifiers went to work on them with all sorts of make-up. Hands, feet and hair were dyed with henna (ancient Egyptian *puker*), a brownish-reddish dye from the willow-herb plant of the same name. The remaining visible parts of the body were tinted with red ochre for a man, and yellow ochre for a woman. Sunken parts of the body, such as the stomach, breasts or cheeks, were stuffed by the Ut priests with little balls of linen soaked into a sticky mass, or with clay, saw-dust or hay. Glass eyes were supposed to look as true to life as possible. Only then did the real embalming begin.

Wine, oil, fats, resins and honey had now to give the emaciated, stuffed body as pleasant an odour as possible. The embalming followed a solemn ritual.

There are only two papyri, independent of each other, in which this ritual is handed down to us; one is preserved in Cairo

Museum, the other in the Louvre. These two hieratic documents from the late Egyptian period are copies of an older original. Unfortunately both are incomplete, and unfortunately neither gives any technical details of the embalming, though certain inferences concerning it can be drawn from the ceremonial direction. A third papyrus, which contains the book of rites for the embalming of the Apis bulls, can be referred to only for purposes of comparison.

The Cairo papyrus fell one day into the hands of the most distinguished researcher, Dr. Elliot Smith. During his activity at Cairo University, Smith had examined thousands of mummies. Incidentally he never spoke of 'mummies'; he always called them his 'patients', and it was indeed as patients that he treated these thousands-of-years-old bodies. He examined some 25,000 skulls for bone deformations, and in 500 that were found in excavations at Giza he detected parodontitis. He was often so immersed in his work that he quite forgot that his patients were beyond any help. He was seen in Cairo one day taking a mummy in a taxi. It was Tuthmosis III, husband of the masterful Queen Hatshepsut, and Smith was on his way from the national museum to a clinic, in order to X-ray his 'patient'.

From the Cairo papyrus Professor Smith and his colleague Warren R. Dawson reconstructed twelve directions for embalming, which are in part very complicated or obscure:

1. Direction to the operator to anoint the mummy's head with frankincense.
2. Direction to take an unguent vase filled with specified ointments such as are used for the *Opening of the Mouth*. An officiant called the 'Treasurer of the God' is to anoint the whole body from the head to the soles of the feet, but omitting the head itself.
3. The next direction is very obscure, and appears to refer to another anointing, and mentions the 'children of Horus', which seems to refer to the separately embalmed viscera.

4. Directions for the 'children of Horus' and for anointing the back with 'fat'.

5. Further directions for anointing and wrapping the back. Some reference is apparently made to filling the skull with medicaments.

6. Directions for gilding the nails and winding the fingers in 'linen of Sais'.

7. Ceremonies performed by 'Anubis the chief of Mysteries' [impersonated by a priest] and 'the Treasurer of the God'.

8. A long section giving directions for the anointing and bandaging of the head, with a detailed specification of the bandages to be used for each part of the head, giving the magical names of each. Thus the descriptions and names of a long series of bandages are given for application to the ears, nostrils, cheeks, brow, occiput, mouth, chin, and neck. The application of these bandages is finished off by affixing a linen band of two fingers' width and anointing the whole with 'thick oil' (doubtless the resinous paste which is so often found upon actual mummies).

9. Directions for further anointing of the head with frankincense and fat, and for enwrapping certain spices.

10. Long directions for anointing and wrapping of the hands. An ointment consisting of 'Amu-flowers 1 part, Resin of Coptos 1, Natron 1.' The bandages are all identified with gods and goddesses, and the vignette at the top of the papyrus shows several deities bringing bandages to the mummy lying on a couch.

11. A similar passage describing bandages, with figures of gods, etc., traced upon them, used for the hands.

12. Directions for the anointing and bandaging of the arms, feet and legs.

'It is difficult to believe,' wrote Elliot Smith, 'that they [the directions] were ever strictly carried out, but there is so little known as to the wrappings of actual mummies that it is unsafe to say whether inscribed bandages and other details of the ritual and verifiable or not.' One thing, however, seems entirely credible: this mummification procedure must indeed have taken three months.

Seventeen days were appointed for the bandaging alone. We find this detail in two papyri which a Scottish lawyer, Alexander Henry Rhind, discovered in the middle of the last century in a private Theban tomb of the 18th Dynasty. The tomb had been occupied in the Ptolemaic period by several mummies. Rhind, who like Lord Carnarvon had gone to Egypt for health reasons and become an excavator there out of boredom, brought to light in west Thebes a whole series of papyri which today all bear his name. According to two of these papyri – one describes the mummification of a man, the other that of a woman – the head was mummified for seven days, the internal organs for four days; the arms and legs required two days each, and chest and back one each. To quote from the hieratic papyrus Rhind No. 1:

The Great Isis, the mother of the god, commands to make the beautiful burial of N. [here follow the name, titles and filiation of the deceased]. Two hundred and six *hin* of fat were boiled as is done for a sacred animal. Thou wast rubbed with balsam by Horus, the lord of the laboratory. Shesmu wound with his fingers the divine bandage in order to enwrap thy body with the wrappings of the gods and goddesses. Anubis as embalmer filled thy skull with resin, corn of the gods. . . cedar oil, mild ox-fat, cinnamon oil; and myrrh is to all thy members. Thy body was invested with holy bandages. Come forth to see the winter sun on the 26th day of Pharmuti [the fourth winter month, from 15th January to 15th February].

Seventy days had gone by since the death. Cleaning and dehydration were begun a day or two after it; these lasted fifty-two days. Seventeen days were taken up with preserving and mummifying. The Ut priests now placed the mummy in its coffin. For a further three days and nights hourly guards stood by the corpse, which had now become Osiris. Then came the day when the dead king was borne to the tomb.

Let us forget time, leap across thirty-three centuries and witness that stirring spectacle, the funeral of Tutankhamun.

Thebes is swarming with people. By the banks of the Nile the boats are crowded together. Hundreds of thousands have thronged in from north and south to attend this event, which for the people is not a sad one. The pharaoh is entering the 'beautiful West'. 'How beautiful,' they say, 'is his lot.' It is one reason for a huge popular festival. Sadness hold sway only in the pharaoh's family, but it is more the sorrow of parting.

The threefold mummiform coffin of the young king, who has departed this life so unexpectedly for everyone, is borne by courtiers on to a Nile barge. Under a canopy, with trappings fluttering in the morning breeze, the bulging coffin shines in pure gold, like a symbol from another world.

The funerary priests murmur their sing-song prayer: 'Hail to thee, Osiris, Lord of Eternity, King of the gods, thou who hast many names and splendid forms and a secret Being in the temples.' Hundreds of thousands look on and avidly draw in the fragrance and the aromas spread by the incense burners and the sacrificial fires on the landing-stage, near the temple of Amun Mut-Khons. Household goods, treasures and foodstuffs are brought out and loaded on to one of the five barges lying ready. Ecstatic cries greet the little statues that are carried past the crowd – domestic servants in miniature, one for every conceivable task, and also for every pleasure: sistrum players, strip-tease dancers, and naked concubines. They are anatomically complete except for the legs, so that they can't run away.

'Helmsman, set course for the beautiful West, for the land of the justified!' calls a priest, who stands in the bow of the first boat. Then one after the other the barges cast off: the boat with the priests; the barge with the dead pharaoh, censed by Sem priests with shaven heads; the widow with relations and friends; the royal household, officials and functionaries; and finally the boat with the treasures, the household goods and

A trumpeter and a drummer lead a religious procession.

food-stuffs. The hundred-thousand crowd remains behind, on this, the living bank of the Nile.

The crowd by which the flotilla is received on the other bank is numerically far smaller, and it is also highly civilised. The people who stand about here in groups, waiting, are 'Inhabitants of the West', tomb-workers, artist-craftsmen, priests of the funerary temples, tomb-guards and officials. They all have their work here; they see the east bank of the Nile only from a distance. Just as the common people from hearsay know only what happens on the west bank, so the westerners know Thebes of the Hundred Gates, with its temple city of Karnak, its golden pylons and obelisks, only from tales.

The roughly-constructed, low wooden sledge on to which the golden mummiform coffin is now lifted gives an almost poor impression. Spanned to it are four oxen. The Sem priest gives a sign and the sledge moves off, sliding gratingly over the sand. Behind it walks Ankhesenamun. She wears a delicate white robe falling in long folds, and utters monotonously sentences learned by heart: 'Woe, woe! I am thy much-loved sister. Why are thou so far from me, thou who tookest such delight in conversing with me and in loving me? Yet this day is a beautiful day, for the happy one is born again in the body of Osiris. . .'

The dusty road, along which Amenophis III, the mighty conqueror, was the last to be drawn to his tomb, twenty-six years before, leaves the fertile, alluvial land behind all too soon. Green fields and pastures and little houses give way to barren rock. Rugged, unfriendly, and cruel, vast blocks of stone lie by the track, which now winds over scree slopes and round spurs of rock. The sledge with the mummy squeaks and groans.

'O misery, O misery,' murmurs Ankhesenamun, 'thou art silent and speakest no word more. Thou, who hadst so many servants, now art thou perhaps in that place where no-one is but monsters with gleaming eyes. Yet this day is a beautiful day; for thou shalt be guarded by the man, the jackal, the ape and the falcon, which are the four faces of Horus. . .'

If we look back, we see, behind the funeral procession with the king's mummy, a second and third procession, which wind like millipedes towards the mountains. They are the Tekenu procession and the Canopic procession. The Tekenu, a ritual figure, is represented by a priest. He lies on a sledge like the mummy, and is covered with the skin of an animal. The sledge is drawn by four men. The Tekenu represents the sun-god in animal form. 'To the West, to the West,' call the sledge-drawers, 'to the land with the pleasant life, to the place where thou shouldst be.' The Canopic procession that follows, with Tutankhamun's internal organs, hardly differs from the Tekenu procession. Here, too, four men draw a sledge. On it stands the Canopic chest. At the end of this third procession come two men, each holding a long stalk of papyrus in his hand.

The entrance to the tomb, prepared for Tutankhamun in all haste, lies nearly opposite the place where, a few years before, Tiye had found her last rest. Glowing on a temporary altar is the sacrificial fire. Meanwhile, those taking part in the funeral procession have ranged themselves round it. Foodstuffs brought along by the servants are put on the fire and burned, along with the valuable vessels. A young bullock, garlanded with flowers, waits to die. The sacrificial priest hurries along with an axe, and strikes the right foreleg off the animal with one blow, as the obscure ritual demands; the bullock falls to the ground and men with axes and knives cut it up while it is still alive. The individual parts are put on the fire. Smoke and stench arise and spread.

Now the men with the grave-goods step forward out of the funeral procession. To the dull beating of sticks on wooden drums, while the sacrificial priests swing censers and sprinkle milk, each steps solemnly to the opening in the ground that leads into the tomb. First comes a procession of statues, followed by bearers of chests and caskets; pieces of furniture are seen, tableware and vessels with unguents and oils.

When the 'nine friends' come forward to take hold of Tutankhamun's coffin, Ankhesenamun throws herself over him and cries, as the ritual prescribes, 'Woe, woe! Cruel is my lament. Thou who didst stroll with me in the gardens on the banks of the Nile, now are thy legs firmly wrapped. Dost thou know me? I am thy wife, thy much-loved sister. . . Joy is with him who now rests in peace. With the *djed* sign [a pillar, symbol of Osiris] will he be able to eat the foods of Osiris. . . O grief, O grief! My body prays for thee, but thy body is quite cold. Yet this day is a beautiful day for the mummy, which bears a scarab in its body. I am thy sister, thou hast forsaken me. Alone I must go home to my house. . .'

Ankhesenamun is led away; the nine men take hold of the coffin; the beating of the drum grows louder; the priests swing high their vessels of incense. 'The god is coming,' cry the 'nine friends' alternately. 'The god is coming.' And so the mummiform coffin, glittering with gold, disappears into the opening to the tomb. It will not see the light of the sun again for another 3,263 years.

The drums spreading grief and devotion fall silent; quickly the scene changes: mats are unrolled, tables set up, food is distributed and drinks are handed out for the funeral feast. Cheerful music is played. Dancers wearing nothing but lotus flowers do their best to brighten clouded faces.

The funerary rites unfolding with the tomb are far from over. The dead king now belongs no more to the living; he has passed into the possession of the priests. Obscure and inexplicable are these ceremonies and customs that are played out inside the tomb a few hours before the vault is closed for ever. As we are shown in the wall-painting in the burial chamber, the aged Ay, Tutankhamun's successor, performed the symbolic act of opening the mouth. And Ankhesenamun it probably was who laid a last bouquet of flowers on the coffin of her beloved husband, the bouquet that was found by Howard Carter.

12 The burden: the Karnak clan and the heretic of Akhetaten

> *Amun was orginally only a simple Theban god, but through the long-standing favour of the pharaohs he became the richest and most powerful god in Egypt. His cult was declared the official cult, whereby practically all the other humbler, subsidiary gods declined into local divinities and their worship was driven back into the provinces.*
>
> Eléonore Bille-de Mot

There were scientists at the time who thought that, after the discovery of Tutankhamun's tomb, the history of the 18th Dynasty would have to be rewritten. This proved to be a mistake, for with all its richness of content, and in spite of its many details that illustrate the life and personality of the child-pharaoh, hardly any new historical facts came to light, and the attempts to write up Tutankhamun, after his rediscovery, into one of the most important pharaohs in Egyptian history had for the most part to be revised.

His position in history, his importance or secondary rating, only become comprehensible if we look at the achievements of his predecessors and their motives. If we do so, one name crops up that overshadows all else: Amun.

Amun ('the hidden one') is not one of the age-old traditional gods, like Ra or Osiris. He first crops up in Thebes in the 11th Dynasty (2133–1991), and he was probably – much like Aten half a millennium later – a new god, to whom, after civil wars and social revolutions, new hopes were attached.

In Thebes, which began to develop at the start of the Middle Empire, a religious vacuum had arisen. So Karnak was built, and the national god Amun gained in importance. The temple of Karnak expanded within a few centuries to become the religious centre of the country, and other, existing sanctuaries were incorporated into it. Above all, Amun, the new national god, had to be integrated into the traditional pantheon.

That did not pass off without difficulties, and sometimes the theologians even used a little violence, as for instance when the sphere of competence which it was sought to attribute to Amun was already occupied by another god; then Amun simply swallowed his convenient forerunner. This was what happened with Min, the god of fertility, and Ra, the all-powerful sun-god. There are representations in which Amun possesses the attributes of both gods, a human body with erect phallus (Min) and a tall crown of feathers with the sun disc (Ra).

Amun of Thebes.

Amun is often depicted as a ram, or with a ram's head on a human body, for to the ancient Egyptian the ram was an animal that suggested power and prestige. Much the same was supposed to be symbolised by the attributes which contemporary artists placed in his hands: a whip, a divine sceptre or curved sword.

In Thebes there were simultaneously three important places of worship for Amun: Karnak, Luxor and Medinet Habu. Karnak was Amun's dwelling-place; in the Luxor temple – the 'Southern Harem' as it was also called – Amun was venerated as the god of fertility; and in Medinet Habu, where there was a temple as early as the Middle Empire, Amun was honoured as a primeval god of creation. Gradually the priests set up a whole chain of temples to Amun, which extended from Lower Egypt (Tanis, Xois, Letopolis) and the western oasis (Siwa, Deir el Hagar) to Upper Egypt (Hermopolis, Dendera, Elephantine) and Nubia (Wadi es-Sebua, Abu Simbel, Amara). With that, Amun had got the better of all the gods.

The centre of his worship, the Rome of the Amun cult, remained nevertheless Thebes, with its temple city of Karnak. Here dwelt the pope of Egypt, the high priest of Amun – also known as the First Prophet of Amun, or Opener of the Door of Heaven – assisted by four deputies. Thebes was the control centre and command post of a predominant state religion.

Thousands of priests and officials were divided up into a perfectly organised hierarchy, which was, economically and politically, the most important factor in the country. There are figures according to which Rameses III had to pay the priests of Amun 32 tons of gold, 1,000 tons of silver and 185 sacks of grain per year. The total assets of the Egyptian temples and priesthood amounted at that time to 750,000 acres of land, half a million head of cattle, and 107,000 slaves. 169 cities in Egypt and Syria paid taxes to the priestly clan.

Akhenaten may have been an intellectual dreamer and a pathological sectarian, but one thing cannot be denied: he was the first and only person in the three-thousand-year history of the people of the Nile who at least made an attempt to end the nepotism of the priests, to impose some check on the priestly clan, and to reduce it to its original function.

Traditionally, the pharaoh was the god Geb's successor on the banks of the Nile, where he had to administer the heritage of the gods Horus and Seth. So it devolved on him also to make appointments to the priestly office, which was originally supposed to be filled by the wisest men in the two lands. But since, in the course of time, temple service developed into a lucrative job, the rush for this office became ever greater, and high priests sometimes even bequeathed to their sons what had once been gained – which in the public service was completely normal.

Warnings such as that of the wise Ani, who said, 'Officials have no children,' remained unheard. The 'holy' life that went on behind the temple walls and on the latifundia of the Amun cult was too tempting. Free board and lodging, a bit of singing

Horus and Seth crown an Egyptian King.

and dancing, a handsome stipend – and all this for life – were indeed not to be despised. Cold baths three times a day and twice at night, the ritual cleansing, could be endured; it was in any case usually a refreshing procedure. And there was also no celibacy.

Is it any wonder that the temples and their attached domains were one day full of these 'holy' men, that this hierarchy gradually developed into a state within the state? 'Raise not the son of an (influential) man above the lesser,' advised Ani, with the king in mind, 'but use a man according to his ability.' Yet in practice things were different.

The Egyptologist Hermann Kees, who has been closely concerned with the life and doings of the ancient Egyptian priests, believes that whether a king accepted the inheritability of the priestly office, or whether he insisted on personal choice and appointment, was determined by the degree to which the families of the officials and priests were dependent on the pharaoh, or whether, conversely, the pharaoh was dependent on them. If he was looking for fresh support for his power in society, then he would thrust aside the old families' rights of succession. If he had gathered a faithful clan around him, then he probably took rights of succession into account. Matters were no different among the priests, according to Kees, from those involving the public officials, for the high priest was not only the 'servant of god', but also as the same time, as administrator of the temple's property, a worldly ruler and economic leader.

By referring to the eternal life, it was an easy matter for the high priest to extort material goods from the pharaoh. So there was no lack of historical models for the Dominican Johannes Tetzel at the beginning of the sixteenth century A.D., who also knew how to turn the preconditions for a pleasant life after death into hard cash. The prestige and importance which the prophets of Amun, to give them their official designation, gathered to themselves can be seen most readily in their richly-appointed tombs and numerous memorial stones that have come down to us.

The 18th Dynasty began thus, with a scandal about a priestess: Queen Ahmes-Nofretari, wife of the founder of the dynasty, Ahmose, received the office of Second Prophet of Amun, hence deputy high priest of the national religion. Although there is an appropriate legal record of the installation of the beautiful queen in her office, the document is silent about the reason for her appointment. Now at that time 'singers' and 'ladies of the harem' did their duty behind the temple walls, but for the chief priest to be represented by a woman was completely out of the ordinary – at least until the 21st Dynasty.

Ahmes-Nofretari, who was later 'deified' by her husband, disposed of her office, however, for a suitable sum in recompense. This took place at a solemn ceremony in the southern hall of pillars in the temple of Karnak, before the assembled council of prophets, the priesthood of Amun, and a large number of royal attendants; Amun himself was called to witness. As compensation, the Queen received 400 bushels of corn, linen cloths and gold and silver, besides arable land. This ensured Ahmes-Nofretari useful pocket-money for the rest of her life.

Such a vast temple-city as Karnak could, in fact, only have arisen under the pressure – at least moral – of the Amun priesthood. Building of the great national temple was begun as early as the 12th Dynasty (1991–1786), but the area first received its character under Tuthmosis I, Hatshepsut, Tuthmosis III and Amenophis III (then later also under Rameses II and Rameses III).

Tuthmosis I, who extended the boundaries of the empire to beyond the Euphrates, reigned too briefly to set his mark on Karnak, but the fourth and fifth pylons, thought to be his creations, give some idea of what he had in mind.

The unfortunate Tuthmosis II, in the four years of his reign, was able to build far less, even, than his father. But he too left behind a visible sign of his intentions, or rather his obligations; he began the so-called obelisk temple, which was completed by Rameses II and extended under Taharka. It was an obelisk from here, over 30 metres high, that was brought by the

Emperor Constantine to Rome in 357, and set up in the Lateran under Pope Sixtus V.

Tuthmosis II's wife and half-sister Hatshepsut, who felt herself chosen to carry on her husband's conduct of affairs, laid her hand on Karnak more than all the men before her. She set up a 'horizon' for Amun, i.e. an inner sanctum; at her behest the eighth pylon rose to the sky, besides the two obelisks that were erected on the occasion of her jubilee. On the base of the vast stone needles, whose transport and dedication are described in the terrace temple of Deir el Bahari, the queen pays her lip-service: 'Concerning the two great obelisks which my majesty has had covered with electrum [75 per cent gold, 22 per cent silver, 3 per cent copper] for my father Amun, that my name may live for ever in this temple, throughout the centuries: they are hewn from a single stone which is of hard granite, with no joints. . . I have shown my devotion to Amun, as a king does to all the gods. . .'

It almost sounds as though Hatshepsut had discharged an onerous duty that had been imposed on her. This prompts a question: is it a coincidence of no significance, or is there method behind it when, not only on Hatshepsut's Karnak buildings but also at Deir el Bahari, the Aten disc with its health-giving rays crops up for the first time?

Hapuseneb, a favourite of Queen Hatshepsut, and his deputy, the Second Priest of Amun, Ipuemre, achieved office and dignity through good connections. Ipuemre's mother was 'great nurse', and Hapuseneb's mother an attractive lady of the harem. Hapuseneb's father had risen to be third lector priest of Amun; Ipuemre's father was a plain 'Mr.' Both Hapuseneb and Ipuemre had imposing tombs cut for themselves in western Thebes, where they and their achievements are skilfully represented.

The careers of the two prophets are exemplary. They were not content with their spiritual dignity. As superintendent of cattle of Amun and as 'one who reckons the payment concerning the heifers for Amun', as 'superintendent of the arable land of Amun', and 'superintendent of all offices of the temple of

Amun', they were the bosses of an organisation that administered properties all over the country and had wage-earners dependent upon it.

Hapuseneb also showed political interests from the beginning; Ipuemre not at first. As a result, Hapuseneb finally laid claim to the political office of vizier, or prime minister, and after the death of Tuthmosis II was able to get the power-obsessed Queen Hatshepsut to dismiss the incumbent vizier. Such a concentration of offices occurred only once more in the 18th Dynasty, when Amenophis III likewise made his high priest, Ptahmose, his vizier.

During Hapuseneb's political rise, Ipuemre held back. He shone more as a scribe and scholar, and saw to the Theban temple buildings; it is known that he was involved in the building of Hatshepsut's valley temple, discovered by Howard Carter. And once at the top of the hierarchy, Ipuemre also

The High Steward Antef hunts hippopotamus with a harpoon.

looked after his sons. The eldest became prophet in the mortuary temple of Tuthmosis III, and the second, thanks to parental connections, managed to become weaving priest of Amun.

Tuthmosis III, who seized power in 1468, achieved importance through his seventeen military campaigns, but he was also a ruler very much after the hearts of the Amun priests. They had brought him to power; now he reciprocated with gold from his Asiatic plundering expeditions. Where Hatshepsut had to trim or abandon her building programme for financial reasons or lack of time, Tuthmosis III made a point of continuing the work.

In the middle courtyard, between the third and fourth pylons, the pharaoh set up two obelisks; he also built the sixth pylon and a granite altar in the inner sanctum. At right angles to the main axis of the temple he created the great banqueting hall, which symbolised the pitching of a tent, 44 metres by 16, with twenty tent-pole columns and thirty-two pillars, and with the charming 'Botanical Room', in which we can still today admire the plants and animals the pharaoh brought back from his Asiatic campaigns, including the chicken. North of this banqueting hall, a further temple shot up, which Tuthmosis III dedicated to Ptah, the creator of the world.

Yet it would seem that the boundless demands of the Amun priests became too much even for this ancient Egyptian Napoleon, for he decided in his old age to dedicate an obelisk to Ra-Harakhte, the rising sun, in a sanctuary east of the Amun temple. The Karnak clan may have taken this as an affront, but there was no open breach, because Tuthmosis III died before the obelisk had been set up. And so the stone needle was left lying near the sacred Lake.

Prince Amenophis, Tuthmosis's son by his favourite wife Merietre, and strictly brought up by his father, could no more escape the pressure of the priesthood than could his predecessors, though his buildings in Karnak were confined to a temple near the Sacred Lake and a small sanctuary between the ninth and tenth pylons. His relations with the priestly clan remain largely obscure.

Connections and hereditary claims ensured that the office-seeking merry-go-round of the Amun priests did not stop in those years either. If the mother of Menkheperreseneb had not been the foster-sister of Amenophis II, i.e. if they had not had the same nurse, her little son would never have risen to be high priest of Amun. At any rate, Menkheperreseneb was one whom 'the king made great when he was a child'.

At the start of this career was the office of Second Prophet, a job for which nothing was needed but connections. He then became High Priest of Karnak, 'Superintendent of the Prophets of Upper and Lower Egypt', 'Superintendent of the Gold and Silver House of Amun', one 'who reckons what is present in the villages of Upper and Lower Egypt', 'Superintendent of the King's Weaving in Upper and Lower Egypt' and 'Chief of the Foremen and Chief Architect'. When, one might ask, did the Right Reverend find time to pray?

Hermann Kees writes that it was typical of these dignitaries that they should feel like temporal lords and be in the thick of life, like men of the court and the army. In contrast to the latter, however, they did not live in material dependence on the pharaoh, and so their decisions were to a great extent their own.

Amenophis-Sise, who married a cast-off playmate from the harem of Tuthmosis IV, did not have to regret his decision. The pharaoh rewarded him with the office of Second Prophet of Amun. As 'Superintendent of the Granaries of Amun' and 'Superintendent of the Gold and Silver House', he managed to supplement his income, and to judge from the representations in his noble tomb he led a life governed by appointments: his installation as priest, which took place in the the Amun temple at Karnak, is almost swamped by his supervision of the harvest-workers and joiners, the sculptors in the king's tomb, the leather-workers and art-foundrymen. His Excellency travelled in a chariot, while attendants with folding stool and sandals ran behind the great man.

There is a whole series of spiritual dignitaries who attained to their high office by a detour through the king's harem.

Meri, a high priest of Amun under Amenophis II, owed his

rise to his mother, who was 'great royal nurse to the lord of the land'. This personal relation to the pharaoh will have played a greater part than the office of his father, who was a high priest of Min in Koptos. Meri again did not let matters rest with his priestly office, but took on the further title of 'Chief and Superintendent of Upper Egypt', one of the most high-ranking officers of the state.

Written evidence from the time of Amenophis II is confined to the glorification of his sporting achievements. If there had been any Olympic Games at the time, Amenophis II would undoubtedly have won all the gold medals. In Memphis one day he gave proof of his ability. The nation's craftsmen brought him 300 bows, which he first tried out by stringing them one after the other, 'in order,' as it states in a hieroglyphic text in Giza, 'to compare the work of the craftsmen and distinguish the bunglers from the masters'. Then the royal exhibitionist selected four bows, had four targets set up, each supposedly as thick as the breadth of a hand, and loosed four arrows at the targets, one after the other, so that they came out again at the back. His bows, it was said, could not be strung by anyone else. Amenophis II was also supposed to be an outstanding rider, an uncatchable runner, and a rower of endurance.

His son Tuthmosis IV, who guided the fortunes of the Nile kingdom for ten years, seems to have held aloof from the Karnak clan. At any rate, it is noteworthy that he did not share the passion for building of his predecessors. He found the Amun empire sufficiently big, rich and powerful; he confined himself to the restoration of temples, and dispensed with the founding of further sanctuaries, without, however, coming into conflict with the national god and his priesthood. A document from Year 8 of his reign, hence from about 1404, describes very graphically how Tuthmosis IV, while visiting Karnak, heard of a rebellion in Nubia. Thereupon the king went to the temple of Amun in the morning, made his sacrifice, and asked the national god what should be done against 'all vagabonds and rebels of another land'. And Amun directed the king, 'as a father speaks to his son'.

Amenophis III, an enthusiastic supporter of the cult of Amun, worships himself.

Tuthmosis IV sought a dialogue with the gods with remarkably frequency. In this Amun obviously came off none too well. But Ra, the sun god, once appeared to the little prince between the huge paws of the sphinx of Giza, which even at the time of Tuthmosis – and this is almost inconceivable – was over a thousand years old. Tuthmosis had gone to a hunting expedition with his team of horses, and had lain down to rest in the burning midday heat in the shadow of the great sphinx. His eyes fell shut and in a dream he heard a voice. 'Look on me, regard me, my son. I am thy father Horus-in-the-Horizon-of-Ra-Atum, who will give thee kingship on earth over the living.' The sun god Ra then prophesied to the prince that he would one day wear the white and red crown, the crown of Upper and Lower Egypt; that he would receive tribute from his own country and from foreign lands; and – here the sun god went wrong – that he would have 'a life with great length of years'.

The prince woke up and went back to Memphis; he sacrificed oxen, flowers and fragrant herbs to Ra, and in memory of this dream caused a huge stone slab to be cut, which was placed between the paws of the sphinx of Giza.

If, under Tuthmosis IV, the tribute which the pharaoh paid

to Amun was kept in bounds, his successor, Amenophis III, tried to make up for all that his father had left undone. He built temples, parks, avenues and palaces to the glory of the national god, not forgetting at the same time to show the necessary reverence to the divine family, the mother Mut and her off-spring Khons. Never since the days of the pyramids of Giza had a pharaoh expended so much on building projects, and if the great Rameses had not come to power a good century later, Amenophis III could claim to rank as the most important architect.

Thebes, the capital of the empire and centre of the Amun cult, received its character through the third Amenophis. He was the last pharaoh to bestow all conceivable honours on Amun and the priestly clan. After him came the revolution, as a reaction to his overdrawn worship of Amun, and even under the restorers – Tutankhamun, Ay, Horemheb and the Ramesides – Amun never regained his former influence.

Amenophis III's funerary temple in western Thebes, of which only the outlines are barely visible today, was dedicated to Amun. Its dimensions were greater than anything that had gone before. It was approached along an avenue flanked by hundreds of jackals, and through a gateway with two 720-ton sculptures, each as high as a six-storey house, each the image of the pharaoh hewn from a single block of sandstone. On a stone slab behind these colossi, Amenophis III made it known that the cream of his army had been drawn on for the construction work. This was unusual, but understandable, for during his thirty-eight year regency the pharaoh's armies were not kept very busy. Tuthmosis III and Amenophis II had conquered so many new territories that the financial officials of the court had their work cut out fixing separate dates for the various countries to pay tribute. Even state visits to foreign lands were a burden to the pomp- and luxury-loving pharaoh; he much preferred to invite the foreigners – especially if they had lovely daughters – to come to him in Thebes, where he had built himself a new palace on the western bank of the Nile, near the necropolis.

Nebmaatre – to give him his royal name, which means

roughly 'the lord of truth is Ra' – was a poor statesman, a passable *bon viveur*, but a bridegroom of genius. 3,200 years before the Austrians discovered marriage as a successful weapon of diplomacy, Amenophis III pursued an expansive marriage policy towards his Asiatic allies: that is to say, he sent for his vassals' princesses and married them, thus saving expensive and time-consuming campaigns. At the same time Amenophis III hardly lived in sexual need. In 1399 he married a very attractive girl named Tiye, the daughter of a priest, Yuya, and a lady of the royal harem, Thuya, whose mummies were discovered by Theodore Davis in 1906 in their tomb in the Valley of the Kings. Tiye, as beautiful as she was clever, knew how to twist the youthful Amenophis III – he was between fifteen and eighteen years old when he married – round her little finger. And she rewarded him with an abundance of children. A crown prince, Tuthmosis, is lost in the records, but of four daughters, Sitamun, Isis, Henuttanebu and Nebetah, the first two later received the title of 'queen', an indication that Amenophis chose them as subsidiary wives. And finally there was the late-comer, Amenophis IV (Akhenaten), who was born in 1376 and was to succeed to the throne.

Tiye had to share her husband with a dozen subsidiary wives and a few hundred ladies of the harem; this she took as occasion to seek her own pleasure elsewhere. It is probable – as we shall see – that Tutankhamun was the fruit of such an escapade. The pleasure-seeking pharaoh knew nothing of that, or else he tolerated it in silence; in any case he was was himself far too deeply involved in affairs of the heart to have made a scandal out of it. He was infatuated above all with the lovely girls of Mitanni, which was a kingdom in what is now Syria. Reigning there in the fourteenth century was a king with the exotic name of Shutarna. This Shutarna had a pretty daughter who had taken the pharaoh's fancy, and so, for a suitable amount of gold and trappings, he sent her to the wonderland on the Nile. In the baggage were 317 ladies of the harem, 'but only the best' proclaimed Amenophis proudly. The lady's name was Gilukhepa.

Gilukhepa's brother Tushratta, who seven years later acceded to the throne of Mitanni, was the father of a daughter called Tadukhepa. Tushratta, who had learned from his father how to make money out of beautiful daughters, sent the pharaoh a picture of Tadukhepa and kept praising her until the pharaoh sent a courier to see the girl for himself. The courier was enthusiastic. He wasn't so pleased, however, when his master's future father-in-law put him under house arrest, because the presents he had bought with him were, in Tushratta's view, mere rubbish. Amenophis sent fresh presents and the deal was settled. Tushratta received all the gold and silver he wanted. Many archaeologists believe that in Egypt the Mitannian princess Tadkhepa adopted the name Nefertiti.

Amenophis III played the same game with the Babylonian King Kadashmankharbe. Although Kadashmankharbe's sister had long since been his, Amenophis wanted to have the daughter as well. That made the Babylonian suspicious. So he sent two envoys to Thebes to see whether his sister was in fact still alive. But the two ambassadors failed to recognise the woman who was presented to them as the sister of their king. This led to a furious correspondence: the Babylonian maintained that the girl had died; the Egyptian accused the envoys of lying. They said they had received no presents in Egypt, yet he, Amenophis, had showered the liars with gifts. They intimated to the Babylonian king that he had called his sister an ugly woman; that too was untrue. The exchange of blows by letter went on for years, and eventually petered out.

Begging letters from the provinces Amenophis III usually left unanswered, or else he sent a shipment of gold as consolation. That was what happened, presumably, when Ribbadi, the king of Byblos, from where Amenophis III got wood for the building of his palace, called for help. Enemy troops stood before the city of Gebal. Seven times, wrote Ribbadi, he bowed at the pharaoh's feet; the king should hasten to send troops, otherwise all must die, and Gebal would be taken. The king of Byblos concluded by swearing, 'Behold, on that day on which thou shalt set forth the whole land shall flock round the

King, my lord.' But nothing is known of any expedition to
Byblos.

The pharaoh had himself glorified in the temple of Luxor as
one who 'turned foreign lands into piles of corpses', who had
banished from them once and for all the origins of strife; who
was steadfast on the battlefield and gallant in close combat; but
only once do we hear about anything concrete, during the
suppression of a rebellion in Nubia. And even then it remains
unclear whether in fact Amenophis III took part in the campaign in person.

It can be regarded as certain that uprisings took place in the
area of the first Nile Cataract in about 1397. They are recorded
on four stone inscriptions, as Semneh, Konosso and Aswan.
According to the first-named source, the army of the viceroy of
Kush, which was under the supreme command of the pharaoh,
'slaughtered' the enemies *on the orders of Amun*'. The might of
Amenophis carried them off.

Since there are no concrete references to the pharaoh's deeds
of war, however, we can probably assume that His Majesty
didn't get his hands dirty in the course of them, especially as the
balance-sheet of the venture turns out to be fairly insignificant.

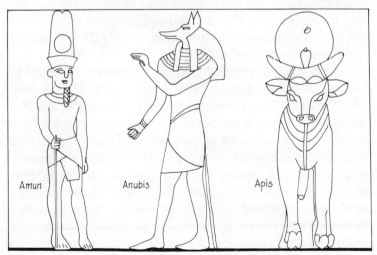

The gods Amun, Anubis and the Apis bull.

A list of booty reads as follows:

Live Nubians	150 heads
Young men	110 heads
Nubian women	250 heads
Nubian attendants	55 heads
Children	175 heads
Total	740 live heads
Hands of these (workmen)	312
Sum of living persons	1052

On the Konosso memorial stone of the same year, however, we learn that Amenophis III came back, 'after he had triumphed on his first victorious campaign against the foreign land of the wretched Kush'. And a stone in Aswan proclaims, 'Bold was he [Amenophis III] in the killing, slaughtering and cutting-off of hands. 30,000 men were taken prisoner.' Whether one, two or three campaigns were involved here, or whether all three inscriptions refer to the same event – recorded perhaps by different authors – is impossible to know, and also not important. What seems significant is the comment on the stone at Semneh that the enemies were killed 'on the orders of Amun'. This means that the political influence of the Amun priests was as great as ever under Amenophis III. The Karnak clan even dictated war and peace.

For his gigantic temple buildings Amenophis III could fall back on a well-tried team. The Superintendent of all Royal Work Projects was a personal friend of the king's, the Wise Amenophis, son of a certain Hapu. 'Come to me, that I may submit what is said to me to Amun-Re in Karnak,' is inscribed on a statue of this architect, which was found, with a companion piece, in Karnak, by the French excavator Georges Legrain. Because of his personal relation to the king, which culminated in his being allowed to build his own mortuary temple in western Thebes, and his readiness to present his subjects' wishes to the king, Amenophis was later reputed to be divine.

Palm column   Lotus column   Papyrus column   Composite column

Tentpole column   Hathor column   Proto-Doric column   Osiris pillar

By the side of the Wise Amenophis stood the architects Suti and Hor, twin brothers. Suti was superintendent of works in the west; Hor directed construction work in the east. So highly did Amenophis III value their achievements that in the solemn processions of the gods in Karnak he allowed them to accompany him in his own procession.

The heart of His Majesty [proclaims a stone tablet from the funerary temple of the great Amenophis] was content with the erection of very great monuments, whose like had not occurred since the dawn of the Two Lands. He did it as his monument to his father Amun, the Lord of the throne of the Two Lands, by setting up for him a lofty temple on the west side of Thebes, a fortress of eternity to the end of time, out of sandstone, faced entirely with gold, the floor made with ritual purity from silver, its gates all of gold, wide and very high, and magnificent in eternity, adorned with a very high monument, richly furnished with statues of the Lord in granite from the island of Elephantine, sandstone and all manner of precious stones, which were carried out magnificently in work for eternity, while its summit shone more than the sky and its rays fell on faces like the sun when it lights up in the morning. . .

Even when allowances have been made for the usual exaggeration of such hymns of praise, we are still left with a marvellous and gorgeous building, unsparing in its use of gold, silver and jewels. This splendour with which Amenophis III surrounded himself and his imperial god Amun finally earned him in history the nickname of 'the Magnificent'.

Like Louis XIV, he liked broad parks with lakes and exotic plants. Even the mortuary temple described above was surrounded by such grounds, for which rare flowers and birds of gay plumage were imported. The attached domain, the farmland with its depots and storehouses, was supposedly overflowing with goods, so that – as Amenophis proudly recorded – their number was not known. The enterprise was run by foreign workers, who were supplied to the pharaoh as tribute from his vassal princes.

The king received his tributes at fixed dates in a garden house that he had built facing the Southern Harem, i.e. the Luxor temple, dedicated to the god Amun. Here, under the watchful eyes of the Amun priests, in the course of a solemn ceremony, the princes of the foreign lands had to deliver 'their silver, their gold, their herds, and the precious stones of their countries in millions, hundreds of thousands, tens of thousands and thousands'.

The temple of Luxor is his work. Not even Rameses II, with his brutal act of building in front of the temple, could destroy the work completely. Amenophis III built his temple in honour of Amun, Mut and Khons, the divine family of Thebes. Before the Rameside reconstruction, this magnificent building was entered through a colonnade, with papyrus columns sixteen metres high. On its outer walls Tutankhamun later immortalised the Opet feast of Luxor. It was Tutankhamun also who completed the associated hypostyle hall. This, in contrast to its antechamber and the sanctuary with the coronation relief, could not be finished during the lifetime of Amenophis III. At the time of Akhenaten the building suffered badly. All the images of Amun, Mut and Khons within reach fell victim to the iconoclasm. Near the scene of desecration Akhenaten erected his temple to Aten, and the visitor notices, as one of the vagaries of history, that the last stones of this same temple to Aten lie today in the shadow of the temple to Amun.

Once a year, in the middle of the period of inundation, the Southern Harem in Luxor was the centre of the worship of Amun. The divine images of Amun, Mut and Khons came up to the Nile from Karnak on three barges. Amenophis III had a great boat built expressly for this two-mile voyage; it was given the name of 'Amun-Re is he with a strong brow'. The cedar wood to build it came from the Lebanon and was transported by each of the princes through whose countries it had to pass on its way to Egypt. The barge was decorated with gold foil on the outside, and on the inside with silver.

To honour Amun, whom Amenophis III called 'the one god', though he didn't let the rest of the pantheon do too badly either, the greatest festival which the empire had ever seen was held. The pharaoh gave offerings daily, indeed, even hourly, and appointed an unheard-of number of priests. In Karnak alone they peopled a whole town. These priests collected sacrificial gifts at every conceivable feast in the calendar. There was not only food and provisions, which, as Amenophis recorded in an inscription on the southern wing of the third pylon at Karnak, he caused to 'gush forth'; at these sacrificial affairs the king also gave gold and silver, genuine lapis lazuli, turquoise, jasper, carnelians, black copper, bronze, lead and dyes. Everything was kept in the priestly treasure-houses, thus increasing the power and influence of the clan. When the king noticed the fatal effect, it was far too late; he could no longer escape the pressure of the priestly caste.

Amenophis III was never a strong personality. His ostentatious appearance and his womanising were by way of compensation for his phlegmatic helplessness. When he came to the throne, he was little more than eight years old, and when he married Tiye not much later, she took the sceptre out of his hands. And behind her again stood her parents Yuya and Thuya. Thuya presided over the harem of the god Amun. Even within the family, Amun had his partisans. Tiye was present at all public functions; she corresponded freely with foreign potentates and had her own power-base among the courtiers. Her tolerance of her husband is probably to be explained only by the fact that she didn't take him quite seriously, and in any case she played the dominant role.

It was no wonder that the third Amenophis had to buy his wives: he was anything but an engaging figure. Victor Loret, who found his badly-treated mummy in the tomb of Amenophis II in 1898, couldn't believe his eyes: the 'Magnificent' measured only 150 centimetres (just under five feet) from top to toe; he had a fat stomach and a full-moon face; he was bald and his incisors were missing. Towards the end of his life he was very ill. Even the arts of the famous Egyptian doctors were of no avail, and Amenophis finally sent for a miracle-working statue from Nineveh. But that too failed to do its duty, and Amenophis III died after a reign of nearly thirty-eight years. The priestly clan of Karnak were sure of themselves: the new pharaoh would be completely under their thumb. But they were to be mistaken.

During the long reign of Amenophis III, the official hierarchy of priests had established the most curious practices. These goings-on, tolerated by his father, obviously gave Akhenaten grounds for his reformation. We can discern for the first time a polarisation in the priesthood: the high priest Meriptah was a man of integrity; he had reached his position without the usual connections, and had even renounced the title 'Superintendent of the Prophets of all the Gods of Upper and Lower Egypt' in favour of the more modest title 'Superintendent of the Prophets of all the Gods of Thebes'. Confronting him were the power-obsessed high priest Ptahmose, who excelled also as a states-man, and finally, in the last years of the reign of Amenophis III, Ramose, who was vizier first and only later assumed the office of 'Superintendent of the Prophets of Upper and Lower Egypt'.

The fourth Amenophis must have followed this development with suspicion. Advisers of an opposition party might also have found him a ready listener – though this wouldn't explain why the young king sent into the wilderness not only the Amun priests but also their gods.

There are indications that the young Amenophis spent some time in Asia. The hundreds of gods between the Nile and the Euphrates, all competing riotously with each other, would have been quite enough to lead a critical young intellectual to think along the lines that – triggered by an external cause – set in motion the revolution of Amarna.

According to the succession, the joint son of Amenophis III and Tiye was destined for the throne. The bright young man was unknown to the priests; he had never been seen on official occasions. Amenophis III made no mention of him on a single document. After graduating from the priestly school at Hermopolis, he was probably brought up at various foreign courts.

Amenophis IV was twelve when he came to power, and he gave the world a sign: he had himself crowned, not at Karnak, the seat of the imperial god Amun, but at Heliopolis, near the old imperial capital of Memphis. He then returned to the palace of Malkata, which his father had built on the left bank of the Nile at Thebes. The sacrifices to Amun were cancelled. This came as a shock to the priests.

Construction-workers came along, and in the midst of the Amun sanctuaries of Luxor and Karnak began to excavate foundations for a temple whose dimensions surpassed even those of the imperial temple. This magnificent building was to be dedicated, not to Amun, however, but to Aten, the sun. The indignant priests raised a storm of protest, but with the young pharaoh it fell on deaf ears. He went even further and made them look ridiculous. The gods they revered were no more than human creations, including their leader Amun; the statues to which they bowed down were hewn stones, no more. There was really only one god, the one that sustained all life, that made the animals grow and the plants flourish, that directed the seasons of the year and, day in day out, banished the night. Although this god was infinitely far, his rays reached down to the earth; this one god was Aten, the sun. He, and he alone, was worthy of worship.

For thousands of years the Egyptians had prayed to their gods and pictured them in human and animal form; priests had encouraged this faith with splendid ceremonial, and now here was this young pharaoh trying to destroy it all. The protest of the priests grew into open conflict. There were doubtless plans to get rid of the pharaoh who had 'gone mad', but Amenophis IV was clever enough to dodge a direct confrontation. When he saw that the temple to Aten on the east bank at Thebes was not to be completed, and when the ground at Malkata grew ever hotter under his feet, he gathered the magnates of the empire round him and sailed three hundred kilometres down the Nile. With him went Nefertiti, his wife who, like her mother-in-law Tiye, never left the pharaoh's side. The beautiful Nefertiti had already given the king, who was just sixteen, three daughters,

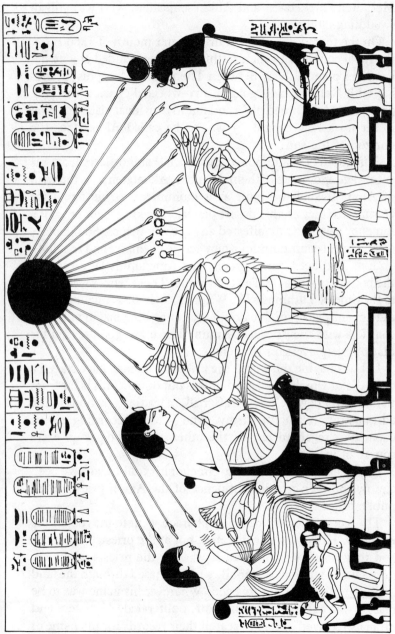

The royal banquet in honour of Tiye, under the rays of the Aten. From the tomb of Huya at Tell el Amarna.

Meritaten, Meketaten and Ankhesenpaaten, who was still in swaddling-clothes.

On the fourth day of the fourth winter month of 1360 B.C., the royal couple with their faithful followers landed at a nameless river plain halfway between Thebes and Memphis. Standing with Nefertiti on a golden, two-wheeled chariot, the king drove round the broad plain and found it an ideal place in which to set up a new capital. It was to be called Akhetaten, the horizon of the sun.

Amenophis IV summoned the officials and officers from his entourage and spoke to them: 'Behold, Akhetaten; it is the wish of Aten. It shall be built as a monument to his name for eternity.' Here, on this desert plateau, the king went on, not a king nor a god had manifested any activity before. So the place offered ideal conditions for a new centre of empire and religion.

'Evil' had been done, proclaimed Amenophis IV on one of the boundary stones of Tell el Amarna. These crimes went back to the time of Tuthmosis IV. What the 'evil' was Amenophis IV did not enlarge upon. No doubt the young king had in mind the conflicts with the priests of Amun. There was good reason for his complete aversion to them.

Let us imagine the worst: the priestly clan may have staged a coup d'état which miscarried or was put down. This is far from unlikely: there were priests, after all, in leading positions in the administration and the army, who – each according to his capacity – regarded one or the other of the jobs as an extra source of income.

But what seemed so 'evil' to Amenophis could also have been simply the ever-growing influence of the Amun priests in all public offices.

The fact is, the revolutionary pharaoh went to the root of the mischief. His wrath was directed, not at the priests, but at the god they professed to serve. It was not the priests who were persecuted, but Amun. Mobile squads chased through the land looking for evidence of this god. Wherever his name was to be read it was cut out, scratched off, obliterated. Ministers and officials received orders to search their records for the name of

Amun and strike it out. The royal scribe was instructed to weed through the foreign correspondence in case one of the Asiatic potentates had used the name Amun in a cuneiform letter; and the scribe did find it, and obediently scratched out what his king no longer wished to see.

Works of art and texts had to be senselessly destroyed by those who received these orders. Some of the name-deleters couldn't even read; they struck out whatever bore even a faint resemblance to the name Amun. As chance would have it, the script-signs that stood for the name of Amun's wife, Mut, were identical with those that stood for the word 'mother'. As a result, all over Egypt, wherever the word 'mother' cropped up, it was blotted out. The king himself set a shining example by casting off his name Amenhotep (Amenophis is the Grecianised version) and calling himself, from then on, Akhenaten ('well-pleasing to Aten'). This took place in Year 5 of his reign, in about 1359, and the absurd thing is that only a few years later the trend went into reverse: Tutankaten changed his name to Tutankhamun. The priestly merry-go-round started up again. The high priest of Aten, Meriere, was out of a job, and so was Panhesi, the 'Second Prophet of the Lord of the Land'.

Meriere's position as high priest was, under Akhenaten, far less important that that of his predecessors. There were two reasons for this. Ay, 'Fan-bearer to the Right of the King', 'Divine Father', 'Commander of the Horse', 'Chief Steward of the Royal Cattle', 'Promised One of his Lord', had united in himself, as the highest-ranking state official and private secretary, all the important offices. Meriere had to content himself with such titles as 'Superintendent of the Treasury', 'Superintendent of the Domains' and 'Superintendent of the Royal Harem of the Great Royal Wife Neferneferuaten Nefertiti'. In addition, the high priest Meriere was under the direct control of the pharaoh. 'I give thee this office,' says Akhenaten in a tomb inscription, 'so that thou shouldst eat the food of the pharaoh, thy lord, in the house of Aten.' Ay, on the other hand, confined himself to politics; his title 'Divine Father' or 'Father of the God' had no religious significance. 'God' referred to the pharaoh.

Akhenaten on the portable lion-throne under the rays of the Aten. In his hands are the ancient pharaonic insignia of authority (crook) and power (flail).

The lay-out of Akhetaten included a great and a small temple to Aten, and between them the royal residence, with store-houses and archives. On the opposite side of the main street, which connected all the buildings to one another, lay the government palace. That was the scene of public life.

Amenophis IV and his beautiful wife attached particular importance to human relationships. They presented them-selves on many official occasions as a happy family; they kissed in front of everybody, something the Egyptians had not seen in a thousand and a half years of history. Together the king and queen inspected the progress of the building works in Akhetaten.

For the vast project, which was conjured out of the floor of the desert in only two years, the pharaoh recruited workmen from the temple domains of Amun. The priests were dispossessed. It may be imagined that this did not pass off without complications. Popular beliefs were undoubtedly deep-rooted in the Egyptians, but even stronger was their awe-inspired relationship with their kings, the descendants of the gods.

Like everything new, the new Aten religion found favour among the people, the more so since the under-privileged, in particular, saw chances of rising in the new capital. The splendid inauguration of Akhetaten, in Year 6 of the reign, seemed to signal a new beginning and a more righteous future, a future without corruption, without cliquishness, without scandals. Who could have guessed that this very epoch would turn out to be the most scandalous in Egyptian history?

It began with a mysterious disease that afflicted the king. As a child Akhenaten had been completely normal, apart from the very pronounced back of his head, but after his seventeenth year he was plagued by fatty degeneration; arm and leg muscles, hips and chest swelled to unusual dimensions and gave the unfortunate king a feminine appearance. Akhenaten's main reaction was to accept the infirmity as sent by god. He was an absolute champion of 'Maat', the truth, and even ordered his chief sculptor, Bak, to represent him as he appeared. That was a revolution no less important than the proclamation of the new Aten religion or the replacement of the hieroglyphs by an everyday script. Never before had Egyptian artists depicted men or gods other than in static attitudes, legs in profile, shoulders and arms from the front. The magic power of representation allowed of no concealment through perspective. Any part of the body that could not be seen in a representation was in danger of being lost.

The original notion of realism was very soon exaggerated by the artists in Akhetaten into a kind of expressionism. Akhenaten and Nefertiti appear to us with long-drawn faces, voluminous thighs and long, thin arms. The colossi which the king caused to be set up in the Aten temple at Karnak show a pregnant, hermaphroditic creature that in no way suggests the founder of a religion or the ruler of a world empire. The 'maat', the very truth that he was seeking, Akhenaten carried *ad absurdum*.

The eccentric king pursued with complete consistency the course he had taken. His ideas were dogma, not only in the sphere of religion. In tombs such as that of the vizier Ramose, which had been begun under Amenophis III but were only completed under Akhenaten, the decoration reflects the clear break in style.

Technically, too, the artists under Akhenaten worked differently from those before them. Hitherto, the relief-sculptors had drawn their subjects and then cut away the stone all round, so that the representation stood out from the wall. Now it was the fashion to chisel the subject, once drawn, into the smooth surface, so that it sank into the wall. As art historians say, raised relief was replaced by hollow relief. There was no obvious reason for this change in the way of working. It was not until a generation later that the unmistakable advantage of the hollow technique became apparent: in contrast to the traditional raised reliefs, the hollow reliefs were difficult to efface. This meant that Akhenaten had an easy time destroying the Amun images of his predecessor; later, with the relics from the heretical period, his successors found things much harder. But did that occur to Akhenaten?

Akhenaten made one decisive mistake: obsessed with the idea of his sun religion, he hardly bothered about politics. While he managed to subordinate art, culture and politics to this idea in his own country, in foreign affairs he let the reins trail. This was more than irresponsible; it was even dangerous, for Egypt was a world empire.

For half a century the Egyptian armies had led a shadowy existence; their effective strength had been reduced, the generals grown old. It was not surprising if there was unrest at the frontiers of the empire. But after two generations of peace the business of war had almost died out in the country. The king's bodyguard was already being recruited from foreign mercenaries.

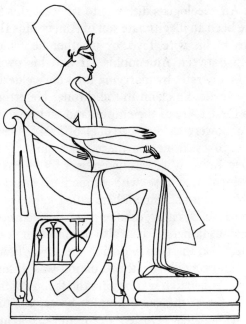

King Amenophis IV (Akhenaten) sitting next to his wife on a settee.

Akhetaten was a small, seemingly safe world, when it should really have been the centre of a universal empire. Up to Year 12 the vassals duly handed over their tribute, and Akhenaten, now the father of six daughters, with his wife Nefertiti, graciously accepted the gold and silver contributions; that was on 21st November, 1352 B.C. After that chaos broke out in Akhetaten.

The series of unfortunate events began with the death of the second-eldest daughter, Meketaten. Bewildered and over-whelmed with grief, Akhenaten and Nefertiti stood at the death-bed of their nine-year-old daughter. We know the scene from a tomb sketch that has been found. Events then followed in rapid succession.

The eccentric king and his beautiful wife, who in thousands of images had presented themselves as one heart and one soul, fell out. Akhenaten married his eldest daughter, Meritaten, to a certain Smenkhare, a man mysterious both in origin and in character. Archaeologists differ as to whether this Smenkhare might have been an illegitimate son of Amenophis III or a lapse on the part of his wife Tiye, or whether he came from the relationship between Amenophis III and his own daughter Sitamun. At any rate, by marrying the king's eldest daughter, Smenkhare secured a claim to the throne. Nefertiti, for fourteen years First Lady of the empire and endowed with all the privileges of power, was stripped of all official duties and placed under house arrest in her northern palace in Akhetaten. The title of Great Royal Wife was taken over by Meritaten, whose husband Smenkhare rose with immediate effect to be co-regent. Akhenaten and Smenkhare ruled jointly.

Since the 12th Dynasty, double regencies had been entirely normal; anxious fathers, driven also by ambition, wanted to see their offspring on the throne during their own lifetime. With Akhenaten and Smenkhare the situation was different. With this measure Akhenaten was buying the favour of the mysterious upstart, for at the same time as he repudiated his wife Nefertiti, Akhenaten revealed his homosexual inclinations. The representations that show the two men in tender embrace can hardly be explained otherwise.

The tangled game reached its climax when Akhenaten, who made no bones about his attachment to Smenkhare, married his third daughter Ankhesenpaaten. Whether this marriage was intended as an alibi, what reasons lay behind it, we do not know. The turbulent life of Akhetaten, however, rapidly came to an end.

Unexpectedly – at least for the writers of history – the designated successor and favourite of Akhenaten died. And before the news had even reached the most distant parts of the country, the dramatic events came to a head: Akhenaten, the founder of Akhetaten, the herald of a new doctrine of salvation, also died, at the age of twenty-nine, after a seventeen-year reign. The empire was faced with the most severe test in its history.

13 The child-king: who was Tutankhamun?

> *I believe Tutankhamun made the
> best possible use of the few years
> for which he occupied the Horus
> throne.*
>
> Pierre Montet

The death of a pharaoh always plunged Egypt into crisis. The start of every reign was a new division of time, marked by her chronology, which began again with Year 1. But this time Egypt had not only lost her king; with the death of Akhenaten the empire was deprived also of its religious model. The Aten religion was as yet too young for its continuity to be secure without this model. The high priests and priests, who had helped the king to realise his ideas, had neither the power nor the authority that were needed to protect Akhetaten from the crisis. So in 1347 B.C. the Egyptians were faced with an uncertain future.

With this unexpected development, the great moment had come for a woman who had already been almost forgotten: Nefertiti. She was, as history shows, not only beautiful but also clever, and was still vegetating in the northern palace of Akhetaten. But to save the throne she needed a man, a man of royal blood.

A letter discovered in the Hittite capital of Hattusha, modern

Boghazköy in Turkey, reflects the desperate situation in which
Nefertiti found herself. The letter ran as follows: 'My husband
is dead, and I have no son. People say your sons are grown up.
If you send me one of your sons, he will become my husband,
for I will not take one of my subjects to make him my
husband.'
The document, as was usual, bore no date and was signed
'The Queen'. There are historians who believe that the letter
could also have been written nine years later by Ankhesenamun, when Tutankhamun died so unexpectedly. This supposition cannot be refuted, but neither can it be proved. It is
rendered more improbable, however, by the fact that in his
nine-year reign Tutankhamun did not correspond either with
the vassal princes or with the Hittite or Babylonian great-kings,
whereas Nefertiti was the sort of intelligent woman, versed in
the ways of the world, who might be thought capable of this
unusual step. For it certainly was unusual. One has only to
imagine the situation: a king's widow was asking her traditional
enemy for the hand of his son.
If the Middle Eastern kings, if the Babylonians, Hittites and
Mitannians, had not been fully occupied at the time in fighting
over border disputes and territorial claims, if any one of them
had led an army against Egypt, the Nile empire would have
fallen into his hands without a fight. But the country was still
living on the fame of the conquerors Tuthmosis III and
Amenophis II. The Hittite king, in answer to the queen's cry
for help, sent his son Zannanza to Egypt, and he was murdered
before he reached the capital, presumably by the partisans of
Ay or Horemheb; but even then the great-king did not intervene. The well-meant alliance between Egypt and the Hittite
empire came to nothing.
Then a name cropped up in history that had not been heard
before: Tutankhaten, a twelve-year-old. In clearing the
antechamber, Carter had already reached the conclusion that
this king must have come to power in his early years and that he
could not have reigned very long, for the grave-gifts were half
those of an adult and half those of a child.

'Our first idea,' wrote Carter, 'was that the king might have kept stored away the clothes he wore as a boy.' But when they examined the pieces of clothing more closely, the excavators discovered that Tutankhamun's royal cartouche had been worked into them, so that he must have already been king as a small boy. The inscription on one box even referred to 'The king's side-lock as a boy.' A wooden chair, which also bore Tutankhamun's name-sign, measured not more than 75 centimetres, in spite of a high back, and could have served as a seat for a ten-year-old at most. The king's slippers and sandals, on the other hand, were all of average size, $7\frac{1}{2}$, and since they also bore a mark of ownership, it seemed to be established that Tutankhamun, who had begun his reign as a child, was on the threshold of manhood when he died.

Without protest or resistance from any side he was crowned king; Egypt had a new pharaoh, and in her chronology it was Year 1 of Tutankhaten.

Where did he come from? What predestined him for this move? Why had nothing been heard of him before?

He was certainly related to the royal house, but who his father was remains a matter of speculation. According to the most recent chronological researches, it could hardly have been Amenophis III. For even if 'the Magnificent' had begotten a son in the thirty-eighth, the last, year of his reign, this son would have been, after the seventeen years of Akhenaten's reign, at least sixteen years old when he ascended the throne. The anatomical investigations of Tutankhamun's mummy, however, leave no doubt that the forgotten pharaoh was at most twenty when he died. And since jar-inscriptions indicate a nine-year reign, Tutankhamun must have acceded to the throne in his twelfth year. So four years are missing.

There is only one theory by which Amenophis III could still have been Tutankhamun's father, though it is rejected by the more eminent chronological researchers. If Akhenaten, during the last years of Amenophis III, had ruled jointly with his father, then Year 34 under Amenophis III would have been at the same time Year 1 of Akhenaten's reign. Such double regencies, however, were always dated with double numbers, hence 'Year 34/1'. That kind of dating is not to be found under Amenophis or Akhenaten. During the double regency of Akhenaten/Smenkhare, on the other hand, the inscriptions 1/14, 2/15, 3/16 and 4/17 crop up repeatedly. This makes improbable the paternity theory with respect to Amenophis III. When Tutankhamun calls him 'my father' on a lion statue in the temple of Soleb, this is no more than a conventional turn of phrase. 'Father' stands here for ancestor, predecessor on the throne.

So the assumption that Tutankhamun was a son of Akhenaten seems very much more realistic. Then, of course, he would have been illegitimate, an escapade of his majesty. Nefertiti was certainly not Tuankhamun's mother, for her family life is fully documented. The birth of a longed-for heir to the throne, which would have had to occur between the birth of the third daughter Ankhesenpaaten and the fourth daughter Nefer-neferuaten Tashery, in Year 5 of Akhenaten's reign, would undoubtedly have been mentioned more than once in documents. Besides, in her letter to the Hittite king, mentioned above, Nefertiti states that she has no son.

The most spectacular interpretation was found by archaeologists in the tomb of Huya, 'Steward of the Household, of the Twofold Treasure-house and Harem of the Great Royal Wife Tiye', in Tell el Amarna. In a wall-relief created in Year 12 of Akhenaten's reign, Tiye and her son Akhenaten sit opposite each other drinking, and the accompanying text speaks of Tiye as 'Mother of the king and great royal wife'. Was there an incestuous relationship between Queen Tiye and her problem-child Akhenaten? Did Tutankhamun spring from the union of Tiye with her son Akhenaten? Historians are still waiting for some chance find that may provide an answer to these questions.

The resemblance between Tiye and Tutankhamun is striking. The full lips, the profile of the nose, the eyes and the prominent cheek-bones make the question of who Tutankhamun's mother was seem almost superfluous. Why should not

Tiye, who was an attractive woman, have had a late love affair after the death of her husband Amenophis III?

Christiane Desroches-Noblecourt, a well-known French archaeologist who has studied this problem, writes as follows:

> It has been suggested that Queen Tiye was barren at the time of Tutankhamun's birth, but in view of the renowned vigour of Egyptian and Nubian women, and the fact that hardly two years earlier she had borne the little princess Baketaten, it is quite likely that she gave birth to the prince when she was about forty-eight. . . assuming that she was married at thirteen.

The role of eroticism among the ancient Egyptians is still an immense field for modern archaeologists, for a strange prudery has so far managed to repress it as a subject of research. On the other hand, for some curious reason, love, desire and passion have been a speciality on their own. In Egypt there are hardly any erotic representations showing the course of personal relations. This could lead one to assume that eroticism was taboo in ancient Egypt. But that would be wrong; all it shows is that eroticism has not come down to us so much in pictorial form (as with the Greeks and Romans) as in written matter. There, at any rate, the authors did not mince their words. The great Turin papyrus shows that pornographic material was already available on the Nile three thousand years ago. We know that as a rule the Egyptian woman preferred the normal position, but that in 'higher' circles coitus a tergo, anal eroticism, autofellatio, fellatio, necrophilia, paederasty and zoophilia were not unknown.

Apart from pornography, the ancient Egyptians made thorough-going use of such aids to stimulation as can be bought today, in plastic, in sex shops; they also used curiously compounded aphrodisiacs and – if all else failed – there were divine sex-counsellors such as Bebon, Bes, Hathor, Qadesh, Reshef and Seth. And so the erotic literature of the ancient Egyptians presents all manner of divine pleasures below the waist. Eye, mouth, hand, snake and arrow have to serve as euphemisms for the sexual organs. But just as often things are called by their names, as for instance when Ra is overcome with delight at Hathor lifting her skirt, or when the hand of the god Atum, which was worshipped as his divine female partner, brings the universe into being in an act of masturbation, or when Isis and Nephthys touchingly exert themselves over the flaccid penis of Osiris.

If the erotic literature of the Egyptians is compared with that of the Greeks and Romans, it is noticeable that the Egyptian woman was unusually permissive, seductive and aggressive in love, and by no means the great endurer that is met in Ovid's *Ars Amatoria* or in Lucian's *hetaera* dialogues. The wife of the state official Potiphar was a sensuous woman who tried by all the arts of feminine seduction to get the innocent Joseph into her bed, and only after vain labours of love accused the young man of making advances.

In the Tale of the Two Brothers, recorded towards the end of the 18th Dynasty in the d'Orbiney papyrus, the wife of the peasant Anubis also made approaches to her young brother-in-law Bata, while her husband was out in the fields. The story went as follows:

The younger brother found the wife of the older one sitting braiding her hair. 'Get up, give me corn,' he said. 'I must go back to the fields, my brother is waiting, be quick.'

But she said: 'Oh, open the granary yourself and fetch as much as you need; I want to finish doing my hair.'

The young man went into the barn and fetched a large vessel for the corn. He poured in barley and wheat and came out. 'How much have you got there on your shoulders?' the woman then wanted to know. 'Three sacks of wheat and two sacks of barley, five altogether,' he replied.

'You *are* strong,' she said. 'I notice every day how strong you are.' And she wished to give herself to him.

So she stood up, took hold of his arm and said, 'Come, let us enjoy each other and sleep together; it is good for you too. In return I will sew you a nice gown.'

But at this base suggesion the young man grew as angry as a leopard. . . or so it says in the story.

Of course, it's only a tale, a fairy-tale; but fairy-tales always reflect a slice of reality. And indeed the peoples of antiquity were taken aback by the far-advanced emancipation of the Egyptian woman. Herodotus was so bewildered by it that he thought everything in the relationship between men and women in Egypt was reversed; that the women went to market and the men stayed at home, and even that the women stood up to urinate, while the men crouched down. That was certainly an exaggeration, but it does point to the fact that the Egyptian woman played a much more active part in corporate life than women in the rest of the world. And that naturally applied also, or specifically, to the erotic sphere.

Where else in the world at that time were there strip-tease displays and dancing-girls? We meet them first during the reign of Tutankhamun's great-grandfather, Tuthmosis IV; a temple scribe under Tuthmosis IV, that is to say, had such a dancing-girl portrayed in his tomb. And after that ladies of this sort were often to be seen in private tombs at Thebes. They can even be admired in the hallowed temple of Luxor, and Herodotus, that modest Greek, thought it was downright obscene.

Where else in the world did the kings treat themselves to so many wives? Rameses II took pride in pleasing four main wives, half a dozen subsidiary wives, and a few hundred professional bedmates. In the harem of Amenophis III, likewise, a few hundred ladies waited upon a sign; officially, he shared bed and board with Queen Tiye, subsidiary wife Gilukhepa, his daughter Sitamun, and subsidiary wife Tadukhepa.

Seen thus, Tutankhamun was a poor specimen. True, he reached only half the age of Amenophis III and only a fraction of the biblical age of Rameses II; but Rameses at sixteen already had two wives and four sons. The French Egyptologist Pierre Montet says, of Tutankhamun's relations with the opposite sex, 'The king and queen led a harmonious married life to the end of their reign, and clearly no other woman acquired the least importance in the king's life.'

Tutankhamun's wife was a woman with a past. When the two were married in about 1347 B.C., it was done above all for reasons of state. Ankhesenpaaten was a royal child, a legitimate heiress to the throne. The third daughter of Akhenaten and Nefertiti was born in about 1360, presumably in Thebes. She moved with her parents to the new capital Akhetaten and there witnessed the early death of her elder sister Meketaten and the marriage of her eldest sister Meritaten to her father's favourite, the strange Smenkhare. At twelve, while her parents' marriage was breaking up, she had to comply with her father's desires. In return, the pharaoh made her a subsidiary wife. The relationship was not without its consequence: Ankhesenpaaten bore a daughter, whom she called Ankhesenpaaten Tashery, Ankhesenpaaten the Younger.

Now Akhenaten had meant Smenkhare to be his successor – Akhenaten was only twenty-five when he gave to his designated successor his daughter Meritaten for wife, and immediately made her First Lady. This was a clear affront to the beautiful Nefertiti, from whom in the meantime Akhenaten had separated. But two years later, when Akhenaten took his twelve-year-old daughter Ankhesenpaaten into his bed of state, she seems very quickly to have stolen a march on her elder sister Meritaten.

This appears from a letter of the Babylonian king Burna-buriash II (1370–1343 B.C.), which was found in the archive of clay tablets of Amarna. In this missive the Babylonian snubs Meritaten, the acting first lady of the state, and sends presents to 'the Lady of Your House', Ankhesenpaaten. In official usage only the queen was addressed thus. Ankhesenpaaten eventually received a chapel of her own in the great temple to Aten in Amarna – just like her sisterly rival Meritaten before her.

The find of a potsherd set the archaeologists in a great stir, for the little piece of terracotta bore the undoubtedly genuine royal titles of Smenkhare and, next to them, the name of the 'Royal Wife Ankhesenpaaten'. This is an example of one of the many little potsherds that have made history. For it says, no less, that Ankhesenpaaten must have been married, not only to Akhenaten, but also to his designated successor Smenkhare, before, at the age of thirteen, she legitimised by marriage Tutankhaten's accession to the throne. An unimaginable strain on the psyche of a girl of school-going age – to say nothing of its physical side! Were the ancient Egyptians monsters, uninhibited sexual bully-boys, who didn't stop even at their own children; men who traded in wives like black-market goods, knocking them down to the highest bidder? At this point it is time for us to look at the question of marriage in ancient Egypt, and especially at the court of the pharaohs.

In pharaonic Egypt there was no going to the altar, no exchanging of rings, and no solemn word of consent; couples simply tried it out with each other. If all went well, the two partners drew up a marriage contract, whether between uncle and niece, cousin and cousin, brother and sister was no great matter; the higher the social standing of those wishing to marry, the freer the relationship. There was no priest to sanction the relationship, and this – considering that the religion of the ancient Egyptians was so closely bound up with everyday life – is strange. Contracting a marriage was apparently regarded as of so little consequence that there was not even a registrar to record it officially. Marriages were celebrated, not sealed; weddings were a private affair and a matter of custom, not of religion or the law. So an Egyptian could marry without further ado a woman of Nubia, Syria or Babylon if she pleased him; the rulers of the 18th Dynasty in particular made industrious use of this.

Although the marriage partners usually came from the same social class, there was no regulation to prevent a rich Egyptian woman from marrying a penniless prisoner-of-war. A marriage deed from the Ptolemaic period, in the light of the unusual number of 'women's things' (household effects such as bed, mirror, oven and crockery) that she brought into the marriage, records the union of a rich woman and a simple soldier, who was living on his meagre weekly pay.

Even in antiquity all this was rather confusing to foreign observers and at times seemed downright suspect. The Greek historian Diodorus, who lived, off and on, in Alexandria, reported in his forty-volume world history that the Egyptians lived polygamously, and that only the priests had to content themselves with one wife. Herodotus of Halicarnassus, on the other hand, in his *History* a few hundred years earlier, was able to report of the Egyptian husband, 'Each of them has only a single wife, as it is among the Greeks.' But here Herodotus was mistaken; the truth is far more complicated.

If an Egyptian contented himself with *one* wife it was not because he couldn't have more. This was not a legal problem, but a material one. Polygamous marriages are known as early as the Middle Empire, even among the middle classes. But with his promise of marriage the man, as the partner who was usually better off, also assumed economic obligations. Marriage deeds, as they come down to us since the 22nd Dynasty, bear witness to a protective conveyance of the man's property in favour of his wife and children. If he had a craving for another woman and wanted to make her officially part of his family, then the second wife had to come after the main wife in the family law, hence also in respect of inheritance. But since a second wife also wanted to be provided for, either the man had to be very rich or the second wife very poor. For this reason it was mainly women of the lower classes, slaves and widows who let themselves become second wives, especially when the marriage with the main wife had been childless. In this case a virgin would rate far higher than a woman with a past.

Normally, the man was the one with the property, and the woman moved in with him. But we also know cases in which the man moved in with a rich wife. A curious form of partnership is what is known as matrilocal marriage. In this the woman continued to live in her parents' house, or set up her own household, and the marriage partner came now and again on a visit. We know nothing further about the cause of this form of cohabitation, but property rights may well have been behind it.

Once the marriage had been consummated and the couple were living together under the regulation of a marriage deed, or rather a deed of partnership, this partnership came under the

protection of the state. That is to say, virginity, consummation
of marriage, and marital fidelity were legally relevant concepts,
and even actionable. There are numerous deeds on the subject
from the period of the New Empire. Thus a man declares on
oath in writing on a potsherd that he had never slept with this or
that woman. In a papyrus text a man is accused of violating
other men's wives. Conversely, a court pronouncement
declares that a husband had caught his wife with another man in
the act of adultery. The adulterer had to swear before the court
never to touch the woman again; as punishment he was
threatened with mutilation of the nose and ears, and exile to
Nubia. But – the frailty of love: the two carried on merrily as
before; the wife even had a child by her lover. In his helplessness the cuckolded husband went again to the court. But again
their worships the judges were merciful; they threatened the
besotted admirer with forced labour on the island of Elephantine, but the threat was not carried out. Jurisdiction over marital affairs was obviously as uncomplicated and loose as the
relationship itself.

If the marriage partners were living apart, they were allowed
to divorce; that is to say, this was not even necessary; for
divorce was not a legal act, but a private one. Grounds for
divorce were: if the wife went with others, if she had no children, if she looked unpleasing, or if the husband wanted to
marry someone else. Then, of course, a maintenance order
came into force for the materially weaker party, usually the
woman. This was actionable, and many a man ruined himself
with his affairs of the heart. 'If thou wilt have friendship endure
in thy house, where thou goest in as master, brother or friend,
wherever thou mayest set thy foot; take care not to come near
women.' So it says in the precepts of Ptahhotep.

It may seem shocking that the thirteen-year-old widow
Akhensenpaaten married the twelve-year-old Tutankhaten. To
the Egyptians of the New Empire, however, there was nothing
at all objectionable about it – even if in actual practice he was
debarred, simply by age, from living with a beautiful woman.
For such an adolescent boy could only enter a partnership-

relationship if he came from a family of good standing, who offered the youngster the necessary financial support. As Ptah-hotep recommends in his book of precepts quoted above, only marry 'when thou art of good standing'.

So it was open to the pharaoh to take a woman unto himself at whatever age he felt inclined. And even if he was so young that, like Tutankhaten or his supposed father Akhenaten, he was not in a position to conduct the business of state himself, then a wife who was usually somewhat older would at least initiate the little king into the mysteries of love.

Tutankhaten married, as we have seen, his presumed half-sister. That too was not unusual at the court of the pharaoh; on the contrary, obsessed by an unprecedented sense of tradition, all the Egyptian kings tried to legitimise their divine inheritance by inbreeding. So Tutankhaten, as the illegitimate son of a king, had need of a legitimate daughter of a king, apart from his youthful age – a marriage of love it certainly was not.

Again, the king of Egypt had to have a wife – even if, as at the end of Akhenaten's time, this was a man. With the widow of his supposed father at his side Tutankhaten could set about restoring the old conditions in Egypt.

The spiritual and cultural chaos that set in with the death of Akhenaten can be read on a memorial stone that Tutankhamun caused to be incised at Karnak. At this time the young king was still living in Memphis, but he was already 'a good ruler who does things of benefit to the father of all the gods'. For, as it says in the hieroglyphic text, 'His majesty ascended the throne at a time when the temples between the delta and the island of Elephantine had fallen into neglect and the sanctuaries become ruins overgrown with weeds. The inner sanctum had disappeared, paths had been trodden through the buildings. Chaos prevailed in the land, for the gods had turned their backs on it. . .'

It was, if one can believe the words of Tutankhamun, who probably had Ay behind him, a godforsaken, wretched time. Pilgrimages, vows, oracles and religious festivals, as necessary to the ancient Egyptians as their daily bread, belonged to the past. This led to universal apathy. Public-building works and projects promoted by the state, the most important source of income for the working population, had not existed since the completion of Akhetaten. There was bitter poverty everywhere.

What was now done in Tutankhamun's name was not only aimed at the restoration of the old religion; it was also a matter of winning back for the pharaoh the trust of the people. To do that, the prime necessity was a programme to provide work, for then as now the same principle applied: well-fed peoples do not make revolutions.

But all peoples need their idols. Akhenaten had abolished them overnight. So far as one can tell, gods to whom the people had prayed were demoted, dismantled, become the nation's laughing-stock. For a decade and a half there had been only one god, the sun, who was moreover amorphous, vague.

The young king restored to his people the almighty Amun. He made a point of declaring that the golden image of Amun, which he caused to be made and decorated with lapis lazuli, turquoise and other precious stones, was bigger than the one that had existed before the Amarna revolution. For the new statue thirteen carrying-poles were needed by the priests; the old one could be raised with eleven.

In his memorandum Tutankhamun went on:

He (Tutankhamun) multiplied their altars of gold, silver, bronze and copper immeasurably. He supplied their work-houses with slaves and slave-girls whom he had captured. He raised the temple tributes. The supplies of gold, silver, lapis lazuli, turquoise and all kinds of precious stones, royal linen, white linen, coloured linen, vessels, were doubled, trebled, quadrupled or increased endlessly.

Akhenaten had closed the temples and estates of the Amun clan; ten thousand people had thereby lost their source of income; many priests had drifted off into the army. Now Tutankhamun had to build up the old Amun hierarchy afresh, and this offered the people fresh chances of advancement. The priesthood was filled with men 'whose names were known', hence morally unobjectionable personalities. They were mostly the sons of fathers whose offices had been snatched from them under Akhenaten. Slave-girls, singers and dancers who had served at the court of Akhenaten were consecrated by Tutankhamun and transferred to the new temple service. They were paid by the pharaoh.

These actions raised the credit of the young king; after the years of decline, a new mood of change could be detected among the people. 'The hearts of the gods and goddesses of this land,' we read on Tutankhamun's restoration stele, 'were in joy, and the lords of the sanctuaries were in jubilation. The lands rejoiced and exulted, laughter resounded throughout the land, for fine things had come to pass. . .'

The old religious festivals were held once more, and for days transformed the whole country into a madhouse. The so-called Opet feast in Thebes was celebrated for twenty days by priests and common mortals, rich and poor, natives and foreigners. Full of pride over this revival, Tutankhamun had scenes illustrating the occasion incised in the walls of the temple at Luxor, where today they still provide eloquent testimony to a stirring spectacle. Amun, the new-old imperial god, in the company of the young king, comes back from Karnak to Luxor. The army and the navy are mustered to accompany the procession for a short distance up the Nile. The soldiers exult. 'How splendid is the good ruler when he has rowed Amun!' Bands of musicians strike up. Dancers display their beauty. Priests slaughter sacrificial animals. There is food and drink, so much after the hearts of the Egyptians.

An important question, which historians have so far been unable to answer, is this: did the Aten cult gradually lose ground to the traditional Amun faith, or did the change take place abruptly? There are substantial pointers to both possibilities, but no proof.

Tutankhamun's chair of state, which – it can be taken as certain – was made at his accession, bears the names and symbols of the god Aten. Oddly enough, the king, during his nine-year reign, did not make a point of destroying this reminder of the heretical period. Besides the throne, he even took with him into the grave a royal fan bearing the names of Akhenaten. This is seen by one school of historians as proof of the tolerance which Akhenaten's successors showed towards the Amarna adventure. In their view, the iconoclasm, which was unsparing even of the written word 'Aten' or 'Akhenaten', only set in under the soldier pharaoh Horemheb and the subsequent Ramesides.

This assumption would have been hard to refute if Arthur Weigall and Theodore Davis had not, in 1907, broached Tomb No. 55 in the Valley of the Kings. There, under the covering of fallen stone, they found a burial shrine, broken and in sections, with the name Tiye, and also a mummy. They naturally thought the body was that of Tiye. According to recent research, however, this opinion proved to be just as false as the view that it was Akhenaten or even Nefertiti that had been found. Anatomists diagnosed the human remains as those of a twenty-year-old man, and archaeologists found a gold leaf in the coffin with the inscription 'Beloved of Ua-en-Re'. Ua-en-Re was one of Akhenaten's epithets. Since the mummy held a royal sceptre in its hands and the royal uraeus was found on the coffin, and since Akhenaten could hardly say that he was beloved of himself, the bones had to be those of Smenkhare.

Smenkhare, whose dubious relationship with Akhenaten has been referred to earlier, was buried under King Tutankhamun in the traditional resting-place of the pharaohs of the New Empire, in the Valley of the Kings. There, during his lifetime, he had begun to build a temple to Amun. The discussions of the archaeologists over the body, which have been going on for decades, are easy to understand. The shrine smashed by the falling stone was indeed originally intended for Tiye. Her name was on a series of finds from the tomb. Two bricks lying in the tomb, however, bore the cartouche of Akhenaten. With that the confusion was complete, and everyone tried to fathom out how this medley of objects could have arisen.

The abandonment of Akhetaten posed difficult problems for Tutankhamun and his advisers. Amongst others, burial-places had to be found in all haste for members of the royal house. Akhenaten had built himself a royal tomb in a wadi some distance from Tell el Amarna, but the traditional ritual required a burial in the Valley of the Kings. If the clique round the young king had dissociated itself from Akhenaten and his supporters, the members of the royal house would indeed have been buried in the places provided for them in Amarna. Instead, a half-finished vault in the Theban Valley of the Kings was taken over as family tomb for Akhenaten, his mother Tiye and his designated successor Smenkhare, and a second, presumably, for Nefertiti and her daughters Maketaten and Meritaten. Tutankhamun felt some obligation to his relations.

Tiye found a resting-place in the confined Tomb No. 55, in a burial shrine prepared for her years before. For the fitting out of a tomb for Akhenaten and Smenkhare, who both died in the same year, 1347, there was little time, just enough for gold mummiform coffins. Grave-gifts, which came from Akhetaten, were available in sufficient quantities.

To one of the radical pharaohs, however, either Horemheb or Rameses II, the lying together of the blameless Queen Tiye and the heretics Akhenaten and Smenkhare seems to have been a thorn in the flesh. He had the sealed entrance to the tomb broken open and Tiye's mummiform coffin taken out. Akhenaten's mummy may have been burned – which in Egyptian eschatology was the most terrible thing that could happen to a person. Only the body of Smenkhare remained in the tomb.

The attempt to remove Tiye's shrine, as well, from the tomb unfortunately failed. Like Tutankhamun's, it had first been assembled inside the burial chamber, and the reburial was obviously supposed to pass off with as little fuss as possible. The doors were already outside, but the side walls of the shrine would not go through the opening, however hard the cemetery officials tried. Their efforts were noticed by Weigall and Davis in the numerous signs of damage. Finally, the sections were left behind. Before the order to withdraw was given, the violators chiselled away from the shrine-sections all symbols and names recalling Aten. On Smenkhare's mummiform coffin the cartouches and the face were struck out; the dead person had lost his identity.

Smenkhare remained in the tomb; Tiye may have been laid in the tomb of her husband Amenophis III. There Howard Carter discovered a small figure of an attendant with her name, such as were placed in the grave with the dead. A faience plate, which was also found by Carter in the Amenophis tomb, bore the name of Rameses II. It seems that it was the great Rameses who ordered this covert affair.

Smenkhare has not received exactly respectful treatment in recent times, either. When James Henry Breasted visited the Cairo Museum in 1919, in order to recover the inscriptions on the coffin of the unfortunate monarch – whom, incidentally, he still took to be Akhenaten – he was taken to the coffin with the obliterated face, but the mortal remains had disappeared. Since Elliot Smith had examined the body, no one had bothered with it any more. Eventually Breasted found it in a labelled box under a table in the Museum store – that is to say, only a few bones were there.

It was a strange experience [wrote the American] to lift his skull from the box, and endeavour to imagine all it must once have harboured. I turned over the lower jaw and found that one wisdom tooth was still embedded in the gum which had partially shrunk away and exposed it. The teeth were powerful and in splendid condition, except that someone had recently let the skull fall and had broken the lower front teeth. I have persuaded the Museum authorities to set an anatomist to work on the body. . .

It remains an open question why Tutankhamun, who had manifestly begun to restore the Amun faith, was in later years assigned to the heretical period and condemned to oblivion. Ay was treated in the same way; he was not enrolled in the official list of kings either. It seems that birth played a part here, and the supposition that Tutankhamun was a son of Akhenaten receives fresh sustenance. Ay's kinship with the royal house – he is thought to be Tiye's brother – may have marked his image as heretic less than the years he spent as educator and adviser to the prince.

Written evidence that could shed light on these obscure problems is lacking, or lying as yet undiscovered in the desert sand. In any case, Tutankhamun did not have a great deal to announce: he conducted no wars, gave rise to no scandals; during his reign there was no great prosperity; only one single temple was built. No, we must resign ourselves to the fact that Tutankhamun was a comparatively insignificant pharaoh.

His greatest significance lay in the fact that he was forgotten, was supposed to be forgotten. If his successors had enrolled him in their lists of kings, grave-robbers in antiquity would have looked for signs of his last resting-place. As it was, this remained unmolested, and illustrates, at least approximately, the splendour, the pomp, with which more significant pharaohs must have been buried. If we compare the size of the burial-places of Sethos I and Tutankhamun, their scale is like that of an English country house to a potting-shed. But Egyptian customs, Egyptian culture, gained new dimensions through this 'modest' discovery, for nowhere else do they present themselves in such untouched and such vivid fashion.

After Tutankhamun came three insignificant decades of Egyptian history, four years under Ay, twenty-eight under Horemheb. Ay is a man who is hard to grasp historically, and his portrait wavers still today. Was he an opportunist, who sacrificed his conscience to his career, or was he a sage, the one and only person who had the fate of his country at heart? Under Akhenaten, he was commander of the chariots and 'Superintendent of all the horses of the lord of the two lands'. In the tomb which he had cut for himself in the rock at Tell el Amarna, but which was never used, he described himself as capable, of strong personality, agreeable, friendly and successful. This is unusual in Egyptian circumstances, and it seems as though Ay was bent on a career at any price. Even under Akhenaten, for whose upbringing he had been responsible, he was no longer the youngest of men. But he had to survive his successor Tutankhamun in order to become pharaoh himself. Before that, he was a grey eminence. Akhenaten had also made him in Akhetaten 'First of the Officials at the head of the subjects'; in addition, he occupied the influential office of 'Scribe to the king', the imposing post of 'Fanbearer to the Right of the King' and the sought-after job of 'Festival leader of the Nine'.

His relation to the Aten faith is not clear. He may not have been so enthusiastic about it as Akhenaten, but he did support the new trend in belief, and zealously held forth in a grave-text: 'Worship the living Aten, that ye may stay firmly in life.'

Under Tutankhamun Ay successfully repeated his role of grey eminence; at any rate, his efforts were now directed against what he had helped to build up under Akhenaten. Now he opposed the Aten faith in favour of the cult of Amun.

After the revolution came the restoration. The gods whose thrones he had been sawing through for years had to be brought back under Tutankhamun with great display.

It is hardly conceivable that this idea was born in the brain of a twelve-year-old boy. The initiative in the first years of Tutankhamun's reign undoubtedly came from Ay. He was conducting the affairs of state for the under-age pharaoh, and so he must also have been the leader of the religious counter-movement. As to the decisive moment in this change of belief, one can only speculate. Was the Aten religion too intellectual? Did it fail to find acceptance among the people? Did the masses revolt against it?

It would be conceivable that Ay yielded to the insistence of the people and remembered the traditional deities. To convince a twelve-year-old of the necessity of this action would not have been so very difficult.

The restoration of the conditions that had prevailed in the heyday of the 18th Dynasty, which was begun so hopefully under Tutankhamun, was a failure; it proved to be impracticable. Tutankhamun was a fickle boy, Ay a feeble old man. Neither of the two could claim that he held the reins of the empire in his hands. The ship of state drifted in the current for over a decade without a helmsman. That it didn't spring a leak was due in the first place to the comparatively quiet course of events. And when the aged Ay died after a four-year reign, the dreaded general Horemheb seized power.

Horemheb, pharaoh by the grace of himself, strove above all to restore law and order. 'His Majesty,' says the Edict of Horemheb, a great slab of stone three metres by five, 'watched at every time of day in order to seek the benefit of the land of Egypt and to strive after excellence. . .'

This Edict of Horemheb was in one a decree for the enforcement of tax laws and a penal code. The gist of its nine paragraphs, worded in great detail, is as follows:

1. The king's tax officials are forbidden to attack a ship bearing the tribute of a vassal. Contraventions will be punished by cutting off the nose or exile.

2. The same applies to attendants of the royal provision store.

3. An attendant of the provision house who robs a vassal of oil-plants or a slave shall likewise lose his nose or be exiled.

4. Soldiers who take an ox-hide from a peasant shall receive 100 blows with a stick and five blood-wounds.

5. If the tribute of a vassal has already been discharged to the inspectors of the queen's household, the desk-scribes of the harem may not demand it a second time.

6. The vegetables for the king's needs may not be gathered by the tribute-collector at random from the garden of a private man, but only from feudal estates.

7. The keepers of the royal monkeys may not draw more than the exact amounts prescribed of vegetables, green stuff and flowers.

From the promulgation of this edict alone we can see that corruption and criminality were widespread. The bureaucratic apparatus, which had not been checked by anybody for years, had been lining its own pockets more and more. It had obviously been quite usual for officials to set their own salaries, for Horemheb emphasised explicitly that he had given each his income and had abolished exceptions. He forbade judges to accept gold and silver.

At the same time a radical purge of the Egyptian bureaucracy seems to have been necessary. Horemheb in person travelled through the land and sought out reliable officials, 'who were accomplished in speech and of good character'. He knew the importance of a well-functioning bureaucratic apparatus; after all, before he ascended the throne he had filled nearly a dozen high offices. He had been 'president of the two lands', 'the true well-beloved scribe to the king', 'chief intendant', 'ambassador of the king in all lands', 'the chosen of the king', 'the trusted of the specially trusted of the king', and he had had himself styled with dubious forms of address, such as 'the two eyes of the king in Upper and Lower Egypt'.

Like Tutankhamun, Horemheb had to legitimise his claim to the throne. To preserve the dynasty's bond of blood, he married a member of the royal family. Ankhesenamun, widowed at least three times (Akhenaten, Tutankhamun, Ay, and perhaps also Smenkhare) seems in the meantime to have died. So the self-appointed pharaoh had to fall back on Princess Mutnedjmet, who is supposed to have been a sister of Nefertiti. Even as a younger sister of the Amarna queen, she must have been about forty years old at the time of her wedding, an age at which Egyptian women usually no longer thought of marriage. Her distant connection with the royal family and her comparatively high age on marrying show, however, how necessary this legitimation was for the upstart Horemheb.

At the end of Horemheb's twenty-eight-year reign, the 18th Dynasty, which had really already become extinct with the death of Akhenaten in 1347, came to its actual end. The head of a military family from the Delta felt called upon to guide the destiny of the empire of the Nile. It was the start of a new period, the age of the Ramesides.

14 Obituary: the quiet end of the discoverer

*There are moments, usually rare
and always brief, when life may be
vividly stirred by some series of
impressive incidents that
successively confront us. To these
we look back with pleasure, whilst
memory loves to contrast their
comparative effect on the mind.
Such experiences occasionally come
to the archaeologist to lighten his
labours and reward his toil.*

Howard Carter

Tutankhamun was in all mouths. Overnight the forgotten
pharaoh had become the best-known Egyptian king – *the* only
pharaoh. His discoverer, on the other hand, fell into oblivion
just as quickly as he had risen to fame; he attached no importance to popularity: quite the contrary. Few people knew that
Howard Carter was still working in the tomb. Alone, with the
help only occasionally of labourers and assistants, he took in
hand the stocktaking and preservation of the contents of the
treasury next to the burial chamber and the annexe opposite the
entrance. Now he could enjoy being alone with his pharaoh, for
another six long years.

After a first brief survey, he had boarded up access to the
treasury and the open view of it, so that – as he said – 'whilst
dealing with the vast material in the Burial Chamber, we might

not be distracted or tempted to disturb any of the objects in this little room'.

In was 1926 when he tackled the treasury, whose contents we have already come to know, and he did so with the same reverence and emotion as he had displayed in working in the burial chamber or in opening the sarcophagus.

Even the most insensitive person, passing this inviolate threshold, must surely feel awe and wonder distilled from the secrets and shadows of that Tremendous Past. The very stillness of its atmosphere, intensified by the many inanimate things that fill it, standing for centuries and centuries as pious hands had placed them, creates the sense of sacred obligation which is indescribable and which causes one to ponder before daring to enter, much less to touch anything.

At the end of 1927, Carter turned to the annexe. In order to get into it he needed help. The low doorway, only 51 inches high and 37 inches wide, whose stonework had been broken through at the bottom by the grave-robbers, was obstructed by parts of the gilded shrine. These heavy sections were now shifted to the northern end of the antechamber. During the earlier stages of the discovery, Breasted and Gardiner had copied and deciphered the seal-impressions in the plaster. This had taken them four days, owing to the poor state of the mortar. The experts managed to read four seal-inscriptions, which ran as follows: 'The King of Upper and Lower Egypt, Nebkheprure, who made images of Osiris and built his house as in the beginning'; 'Nebkheprure-Anubis triumphant over the "Nine Bows" '; 'Their Overlord, Anubis, triumphant over the four captive peoples'.

The inscriptions are particularly interesting to historians. The first, reflects in a few words, Tutankhamun's historical significance. This seems indeed to have been confined to the fact that the king caused new images of the gods to be made and that he re-introduced the numerous sacrifices. The reference to his having triumphed, as Anubis (the god of the dead), over the 'Nine Bows' and the 'four captive peoples' is a customary turn of phrase. It means that Tutankhamun had gained the upper hand over his enemies. And that referred as much to the religious offenders in his own country as to enemies in foreign lands.

When Carter had cleared half the walled-up entrance, he saw what he had glimpsed five years earlier through the opening made by the grave-robbers: an indescribable confusion of bedsteads, chairs, stools, footstools, hassocks, game-boards, baskets, alabaster vessels, jars, boxes, toys and weapons. The whole place was more like a rubbish dump than a store-room or armoury.

This room, four metres by two and a half, which, after the incursion in pharaonic times, could be entered through the low hole in the wall, had not been tidied up by the necropolis officials. As Carter wrote, 'There was hardly an object that did not bear marks of depredation.' A chair lay upside down, bedsteads stretched across the room, bits of stone that had been knocked loose in breaching the wall had shot into the room and destroyed delicate vessels, a little table on high legs was miraculously undamaged, and in between was a fan, a sandal, a fragment of clothing, a glove. 'The scene, in fact,' wrote Carter, 'seemed almost as if contrived, with theatrical artifice, to produce a state of bewilderment upon the beholder.'

Part of the blocking wall still remained; Carter dared not clear it completely because by doing so various grave-gifts, leaning against the inside of the wall, would have been destroyed. The excavator was now faced with the task of removing each time, from this gorgeous game of spillikins, the uppermost object, in such a way that the rest of the piled-up antiquities did not collapse on top of one another.

First of all, to create standing-room and later a narrow access to the rest of the room, Carter leant over the sill, which was more than three feet above floor level, his legs held by two assistants. Eventually he extended his reach by putting a sling under his arms; with the rope held by three or four men, he hovered over the pharaonic treasure like a dragonfly, until he had cleared a safe place in which to stand. It was unusually laborious, because the various objects couldn't just be picked up; each had first to be photographed and numbered, and its position recorded.

Although to begin with this exacting work seemed as pointless as it was hopeless, soon, behind the chaos, the original system became discernible. With the vigilance of a detective, Carter secured all the traces of the grave-robbers, noted, analysed, deduced, and then made known the results of his reflections.

Tutankhamun's tomb had been visited twice by marauders, with different intentions. At the first break-in, the bandits had been interested only in gold, silver and bronze; for that, all four rooms were ransacked. The subsequent robbers had eyes only for the valuable unguents and oils, which – as initiates knew – were always kept in the store-room of a tomb. So they concentrated on ransacking that little chamber, and they did so thoroughly. The burial chamber and the treasury were spared; the antechamber, on the other hand, was also searched. This was done because, contrary to custom elsewhere, unguent vessels had been deposited there, too. The store-room, that is to say, had already been walled up when the last grave-gifts for the room were brought along. Ay seems to have been in a hurry. So food offerings in egg-shaped containers were piled on top of one another under a bed in the antechamber. Carter thought they might have been put aside somewhere, together with the unguents and oils, been forgotten, and only discovered after the masons had already closed the store-room.

It seems to us quite incomprehensible that people should have taken the risk of breaking into a pharaoh's tomb merely to rob it of oils and unguents. But it must be borne in mind that in pharaonic times aromatic ingredients were uncommonly expensive; their value was altogether comparable with that of gold and silver. In the store-room Carter found forty pottery jars and thirty-five heavy alabaster vessels. Their contents had cost a fortune.

That the robbers in the second break-in intended to take only the valuable unguents and oils seems to be established, for they had come with water-skins, into which they decanted the coveted liquids for ease of transport. Carter found some of these 'profane' containers, which were so out of place in a pharaoh's tomb, in the entrance passage. The robbers had obviously been disturbed, and in their haste to get away had left a few filled skins lying there. Since all the seals of the jars had been broken open, it can be assumed that the robbers filled their skins.

This second, deliberate raid raises the question whether the marauders were not the same on both occasions; whether on their first visit, when they took all the solid gold and silver within reach, they did not hit on the idea of the skins and then tried their luck a second time. Incidentally, today, in the age of modern criminology, the bandits would hardly have stood a chance, for on the inside walls of several alabaster vessels that had contained unguents or viscous oils, Carter found distinct fingerprints. They had been preserved for more than 3,000 years.

The longer work went on in Tutankhamun's tomb and in the laboratory in the Valley of the Kings, the louder became the criticism of Howard Carter. He was accused of eccentricity; he was working only for his own pleasure; the tomb was still not open to the public. The rumour went round that in the salvage work more than half the contents of the tomb had been destroyed. Carter defended himself; less than a quarter of the valuable finds had been lost, and neither he nor his associates were to blame, but moisture, which had been finding its way into the tomb for thousands of years. Treasures which at first glance looked 'as new' could not even be touched, or they disintegrated. Ingenious preparatory work was needed, and that took time, a lot of time.

How moisture could have got into the tomb remains a mystery. Carter believes that water had seeped in from above through fissures in the limestone rock. Water, in the dried-up Valley of the Kings? The excavator, who had worked in the Valley for nearly four decades, in fact remembered four downpours during that time, in the spring of 1898, in the late autumn of 1900, and in October and November of 1916. They were of such violence that cascades rushed out of the ravines. After an hour, nature's spectacle was over. Such thunderstorms may have been the cause of the moisture in the tomb, and hence of the decay of numerous treasures.

Criticism and pressure could not unsettle Howard Carter. Cautiously he went on with his job. He knew that the Tutankhamun enterprise was his life's work.

This enterprise lasted a full ten years, ten years of discovering, recording, preserving, evaluating, transporting; ten years of heavy physical labour; ten years of stuffy atmosphere and heat; ten years of concentrated mental work; ten years of tiresome visitors, hindrances, political quarrels; ten years in which there had been five changes of government, and as many ministers responsible for the excavations.

In 1930 the Wafdists, a movement of nationalist and anti-British aspirations that had come to power in 1927, imposed an export ban on all finds, even duplicates, from the tomb of Tutankhamun. This was contrary to the agreement made with the administrators of the Carnarvon estate, who had been promised duplicates from the tomb-treasures. The heirs, it is true, now no longer showed any great interest in finds. The Carnarvon collection, one of the most important private collections of Egyptian art, was auctioned in 1926, at the instigation of Carnarvon's widow, and acquired by the Metropolitan Museum of Art in New York.

The financial costs of the Tutankhamun enterprise were estimated by Howard Carter and the responsible Egyptian authorities at £36,000. This amount was remitted by the Egyptian government to Lady Almina of Carnarvon in the autumn of 1930. The Metropolitan Museum of New York received £8,000 for its collaboration. With that everything was officially wound up. The Egyptians expected Carter to go home. But Carter couldn't leave off.

Still standing around the antechamber to the tomb were the huge sections of the four shrines. Government agencies had not been particularly anxious to transport them to Cairo, for there was no room available at the Museum. Carter himself bore part of the cost of preparation and transport. He felt responsible for 'his' tomb, and gave it up only after the last piece had been duly catalogued, prepared and salvaged.

When he returned to London in 1932, after forty years of excavating activity in Egypt, Howard Carter was a sick man. The extreme desert climate, the trying work below ground, and, above all, the excitements and quarrels over the discovery of the century had ruined his circulation. He was fifty-eight years old, but his movements were those of an old man. Secluded in his house in Albert Court, he led the cheerless existence of a hermit. He felt quite clearly that he had fulfilled his task; he could now no longer make any real sense of his existence. As always in his life, he was alone; an age avid for sensation had already forgotten him.

The only person to take any notice of him in the last years of his life was his niece Phyllis Walker. She implored her Uncle Howard to sort out the thousands of cards on which he had recorded the Tutankhamun enterprise, down to its smallest detail. But Carter was tired; his own work had grown beyond him. An analysis of the card-indexes would have meant his starting the work all over again from the beginning, and for that he no longer had the strength – or the money. He estimated the costs of a scientific publication of the treasures of Tutankhamun's tomb at £30,000; today it is still overdue.

The three books that he wrote on the progress of the salvage work were translated into German and Dutch. The royalties on these were his only source of income in his last years. Scholars smiled at them, because they were unscientific, written for the masses; the general public was disappointed because Carter had confined himself to a harmless description of the contents of the tomb and had scrupulously avoided going into personal details and all the complications that had once been on every lip. This too gave Carter cause for bitterness.

So it was that only a few people took note when Howard Carter died on 2nd March, 1939. *The Times*, which had marketed his reports throughout the world, announced his death the following day in the obituaries on page sixteen:

> Mr. Howard Carter, the great Egyptologist, who gained fame for his part in one of the most successful and exciting episodes in the annals of archaeology, the discovery and exploration of the tomb of Tutankhamun, died at his London home, Albert Court, S.W., yesterday. . . To have found the tomb at all was a triumph, but to have found it intact was beyond the wildest dreams of Egyptologists, as Royal tombs had been so often the prey of the ancient robber. The discovery stirred the whole civilised world more perhaps than any other archaeological success had ever done.

His funeral was a modest affair. Only a handful of people paid their last respects to the one-time hero of the nation. Among them was the only woman who had ever meant anything to him, and who was for him so unattainable, Carnarvon's daughter Evelyn.

Carter's records were made available for research. Phyllis Walker, who died in May 1977, presented them to the Griffith Institute, attached to the Ashmolean Museum in Oxford. There they are being analysed by experts, along with the notes of Percy E. Newberry, Arthur Mace, Alan Gardiner and Alfred Lucas. Archaeologists from all over the world, who in the meantime have filled libraries with doctoral theses on the subject of Tutankhamun, turn to them with gratitude again and again.

Right down to the most recent times the early death of the forgotten pharaoh has occupied scholars from all over the world. What did the twenty-year-old Tutankhamun die of? The findings of Dr. Derry's autopsy gave no information on the subject. Historians, however, take the view that a clarification of the cause of death could provide important indications for the writing of history. In November 1968, a group of nine British researchers travelled to Luxor to unveil the secret, with the help of the most modern technology. Dr. George Harrison, Professor of Anatomy at the University of Liverpool, took Tutankhamun's mummy out of its sarcophagus and made countless infra-red photographs of the human remains of the dead king. 'I anticipate,' said Professor Harrison, 'that the photographs will bring to light some very interesting facts.' The result of the three-day investigation was a sensation: Tutankhamun had a hole in his head at the level of the left cheek, such as might have been caused by the point of an arrow or a spear, but also by a fall.

Was it murder or an accident? The forgotten pharaoh took this secret with him into the grave.

Appendices

Tutankhamun
1347–1338

Name at birth: Tut-ankh-Aten ('Absolute in life is Aten')
Change of name to Tut-ankh-Amun ('Absolute in life is Amun')

Coronation name: Neb-khepru-Re ('Lord of transformations is Re'); in Babylonian letters, Niphururia or Niphurira.

Personal data: Height 1.68 metres (5'6")
Blood group A2
Shoe size $7\frac{1}{2}$

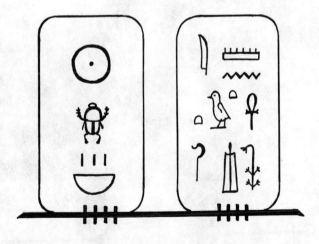

Neb-khepru-Re.   Tut-ankh-Amun.

Year B.C.	Regnal year	Age
1347	0	11
1346	1	12
1345	2	13
1344	3	14
1343	4	15
1342	5	16
1341	6	17
1340	7	18
1339	8	19
1338	9	20

The pharaohs of the 18th to 20th Dynasty
(according to Erik Hornung)

18th Dynasty	certain		probable	
Ahmose	1559/45	– 1534/24	spring 1552	– summer 1527
Amenophis I	1534/24	– 1514/04	summer 1527	– 22.3.1506
Tuthmosis I	1514/04	– 1501/1491	23.3.1506	– December 1494
Tuthmosis II	1501/1491	– 1490	December 1494	– 30.4.1490
Hatshepsut	1.5.1490	– 1469/68	30.4.1490	– 30.1.1468
Tuthmosis III	1.5.1490	– 14.3.1436		
Amenophis II	16.11.1438	– 1412/11	16.11.1438	– September 1412
Tuthmosis IV	1412/11	– 1405/02	September 1412	– 6.6.1402
Amenophis III	1405/02	– 1367/63	7.6.1402	– August 1364
Amenophis IV (Akhenaten)	1368/63	– 1351/45	August 1364	– February 1347
Smenkhare			early 1351	– end of 1348
Tutankhamun	1351/45	– 1342/36	February 1347	– early 1338
Ay	1342/36	– 1337/31	early 1338	– 1334
Horemheb	1337/31	– 1307/01	1334	– end of 1306

19th Dynasty

Rameses I	1307/01	–	1306/00	end of 1306	–	1304	
Sethos I	1306/00	–	1290	early 1304	–	2.6.1290	
Rameses II	June/Nov. 1290	–	summer 1224	3.6.1290	–	12.7. 1224	
Merenptah	summer 1224	–	1211/04	13.7.1224	–	January 1204	
Amenmesse	1211/04	–	1206/1199	January 1204	–	December 1200	
Sethos II	1206/1199	–	1200/1193	December 1200	–	October 1194	
Siptah ⎫	1200/1193	–	1192/85	October 1194	–	early 1188	
Tausret ⎭				October 1194	–	1186	

20th Dynasty

Sethnekht	1192/85	–	1190/83	1186	–	6.3.1184	
Rameses III	1190/83	–	1159/52	7.3.1184	–	16.4.1153	
Rameses IV	1159/52	–	1152/45	17.4.1153	–	January 1146	
Rameses V	1152/45	–	1147/40	January 1146	–	October 1142	
Rameses VI	1147/40	–	1140/33	October 1142	–	spring 1135	
Rameses VII	1140/33	–	1133/26	spring 1135	–	1129	
Rameses VIII	1133/26	–	1130/23	1129	–	June 1127	
Rameses IX	1130/23	–	1112/05	June 1127	–	summer 1109	
Rameses X	1112/05	–	1103/1096	summer 1109	–	May 1099	
Rameses XI	1103/1096	–	1073/66	May 1099	–	1070	

Discoverers and finding-places of the kings of the 18th Dynasty (1552–1306)

King	Discoverer	Finding-place of mummy	Tomb
Ahmose	–	Deir el Bahari	unknown
Amenophis I	Howard Carter	Deir el Bahari	Dra Abu el-Naga
Tuthmosis I	Victor Loret	Deir el Bahari	Valley of the Kings No. 38
Tuthmosis II	Attribution not certain	Deir el Bahari	Valley of the Kings No. 42
Hatshepsut	Howard Carter	Tomb of Amenophis II	Valley of the Kings No. 20
Tuthmosis III	Victor Loret	Deir el Bahari	Valley of the Kings No. 34
Amenophis II	Victor Loret	Tomb of Amenophis II	Valley of the Kings No. 35
Tuthmosis IV	Howard Carter	Tomb of Amenophis II	Valley of the Kings No. 43
Amenophis III	Napoleonic Expedition	Tomb of Amenophis II	Valley of the Apes, No. 22
Amenophis IV	?	–	Tell el Amarna

Discoverers and finding-places of the kings of the 18th Dynasty (1552–1306) (continued)

King	Discoverer	Finding-place of mummy	Tomb
Smenkhare	Theodore Davis	Tomb of Tiye	Valley of the Kings No. 55
Tutankhamun	Howard Carter	in his own tomb	Valley of the Kings No. 62
Ay	?	—	Valley of the Apes No. 23
Horemheb	Theodore Davis	—	Valley of the Kings No. 57

General bibliography

Bille-de Mot, Eléonore: *Die Revolution des Pharao Echnaton*, Munich, 1965

Blackman, Aylward: *Das hunderttorige Theben*, Leipzig, 1926

Blackman, Aylward: *Luxor and its Temples*, London, 1923

Bratton, F. Gladstone: *A History of Egyptian Archaeology*, London, 1967

Breasted, Charles: *Pioneer to the Past*, New York, 1947

Breasted, Charles: *Vom Tal der Könige zu den Toren Babylons*, Stuttgart, 1950

Brugsch, Heinrich: *By Nile and Tigris*, London, 1920

Budge, Wallis: *Tutankhamen. . .*, London, 1923

Bulletin of the Metropolitan Museum of Art XXXV (1940), New York, 1940

Carter, Howard, and Lord Carnarvon: *Five Years' Exploration at Thebes*, London, 1912

Carter, Howard: 'A Tomb Prepared for Queen Hatshepsut and Other Recent Discoveries at Thebes', *Journal of Egyptian Archaeology IV*, 1917

Carter, Howard: *The Tomb of Tut-ankh-Amen*, London, 1923

Carter, Howard: *Tut-ench-Amun, ein ägyptisches Königsgrab*, Leipzig, 1927

Cottrell, Leonard: *The Lost Pharaohs*, London, 1951

Cottrell, Leonard: *Das Geheimnis der Königsgräber*, Baden-Baden, 1952

Cottrell, Leonard: *The Secrets of Tutankhamon*, London, 1965

Daniel, Glyn: *A Hundred and Fifty Years of Archaeology*, London, 1975

Davis, Theodore M. (*et al.*): *The Tomb of Hatshepsitu*, London, 1906

Davis, Theodore M. (*et al.*): *The Tomb of Siphtah*, London, 1908

Davis, Theodore M. (*et al.*): *The Tomb of Queen Tiyi*, London, 1910

Davis, Theodore M. (*et al.*): *The Tombs of Harmhabi and Touatankhamanou*, London, 1912

Davis, Theodore M. (*et al.*): *The Tomb of Iouiya and Touiyou*, London, 1907

Dawson, Warren R.: *Who was Who in Egyptology*, London, n.d.

Desroches-Noblecourt, Christiane: *Tutankhamen*, London, 1963

Edwards, Amelia: *A Thousand Miles up the Nile*, London, 1877

Erman, Adolf: *Mein Werden und mein Wirken*, Leipzig, 1929

Gardiner, Alan: *My Working Years*, London, 1962

Gardiner, Alan: *Tutankhamun's Painted Box*, Oxford, 1962

Helck, Wolfgang: *Urkunden der 18. Dynastie*, Berlin, 1961

Hornung, Erik: *Untersuchungen zur Chronologie und Geschichte des Neuen Reiches*, Wiesbaden, 1964

Illustrated London News: 27th June, 1925; 6th February, 1926, London

Kees, Hermann: *Das Priestertum im ägyptischen Staat*, Leyden/Cologne, 1953

Leek, F. Filce: *The Human Remains from the Tomb of Tutankhamun*, Oxford, 1972

Naville, Edouard: *Memoir of the E.E.F.: The Temple of Der el-Bahari*, London, n.d.

Petrie, Flinders: *Tell el-Amarna*, London, 1894

Petrie, Flinders: *Seventy Years in Archaeology*, London, 1931

Redford, Donald B.: *History and Chronology of the Eighteenth Dynasty of Egypt*, Toronto, 1967

Riesterer, Peter: *Der Grabschatz des Tut-ench-Amun*, Berne, 1966

Sayce, A. Henry: *Reminiscences*, London, 1923

Smith, Elliot, and Warren R. Dawson: *Egyptian Mummies*, London, 1924

Smithsonian Institute: *The Opening of the Sarcophagus of Tutankhamun*, June, 1972

Sudhoff, Karl: *Archiv für Geschichte der Medizin*, Vol. 5, Leipzig, 1911

Times, The: 30.11.1922; 1.12.1922; 4.12.1922; 9.12.1922; 18.1.1923; 30.4.1923; 3.3.1939, London

Weigall, Arthur: *A History of Events in Egypt from 1798 to 1914*, Edinburgh, 1915

Weigall, Arthur: *Tutankhamen and Other Essays*, London, 1932

Woolley, Leonard: *The City of Achenaten Excavations of 1921 and 1922 at Al-Amarneh*, London, 1923

Woolley, Leonard: *Digging up the Past*, London, 1930

Woolley, Leonard: *Dead Towns and Living Men*, London, 1954

Woolley, Leonard: *As I Seem to Remember*, London, 1962

Woolley, Leonard: *Spadework Adventures in Archaeology*, London, 1975

Notes on the sources

Chapter 1 Howard Carter: the apprentice excavator.
The opening quotation comes from Howard Carter's book *The Tomb of Tut-ankh-amen*, London, 1923. Flinders Petrie described his excavations at Tell el Amarna in his scientific work *Tell el-Amarna* (London, 1894) and in his memoirs *Seventy Years in Archaeology* (London, 1931). The quotations are taken mostly from the first-named work. How Petrie struck others can be read in Charles Breasted *Pioneer to the Past* (New York, 1947). Carter's childhood is outlined in the obituary of him by Percy E. Newberry in the *Journal of Egyptian Archaeology XXV*, 1939. The quotation from Leonard Woolley on field archaeology comes from Ch. 1 of his book *Digging up the Past*, London, 1931.

Chapter 2 Gold rush: the battle for the past
On Deir el Bahari, see Edouard Naville, *The Temple of Der el-Bahari: its Plan, its Founders, and its First Explorers*, London, 1894 (12th Memoir of the Egypt Exploration Fund). Jean-François Champollion reports on Deir el Bahari in *Lettres écrites d'Egypte et de Nubie*, No. 15. On the life of Heinrich Brugsch, see *Mein Leben und mein Wandern*, Berlin, 1894. The quotation from Kurt Sethe is from *Der Alte Orient: Kurt Sethe, Die Ägyptologie*, address to the Vorderasiatische Gesellschaft on 3rd January, 1921, Leipzig. On the erotic aspects of the younger Brugsch, Adolf Erman writes in *Mein Werden und mein Wirken*, Leipzig, 1929. The grotesque idea of 'one last pleasure' for the

dying Mariette is recounted in Heinrich Brugsch, *Mein Leben und mein Wandern*, Berlin, 1894, where the dialogue and the quotation may be found. The Sayce quotation comes from Henry Sayce, *Reminiscences*, London, 1923. On patronage, see the mentioned address by Kurt Sethe. Howard Carter's description of the Valley of the Kings comes from his book *The Tomb of Tut-ankh-Amen*, London, 1923. 'Herr Franz' is referred to by Adolf Erman in his memoirs, see above. The clearing of the tomb of Hatshepsut is fully described in Theodore M. Davis, *The Tomb of Hatshopsitu*, London, 1906. This work also contains Howard Carter's contribution, *Description and Excavation of the Tomb of Hatshopsitu*, from which the quotations are taken. On life in Luxor at the end of the last century, see Amelia Edwards, *A Thousand Miles up the Nile*, London, 1877.

Chapter 3 Saqqara: the end of a career
The 'Carter case' is described by his friend Percy E. Newberry in the *Journal of Egyptian Archaeology XXV*, 1939. On the Yuya/Thuya tomb, see Theodore M. Davis, *The Tomb of Iouiya and Touiyou*, London, 1907. The meeting with Breasted is described by Charles Breasted, *Pioneer to the Past*, New York, 1947. The night ride to the Nile is also described there. The quotations in connection with the Horemheb tomb and the Tutankhamun cache come from Theodore M. Davis, *The Tombs of Harmhabi and Touatankamanou*, London, 1912.

Chapter 4 The Earl of Carnarvon: a lord and his lackey
For the characterisation of Lord Carnarvon the following were used: the obituary in *The Times* (30.4.1923); a 'Biographical Sketch of the Late Lord Carnarvon' by Lady Burghclere in Vol. I of Carter's book *The Tomb of Tut-ankh-Amen*, London, 1923; the obituary by John G. Maxwell in the *Journal of Egyptian Archaeology IX*, 1923; information in Warren R. Dawson's *Who was Who in Egyptology*, London, n.d.; and interviews with the 6th Earl of Carnarvon. On the excavations, see Howard Carter and Lord Carnarvon, *Five Years Exploration at Thebes*, London, 1912. Carnarvon's purchase of stolen property is

described by Leonard Woolley in *As I Seem to Remember*, London, 1926, where the dialogue is recorded.

Chapter 5 First World War: the King's Messenger
An account of the Hatshepsut tomb is given by Carter in the *Journal of Egyptian Archaeology IV*, 1917. An outline of the modern history of Egypt may be found in Arthur Weigall, *A History of Events in Egypt from 1798 to 1914*, Edinburgh, 1915.

Chapter 6 The discovery: the pharaoh's last secret
The initial telephone conversation between Lord Carnarvon and Alan Gardiner is reported by Leonard Cottrell in his book *The Lost Pharaohs*, London, 1951. The humiliating interview between Carter and Carnarvon was related by Carter to his friend James Henry Breasted, whose son reproduces it in his book *Pioneer to the Past*, New York, 1947. James Henry Breasted was in England at the time to receive an honorary doctorate at Oxford. During this time he was also party to the episode with the canary. The circumstances of the finding of the tomb are described by Carter himself in his book *The Tomb of Tut-ankh-Amen*, London, 1923. Carnarvon's letter to Wallis Budge is reproduced in the latter's book *Tutankhamen. . .*, London, 1923. The information about Carter's fellow-worker Arthur C. Mace is taken from the *Journal of Egyptian Archaeology XV*, 1929. The first meeting between Breasted and Carter after the discovery, and the Breasteds' first sight of the tomb, are described by Charles Breasted in his above-mentioned book. The discussion of the sale of press rights is recorded in Leonard Cottrell, *The Lost Pharaohs*, London, 1951. 'Tutankhamen Ltd.' was in the *Daily Express* for 10th February, 1923. The reply by *The Times* appeared on 16th February, 1923. The clearing of the wall and the comments of those present comes from Cottrell's book, already mentioned. On the Antiquities Law and Alan Gardiner's attitude, see *The Times*, 4.12.1922. The Egyptian Law No. 14 is discussed in detail by Henry George Lyons in the *Journal of Egyptian Archaeology I*, 1912, pp. 45–6.

Chapter 7 Preserving the evidence: the mysterious life below
ground
The opening quotation from Alan Gardiner is in Leonard
Cottrell, *The Lost Pharaohs*, London, 1951. Carter's card 48D
is also taken from there. The contents of the chest are described
by Carter in his chapter 'Work in the Laboratory', *The Tomb of
Tut-ankh-Amen*, London, 1923, Vol. I. Alfred Lucas wrote
Appendix II to Vol. II of this work, in which he describes,
amongst other things, the bacteriological examination of the
tomb. The visits of the illustrious to the tomb are described in
Arthur Weigall, *Tutankhamen and Other Essays*, London, 1923.
The words of the priest Neferhotep may be found in Adolf
Erman, *Die Literatur der alten Ägypter*, Leipzig, 1923.

Chapter 8 Carnarvon's death: curse or legend?
The opening quotation comes from Arthur Weigall, *Tutankhamen and Other Essays*, London, 1923. Carnarvon's last letter
was mentioned by J. G. Maxwell in his obituary of him (*Journal
of Egyptian Archaeology IX*, 1923). The episode with the cobra
is related by Charles Breasted, *Pioneer to the Past*, New York,
1947. The Nekhebet curse was the subject of an interview
which the author had in April 1977 with the Director-General
of the Egyptian Museum in Cairo, Dr. Ali Hassan. Information
about the 6th Earl of Carnarvon comes from the author's
correspondence with his lordship and from a German broadcast
by Margret Dünser in February 1978. Details of the electricity
failure are in Christiane Desroches-Noblecourt, *Tutankhamen*,
London, 1963. Carter's absence at the funeral is attested by the
6th Earl of Carnarvon in a letter to the author of 29th April,
1978. The Maxwell quotation is from his obituary of Carnarvon
in the *Journal of Egyptian Archaeology IX*, 1923. The quotation
about Professor La Fleur may be found in Charles Breasted,
and the Mehrez quotation in Philipp Vandenberg, *Der Fluch
der Pharaonen*, Berne, 1973, which also features the episode
with Dr. Ezzedin Taha. Arthur Weigall relates his experience
with the mummy in his work quoted at the start of the chapter,
also the story of the proposed play.

Chapter 9 The Burial Chamber: treasures for eternity
The opening quotation is from Carter, *The Tomb of Tut-ankh-Amen*, London, 1923, Vol. II, Ch. 3. Also from there are the Gurgar letter and the Carter quotations in connection with the opening of the shrines and the sarcophagus. The pigments in the tomb are reported on by Alfred Lucas in Appendix II of Vol. II of Carter's book. The opening of the coffin and the political quarrels are described both by Carter and Charles Breasted in their mentioned works.

Chapter 10 Carter's triumph: face to face with Tutankhamun
The opening quotation is taken from Douglas E. Derry's report on the mummy, reproduced in Appendix I of Vol. II of Carter's work, *The Tomb of Tut-ankh-Amen*, London, 1923. The exchange of letters with the Ministry of Public Works may also be found there, in the Preface. The cited issue of the *Illustrated London News* was for 27th June, 1925. The examination of the mummy is described by Howard Carter in his diary, extracts from which appear in Filce Leek's, *The Human Remains from the Tomb of Tutankhamun*, Oxford, 1972. The Carter quotation, 'Familiarity can never entirely. . .', comes from Vol. II, Ch. 5, of his book. The coffin nails and the resinous matter are discussed by Alfred Lucas in Appendix II of the same volume of Carter. The quotations from Carter's diary are taken from Leek, as above. The Derry quotation is from Appendix I, as above.

Chapter 11 The mummifiers: reconstruction of a
transformation
The opening quotation comes from Chistiane Desroches-Noblecourt, *Tutankhamen*, London, 1963. The Carter quotation is from Vol. II, Ch. 5, of his book. Labib Habachi's theories may be read in an article in the *Los Angeles Times*, which was reprinted in the *International Herald Tribune* for 2nd March, 1978. The source of light for the tomb-workers is described in *Lexikon der Ägyptologie*, Wiesbaden, 1973. Herodotus's account of mummification is from *Historien II*,

Munich, 1961, translated by Dr. Eberhard Richtsteig. Prof. Karl Sudhoff's experiment in mummification is set out in *Archiv für Geschichte der Medizin*, Vol. V, August 1911, No. 3. The papyri concerned with the embalming ritual are Papyrus Bulak No. 3 and Papyrus Louvre No. 5158 – the third papyrus is the demotic Papyrus Vienna No. 27. The translations from the papyri come from Elliot Smith/Warren R. Dawson, *Egyptian Mummies*, London, 1924. The funeral texts are from the *Lexikon der Ägyptologie*, Wiesbaden, 1973 (*'Bestattungsritual'*) and Albert Champdor, *Das Ägyptische Totenbuch in Bild und Deutung*, Berne, 1977.

Chapter 12 The burden: the Karnak clan and the heretic of Akhetaten

The opening quotation is from Eléonore Bille-de Mot, *Die Revolution des Pharao Echnaton*, Munich, 1965. Details of Amun are taken from the *Lexikon der Ägyptologie*, Wiesbaden, 1973. Figures concerning the wealth of the priests are mentioned by Jürgen Thorwald, *Macht und Geheimnis der frühen Ärzte*, Munich, 1962. On the priests in general: Hermann Kees, *Das Priestertum im Ägyptischen Staat*, Leyden, 1953. All stele inscriptions are after Wolfgang Helck, *Urkunden der 18 Dynastie*, Berlin, 1961.

Chapter 13 The child-king: who was Tutankhamun?

Opening quotation: Pierre Montet, *Das Leben der Pharaonen*, Herrsching, n.d. Concerning Tiye, Christiane Desroches-Noblecourt gives an account in her book *Tutankhamen*, London, 1963. On eroticism among the ancient Egyptians, see *Lexikon der Ägyptologie*, Wiesbaden, 1973. Stele texts are according to Wolfgang Helck, *Urkunden der 18. Dynastie*, Berlin, 1961. The encounter with Smenkhare is quoted by Charles Breasted, *Pioneer to the Past*, New York, 1947.

Chapter 14 Obituary: the quiet end of the discoverer

The Carter quotation at the beginning of the chapter comes from the Preface to Vol. II of his book, *The Tomb of Tut-ankh-*

Amen, London, 1923. The reference to the boarded-up Treasury is taken from Ch. 1 of Vol. III of his book. The quoting of Prof. Harrison comes from the *International Herald Tribune* for 8th December, 1968.

Index